And This Is My Friend

Also available from Bloomsbury:

Black Performance Practice as British Musical Theatre
9781350119635

British Musical Theatre since 1950
9781472584366

Broadway Swings
9781472590008

A Critical Companion to the American Stage Musical
9781472513250

Doing the Time Warp: Queer Temporalities and Musical Theatre
9781350151703

An Inconvenient Black History of British Musical Theatre
9781350119635

LGBTQ* identities and queer representations in
contemporary musical theatre
9781350119543

Musical Theatre
9781474267007

And This Is My Friend Sandy

Sandy Wilson's The Boy Friend,
London Theatre and Gay Culture

Deborah Philips

methuen | drama

LONDON • NEW YORK • OXFORD • NEW DELHI • SYDNEY

METHUEN DRAMA
Bloomsbury Publishing Plc
50 Bedford Square, London, WC1B 3DP, UK
1385 Broadway, New York, NY 10018, USA
29 Earlsfort Terrace, Dublin 2, Ireland

BLOOMSBURY, METHUEN DRAMA and the Methuen Drama logo are
trademarks of Bloomsbury Publishing Plc

First published in Great Britain 2021
Paperback edition published 2023

Cover design: Louise Dugdale
Cover photo by John Pratt/ Keystone Features/ Getty Images

A catalogue record for this book is available from the British Library.

A catalog record for this book is available from the Library of Congress.

ISBN: HB: 978-1-3501-7421-4
PB: 978-1-3503-3505-9
ePDF: 978-1-3501-7423-8
eBook: 978-1-3501-7422-1

Typeset by Deanta Global Publishing Services, Chennai, India
Printed and bound in Great Britain

To find out more about our authors and books visit www.bloomsbury.com
and sign up for our newsletters.

This book is for Ursula Harby and for Reginald Woolley, who loved the Players' Theatre and The Boy Friend.

With thanks to the Players' Theatre Company for permission to reproduce the photographs and the Players' programme.

Contents

List of figures   viii

Acknowledgements   ix

1   And this is my friend Sandy . . .   1

2   Mapping theatreland: Soho, the West End and
    homosexual law reform   23

3   The Ivy League: Binkie Beaumont, Noël Coward, Ivor Novello
    and Terence Rattigan   39

4   'Oh! The Fairies': The Players' Theatre Club   57

5   'That certain thing called The Boy Friend': The
    1953 production of *The Boy Friend*   73

6   'What next?': After *The Boy Friend*   91

7   Queer utopianism: *Valmouth*   109

8   'A walpurgisnacht of self-indulgence': The Ken Russell film
    of *The Boy Friend*, *His Monkey Wife*, *The Clapham Wonder*
    and *Aladdin*   129

Conclusion   147

Afterword   157

Notes   159

Bibliography   169

Index   177

Figures

4.1 'Late Joys'; programme, The Players' Theatre Club   56
8.1 *The Boy Friend*, directed by Ken Russell, 1971   128

Acknowledgements

Theatre is a collective project, and I have been supported in writing about it by a host of knowledgeable and generous people. This book was made possible by a grant from the Andrew W. Mellon Foundation to study Sandy Wilson's archives at the Harry Ransom Center at the University of Texas at Austin. The staff of the Harry Ransom Center, from the conservationists to the receptionists, are to be thanked for making the research process so pleasant, particular thanks are due to the drama curator Eric Colleary, who went beyond his brief to share his extensive knowledge of theatre history. Also thank you to my fellow fellows for making the experience such fun, especially Loois Van Kessell, who kept me up to scratch with queer theory.

At the British Library, thanks are due to Andy Linehan, the Popular Music curator, who again went beyond his job description in sharing his comprehensive knowledge of popular music, and to Steve Cleary, curator of Drama and Literature. Special thanks are owed to the late Dave Laing who shared his unrivalled knowledge of popular music and to Val Wilmer, who knows so much about jazz and popular culture. Thank you to the Production team at Bloomsbury, to my most sympathetic editor Don O'Hanlon, to Meredith Benson who helped with the images, to Mohammed Raffi for his meticulous proof-reading and to Sophie Beardsworth. Particular thanks to my own publishing support group – Steve McCubbin who valiantly scanned the pictures of my mother and Reginald Woolley and Elspeth Broady who took on the indexing. And to Françoise Jaouën, who assisted in translating the Proust quotation. Thanks are also due to Bill Halson of the Players' Theatre Club for permission to reproduce images from Players' publications, and for the details of the Players' beginnings and to Sandy Wilson's friends, Paul Guinery and Rexton S. Burnett, for refining my knowledge of Wilson's work and career. And thank you to Chak Yui who makes a great Manhattan.

My neighbour Gary Yershon burst into song when I asked him at a resident's meeting what he knew about Sandy Wilson. He very kindly reassured me over coffee that I was on the right lines and put me in touch with Colin Sell who was immensely generous with his memories of Sandy Wilson, and in providing me with programmes and with scripts. Colin Sell in turn put me in touch with Barry Cryer whose memories of the Players' Theatre and of revue in the 1950s were immensely important. Colin Sell also gave me contact details for Patricia Michael who had played Polly in the original *Divorce Me, Darling!* (she is one of the dedicatees in *Sandy Wilson*

Thanks the Ladies) and she graciously shared her memories of the Players' and Sandy Wilson over lunch at the Oyster Bar at Grand Central Station.

My friends have been living with this project for a very long time and are now getting fed up with having to burst into 'It's Never too Late' whenever we meet. Carole Woddis, Jessica Higgs and Ian Haywood, along with William McElvoy and Dimitris Papanikolaou, have been constant sources of references, ideas and support. Nigel Pugh and Adam Wide have shared their memories of *The Boy Friend* and were kind enough to let me repeat the story of their simultaneous coming out at the Players' Theatre. Justin Fleming and Fae Brauer, with Neil McWilliam and Olga Grlic, were good enough to sit with me through Ken Russell's film version of *The Boy Friend*.

More than anyone, I owe thanks to Garry Whannel who has been on side with this book every step of the way, from Austin, Texas, to North Marston, Buckinghamshire.

And this is my friend Sandy . . .

Bona to vada your dolly old eek

Round the Horne

From 1965 to 1968, BBC radio broadcast the programme *Round the Horne* which weekly featured a sketch with Kenneth Williams and Hugh Paddick,[1] each episode was introduced with Williams saying 'I'm Julian, and this is my friend Sandy.' Julian and Sandy were unabashedly camp, and brought Polari, the coded language of a gay subculture,[2] to a mainstream audience. 'Julian' was a reference to Julian Slade, the writer and composer of *Salad Days*, and 'Sandy' to Sandy Wilson, the writer and composer of *The Boy Friend*.[3]

The Boy Friend and *Salad Days* were *the* hit musicals of 1953 and 1954, *Salad Days* eventually outstripping *The Boy Friend* as the longest running musical in the West End. According to Mander and Mitchenson's survey of musical comedy:

> The two phenomena of 1954 were *Salad Days*, written as an end-of-season romp, by Dorothy Reynolds and Julian Slade for the Bristol Old Vic Company, which unexpectedly became a record runner at the Vaudeville, and *The Boy Friend*, a brilliant nostalgic pastiche of the 1920s which, after two tentative starts at the Players' Theatre, settled in . . . at the Wyndham's Theatre. (Mander and Mitchenson, 1969, p. 35)

Both musicals had originated in small-scale productions, originally intended as Christmas entertainments for independent theatres from outside the West End, *Salad Days* at the Bristol Old Vic and *The Boy Friend* at the Players' Theatre Club, known for its staging of nostalgic Victorian music hall. *Salad Days* and *The Boy Friend* both pastiched the music and styles of the 1920s, and both writers had come from a background in university drama clubs, Slade with the Cambridge Footlights[4] and Wilson with the Oxford Experimental Theatre Club, each had gone on to write for revues. And both musicals were written by gay men in the context of a post-war Britain in which sexual acts between men were both illegal and demonized.

Sandy Wilson (or rather, his most famous work, *The Boy Friend*) is regularly cited as a footnote in surveys of 1950s theatre.[5] Wilson, however, merits more than a footnote in the history of musical theatre; he wrote what was to become one of the most loved and performed musicals and has a back catalogue that is widely remembered and revived. He is also a figure who provides a focus for a culture and a sensibility at a significant period in British gay history. Wilson's trajectory represents a transitional moment in the history of the British musical, in British theatre and in modes of homosexuality. As a composer he begins by being in thrall to the glamorous and romantic works of Noël Coward and Ivor Novello and ends with musical adaptations of fiction, largely written by gay men, for the stage. As a young man he came into his professional own at a time when sexual relations between men were illegal; he modelled himself on the covert homosexuality of Coward and Novello and their generation. Wilson ended his life, if somewhat uncertain of the strategies of the Gay Liberation Front, certainly supportive of the cause. An undated lyric in Sandy Wilson's file of 'Songs and Sketches' is titled 'Why did it have to be gay?' and expresses an understanding of the need for change, but also rueful regret for the discreet camp of closeted homosexuality:

'Why did it Have to Be Gay?'
I remember the days, not long ago,
When one sometimes used to hear
A person say 'He's Bent' or 'so'
Or 'one of those' or 'Queer'
They were none of them nice expressions

And I'm rather glad they went . . .
In my old-fashioned way,
I'm all for hi-de-ho and also hi-de-hey.
But something has gone for ever,
And though you may think I'm absurd
I could smack the head of whoever said,
'Gay's the Word!'
                                    (undated lyric, Sandy Wilson archive)

It was Ivor Novello who coined the phrase 'Gay's the Word'[6] as the title of his last musical in 1951, as Wilson knew full well as an admirer and biographer of Novello. Wilson's lyric articulates a resentment at the derogatory terms used for gay men, but also a wistfulness for a time at which 'gay' was a coded word, which must have resonated with the generation of men who attended the revues for which this lyric was written.[7]

Wilson's life appears to follow a conventional narrative of the successful songwriter; public school, Oxford, a move to London and a hit musical in 1954, but his life was less straightforward than his autobiography or that life history would suggest. There is little in Sandy Wilson's archive about his childhood or schooldays, the only item from that period is a scrapbook with pasted images of New York, Paris and Hollywood stars (suggesting his youthful aspirations). There are very few letters from his immediate family; Wilson's archiving begins from the collection of programmes from productions he was involved in, starting with the revues he scored at Oxford. The only information available about his childhood is from his 1975 autobiography, which ends with the production of *The Boy Friend*, and gives an unapologetically show-business and resolutely optimistic account of his life. The narrative is focussed on his theatrical career; it neatly glosses over any personal details, eschews anything painful and alludes only very tangentially to his relationships with men.

Wilson seems to have had a relatively untroubled time at public school, at university and in the army, as he blithely recounts in the autobiography. His progress, through public school at Harrow to Oriel College, Oxford, would appear to be one of privilege, but it is clear that his access to education was a struggle for him and for his family; his early childhood was troubled by family tensions and constant house moves brought on by the Depression. Like his heroes, Coward and Novello, Wilson was not born into wealth, but had to make his own way; he may have possessed family connections and cultural capital, but there was not enough financial capital to support his family's ambitions.

The only son in a family of three sisters (to whom he remained close throughout his life) Wilson was born Alexander Galbraith Wilson in 1924, to a genteelly impoverished family, with the aspiration, but not the wealth, to send him to public school. Wilson's father came from a Scots family who had made money in woollen mills, and had himself been to Harrow, 'where he distinguished himself in games and was made captain of the school football team' (Wilson, 1975a, p. 11). George Wilson was sent, as befitted the youngest son of a gentleman of the period, to India, where he worked for a shipping company and where he met Wilson's mother, Elsie Humphrey. The family fortune dwindled during the Depression, as did that of the shipping company, and the family finances, and Wilson's parents' marriage, were clearly strained. The family returned to Britain to an aunt's house in Stirling, then moved to Manchester, to Sale in Cheshire (where Wilson was born), and eventually to London.

Wilson's childhood reminiscences are dominated by his visits to the pantomime and to films. On moving to London, the young Wilson mapped the city through its theatres and cinemas:

Down St Martin's Lane . . . was the Duke of York's, and, opposite it the
Coliseum. Round the corner and . . . there was the Garrick. Across
the road to Leicester Square . . . and beyond lay Piccadilly Circus and
Shaftesbury Avenue with another whole row of theatres to be explored.
By the time I was ten I knew my way all round the West End and could
reel off exactly what was on at each theatre and cinema and who was in
it. (Wilson, 1975a, p. 32)

Although clearly happy in London, Wilson was sent, under the auspices of a
family friend, to Elstree preparatory school to be 'groomed' for the Harrow
scholarship, the only way in which he could follow his father to public school:
'There was a place waiting for me at the Headmaster's House, Harrow. But
it was rapidly becoming obvious that I could only take it up if I . . . won a
scholarship and a substantial one at that' (Wilson, 1975a, p. 33). At Elstree
there is a faint suggestion of homoerotic feelings as he recounts his daydream
of rescuing 'my current hero . . . a fair-haired boy in an upper form' (Wilson,
1975a, p. 35), but his most significant friendship is with another boy, Charles
(who remained a friend for the rest of their lives, and who is interviewed for
Wilson's autobiography). Charles shares Wilson's passion for cinema, together
they spend their holidays at the cinema and theatre, read film magazines and
set up a Drama Society at the school. In a passage which rather over neatly
maps on to the history of *The Boy Friend*, Wilson fantasizes about becoming a
writer of musicals: 'my favourite fantasy was set in the future. . . . I wrote and
composed a musical show which was a hit in the West End and then went to
Broadway' (Wilson, 1975a, p. 36).

The graft and ambition that it must have taken to take the entrance
examination, and his eventual success at winning a Harrow scholarship are
underplayed in the autobiography; he briskly notes only: 'I was a scholarship
boy, I had worked extremely hard to get there, and it was what my family
wanted for me, so that was that' (Wilson, 1975a, p. 54). Instead, Wilson lists
all the plays and films that he and Charles went to together, some among
them rather improbably adult for boys of prep school age. This period in
Wilson's life is written with an eye to his later status as a man of the theatre;
he is keen to demonstrate his immersion in popular theatre, music and film.
Wilson's childhood, by his own account, is largely framed by the glamour
of theatre and cinema, which overshadows everything, including his father's
serious illness and his mother's fragile health. Wilson senior's death and
funeral takes up a paragraph, rather less than the space he devotes to his
reading of the coverage of West End Theatre in *Vogue* and *Life* magazines.

Once at Harrow, Wilson joins the Film Society, avoids football (he does
not follow his father as captain of the football team) and learns to play the

piano. He reads Noël Coward's autobiography, and clearly sees him as a role model for his future career: 'I was amazed and envious to read how early he had started his career and how soon he had been successful . . . . He acted, wrote plays, composed songs – all the things I wanted to do. If I was to follow in his footsteps, there was no time to be lost!' (Wilson, 1975a, p. 56). His theatre-going during the school holidays extended to attending revues, among them one with Joan Sterndale Bennett and Vida Hope,[8] who were both stalwart performers at the Players' Theatre Club; he also sees Hermione Gingold,[9] for whom he would later write his first revue songs. He attends the Late Joys at the Players' Theatre (which would become the producing venue for his greatest success, *The Boy Friend*), where he feels 'peerlessly adult' in his first dinner jacket (Wilson, 1975a, p. 59).

In 1938, among the lists of plays and films, there is some recognition that global politics would encroach on Wilson's enclosed world: 'back in 1938, the current decade was having its troubles' (Wilson, 1975a, p. 56), as Wilson grudgingly acknowledges the impending war that would shape his entire generation. The 'phony war', months before the outbreak of fighting in the Second World War between September 1939 and May 1940, sounds the first alarm: 'we were all of us thoroughly scared' (Wilson, 1975a, p. 57). This does not, however, impinge on Wilson's playgoing or interest in the theatre; he begins to write his own plays, and produces his own version of *Frankenstein* at Harrow. With the award of another scholarship he takes up piano lessons and begins to write his own songs. The beginning of the air-raids is marked, for Wilson, by the closure of his beloved theatres and cinemas, and he does take note when his charity production is interrupted by the sound of fighter planes and distant gunfire (Wilson, 1975a, p. 67).

Wilson's progress throughout the war is erratic, unmarked by heroism, and his experience is dealt with briskly and briefly in the autobiography: 'I spent three years in uniform and, while there were periods of discomfort and depression, on the whole I disliked it much less than I expected' (Wilson, 1975a, p. 77). His first response to the war effort is to take up the War Office's appeal to the public schools for students to learn Chinese and Japanese for the Far East campaign. Based at the School of Oriental and African Studies in central London, he takes advantage of its proximity to the West End and spends much of the time going to the theatre and cinema. Focussing on producing a revue rather than his studies, he fails to learn any Japanese, and is permitted to leave. On being called up to the army he is sent for military training, and requests to be a front line cook, but his Harrow education means that he is assigned to the Royal Army Ordnance Corps as a clerk, a post which consists largely of filing.

Having never before travelled beyond Paris, Wilson is sent to Egypt and then to Iraq, where his filing duties continue. He meets men from outside his own public school-educated milieu, which convinces him to become, for the first time and from then on, a Labour voter. While in the army he composes music, plays the piano in the mess, edits a newspaper for the base, which includes his own caricatures of 'Camp Characters' ('camp' ostensibly referring to the army base) (Wilson 1975a, p. 94). The army was, for many of Wilson's generation, a time which afforded men the experience of performing, and, with the absence of women in most army units, often performing in drag. Spike Milligan, Frankie Howerd and Kenneth Williams were among the many British comedians whose first experience of performance was in the Armed Services. According to Matt Cook, drag was an integral part of wartime entertainment for all male troops; he describes drag as 'a staple of troop entertainment . . . . In these shows, performers were often obviously male, but there were also sometimes more genuine attempts to pass as female . . . . Drag in the forces did not need to compromise the manliness and presumed "normality" of those involved' (Cook, 2007, p. 148). Wilson's theatrical Aunt Virginia does open up an opportunity for him to be transferred to ENSA (Entertainments National Service Association), but Wilson's clerical duties are deemed to be so important to the war effort that he is not permitted to take this up.

Wilson's description in the autobiography of his experience of wartime service is one largely of tedium. This is echoed in the first version of an unpublished novel in which Wilson's protagonist, Colin Holt (clearly a thinly disguised version of Wilson himself), reflects on the experience of army life:

> It had represented for him a period of bored drudgery which he had enjoyed thinking were the best years of his life. As soon as his release came through, a few days before the Oxford term started, he had felt a sense of emancipation, of glorious independence. (*Oxford's Not What it Used to Be*, first version, unpublished, undated manuscript, p. 1, Sandy Wilson archive)

Wilson had failed his first scholarship examination to Oxford (the only way he could attend was with a scholarship) but was later awarded a School Scholarship. His new-found democratic spirit would not allow him to take the exemption from war service accorded to students, and he finally went up to Oxford as an ex-service undergraduate at the end of the war. His autobiographical account of arriving at Oxford echoes the 'glorious independence' that Colin expresses in the novel:

> For the first time in my life I felt no responsibility to anyone or anything but myself. Until then I had done everything because it was expected

of me – by the family, by the various schools I had beer   ∞
Army; now I suddenly discovered that I need please nobo
(Wilson, 1975a, p. 101)

Unstated, but implicit, is that the freedom Oxford offered was in part a sexual freedom. Oxford at the time was, like a male public school, an overwhelmingly male world.[10] O'Connor here describes an Oxford generation before Wilson, but, bolstered by images of Evelyn Waugh's 1945 *Brideshead Revisited*, Oxford retained a sensibility of homoeroticism in the post-war period:

> Oxford in the 1930s was almost entirely a society of men. Of 1,750 undergraduates only 250 were women. Many freshman undergraduates, like Rattigan, had progressed straight to university from public schools . . . . Homosexuality, or the appearance of it, was part of the Oxford aesthetic culture. (O'Connor, pp. 130–1)

Robert Hewison has pointed to the powerful influence of *Brideshead Revisited* on a generation of ex-servicemen from the Second World War, of whom Sandy Wilson was one:

> The universities were especially crowded immediately after the war because of the large numbers of ex-service personnel. . . . It was during this period . . . that Evelyn Waugh's nostalgic evocation of a lost, sybaritic, 1920s Oxford had its most poignant, and pernicious effect . . . succeeding generations of undergraduates have been misled into trying to recover a lost and probably never-existent Eden, oblivious of the social values it represented. (Hewison, 1981, p. 46)

The period of the 1920s is the setting for *The Boy Friend* and also for the first book of *Brideshead Revisited*, in which Charles Ryder and Sebastian Flyte meet as students at Oxford. Titled 'Et in Arcadia ego' the sequence represents a lost time of youthful, homoerotic love, before the advent of family, marriage, Catholicism, addiction and divorce later in the novel. Sandy Wilson was already nostalgic for that 'lost sybaritic' Oxford while he was himself a student there; his unpublished novels are both titled *Oxford's Not What It Used to Be* (this was also the title of a song he wrote for an Oxford student revue) and wistfully invokes an imagined Oxford. Oxford is, in Wilson's autobiography and in his unpublished novels, a utopian world, dominated by the theatre and a glamour that seemed to promise an optimistic post-war future. Colin's first night at Oxford seems full of potential and possibilities : 'he had lain awake in his small bedroom in St. Jeremy's college and thought of the future – a free, energetic future full of ambitions attained and dreams realised' (*Oxford's Not What it Used to Be*, first version, unpublished, undated manuscript, p. 1, Sandy Wilson archive).

Like Rattigan, Wilson had progressed straight from an all-male public school (in both cases, Harrow) to an all-male Oxford college, but he had a wide range of friendships. It is to his credit that Wilson clearly developed close friendships with the few women undergraduates then at Oxford, as is clear from letters that continued until the end of his life. There is an episode in both versions of his unpublished novel in which a woman friend becomes pregnant before finals and Wilson's alter ego gallantly proposes, an incident which is confirmed as true in private letters. Wilson kept this real episode out of his autobiography, much to the relief of the woman concerned; she has since married, her son is at boarding school and unaware of his history and she remains touched by his kindness and discretion (unsigned, undated letter, 1975, Sandy Wilson archive). Julian Slade writes to Sandy Wilson in 1989 after a party, at which he had met Wilson's Oxford friends of both genders: '. . . enjoyed your Oxford chums and hearing about those revues which I'd love to have seen' (letter from Julian Slade, 1989, Sandy Wilson archive).

Those revues were staged by the Oxford University Experimental Theatre Club (ETC), which was at the centre of Wilson's experience of university and the focus of his friendship group; he was also a member of the Oxford University Dramatic Society (OUDS), where he hung out in the coffee bar with the 'University's Theatrical Clique' (Wilson, 1975a, p. 107). Terence Rattigan and George Devine, the first director of the English Stage Company, were of a previous Oxford generation who had been involved in OUDS. Many of those Wilson met through OUDS and the ETC would remain friends for life, some he would later encounter in his professional career. Undergraduate members of the ETC of Wilson's generation included those who would go on to make careers in revue (Donald Swann, later of Flanders and Swann, and Wilson himself), and those who would be central to the Royal Court Theatre's reputation for avant-garde drama (Tony Richardson, John Schlesinger, Lindsay Anderson and Kenneth Tynan).

A note in the programme for the revue *Oxford Circus* at the Oxford Playhouse in 1948 describes the Theatre Club: 'The Oxford University Experimental Theatre Club was founded in 1937 in order to produce plays of an unusual and non-commercial nature. Its senior members are Nevill Coghill and Robert Levens' (*Oxford Circus* programme, Playhouse Theatre Oxford, 1948). The ETC was clearly something of a haven for gay men, if Wilson is reluctant to publicly acknowledge that; in his autobiography Wilson remembers 'most of us were still bound by old-fashioned taboos where sex was concerned' (Wilson, 1975a, p. 113). Nonetheless, many of the members of Wilson's generation would later become prominent gay figures, among them John Schlesinger, Peter Wildeblood and Tony Richardson. Nevill Coghill, the 'senior member' of the ETC, was Professor of Rhetoric and a Chaucer and Shakespeare scholar; while he had married and fathered a child, he later separated from his wife and led a 'quietly homosexual life' in his Oxford rooms (see Price, p. 128). Coghill had directed Shakespearean productions for OUDS, and developed the ETC as 'a more adventurous group than the OUDS, and also one that gave women equal opportunities' (Carpenter, p. 145).

While Wilson was largely involved in revue at Oxford, it was his contemporary Kenneth Tynan, who was more concerned with 'serious' theatre, producing Maxwell Anderson's 'tragic' verse drama, *Winterset*, under the auspices of ETC in 1948, with Wilson appearing in a small part. Wilson writes to Kathleen, Tynan's widow, sometime in the 1980s, of his rivalry with Tynan at Oxford: 'Another reason why we were not too close at Oxford may have been that we were, in a sense, rivals for the limelight. By the mid-1950s, when he had married Elaine, we had both "made it" – but in quite different fields' (undated letter, Sandy Wilson archive). A 1991 letter from Kathleen Tynan, thanking Wilson for his condolences on Tynan's death, makes it clear that it was an important friendship: 'Kenneth's friendship with you gave him much pleasure and delight. We often played "The Boy Friend"; and "Divorce Me Darling"' (Letter from Kathleen Tynan, 29 July 1991, Sandy Wilson archive). It is the first meeting with Tynan that introduces Wilson to the term 'queer', although he had very likely encountered it in the army he claims he did not know what it meant as a student. His friend Heather asks his opinion of Tynan, to which Wilson responds: '"He's very *queer* isn't he?" (Wilson's emphasis) . . . Then she said "Do you know what queer means?", and I said "No". I was that innocent' (Wilson 1975a, p. 109).

A line in Wilson's unpublished novel suggests the level of performativity that he and his contemporaries felt obliged to enact while at Oxford; one of the protagonist's woman friends says: 'It's only an act. We all have to put on acts up here, otherwise no-one would take any notice of us, you know' (*Oxford's Not What It Used to Be*, first version, undated manuscript, p. 40, Sandy Wilson archive). Nonetheless, Wilson had a successful time at Oxford, if not academically (he emerged with a third-class degree), then socially and professionally; theatre was at the centre of his student experience and ambition. He was crowned an *Isis* (the Oxford student newspaper) 'idol' in 1947 and became secretary of ETC. In a talk given to the Theatre Club of which he had once been secretary, Wilson acknowledged the advantages that being at Oxford and Cambridge conferred on theatrically ambitious students, noting that West End producers took an interest in what Oxbridge student theatre groups were doing: 'You stand a better chance of having your musical seen by a management if you stage it right here in Oxford. Tom Arnold[11] or Jack Hylton[12] seem quite glad to jump into their Daimlers and roll off to a University town' (talk to the ETC, 5 May 1955, Sandy Wilson archive). The ETC productions, and Wilson, had attracted attention from professional producers while he was still a student; Peter King, a fellow student, acted as the business manager for the revue *Oxford Circus* which was produced at the professional theatre, the Oxford Playhouse, in 1947. *Oxford Circus* featured Peter Wildebood, Donald Swann, Kenneth Tynan and Lindsay Anderson among 'Les Boys' of the cast, with Wilson and Donald Swann accompanying on the piano. King later organized for Wilson to put on a show based on material done for the ETC at the Playhouse theatre in London for one night.

Despite the nostalgic glow that Oxford represents in Wilson's novels and autobiography, he leaves Oxford in 1948 after two years, with little regret: 'I was not particularly afraid of the future, in fact I was eager to get going, to move on' (Wilson, 1975a, p. 126). He was multi-talented; not only did he write both the libretto and the music for musicals and revues, he could also draw beautifully; at school he had taken classes at the Art School, and briefly considered becoming a fashion artist (Wilson, 1975a, p. 54). His witty and charming illustrations accompany the first published volume of the play text of *The Boy Friend*. Wilson arrived in London armed with his degree from Oxford, a reputation as a writer and composer from his work in the ETC revues, with experience of acting and assisting in university productions and with an address book full of contacts. On the advice of the impresario Bronson Albery,[13] after an introduction from his Aunt Virginia, Wilson undertook a course in Production at the Old Vic. There he learned stage craft, lighting, carpentry and directed a revue. Like Coward and Novello, Wilson was reared in musical theatre and revue; he had spent his childhood and teenage years attending shows in the West End, going on to produce and write his own at Harrow and at Oxford.

In his *Good Time Guide to London* Aldor knowingly refers to the sophistication of the audience for revue, and to the frissons that the form offered:

> Sit back, cigarettes glowing in jewelled holders. . . . A little French song – you understand the 'double entendre'? *Of course.* A risqué joke, a shiver of wild delight. A smile that means – *you* know – but everything. A clamorous cleavage from the States; a dusky, almost *completely* naked dancing girl; a little touch of ballet: a soufflé of charm – sophisticated, rare, created for the gourmet, the connoisseur. (Aldor, p. 271)

Revue theatres were spaces that resisted the conventions of conformist 1950s culture, as Aldor implicitly suggests: 'If you want to eat late, to drink the morning in, to dance, you have to move into a world of its own, a "little London" hedged about by convention, fashion, and laws made by a patronising, conformist minded government' (Aldor, p. 274). Small theatres were an intrinsic part of that 'little London', and, as private clubs, could evade the edicts of the Lord Chamberlain and, to an extent, protect their clientele. Wilson refers in his autobiography to the late 'blossoming' of revue in London in the 1950s and the little theatres that staged it (among them the Players' Theatre Club); it was in those intimate revues that he made a 'slender but adequate living' (Wilson 1975a, p. 130) for the next five years. As Wright explains, Wilson's skills were well suited to the revue form: 'The originality of his ideas, the cleanliness of his lyrics and simplicity of his music made him a natural for revue material when revue was about to embark on the last phase of its golden age' (Wright, 2010, p. 72). Wilson's time in Oxford and his arrival in London coincided with that 'golden age'.

Laurier (Laurie) Lister, the revue producer, and Hermione Gingold had both attended the one night staging of *Oxford Circus* at the Playhouse theatre in London. Lister was about to produce *Oranges and Lemons* in 1948 at the Lyric Theatre, Hammersmith, and invited Wilson to contribute material. *Oranges and Lemons* saw the first appearance in revue of Michael Flanders and Donald Swann. Swann had been a fellow member of the ETC and part of *Oxford Circus*; Flanders and Swann were to keep the revue format going through the late 1950s and into the 1960s with their successful shows, *At the Drop of the Hat* (1957) and *At the Drop of Another Hat* (1963), both of which had an extended life as recordings. Gingold invited Wilson to write a song for a revue which she had devised, *Slings and Arrows*, in 1949 at the Comedy Theatre. A woman friend who is cast in the show also asked Wilson to write a song for her, 'Thanks Mr Rank', another friend auditioned for the revue with one of Wilson's songs, 'Taken as Red', and all three are included. For Gingold, Wilson wrote 'Come for a bathe at Brighton' which she sang with a chorus of bathing boys (a precedent for 'Sur le Plage' in *The Boy Friend*). With three songs in a successful West End show with an established star, and with *Oranges and Lemons* on tour before coming to the West End at the Globe theatre, Wilson is 'established, albeit precariously, as a revue lyricist and writing had become a full-time occupation' (Wilson, 1975a, p. 136).

Wilson moved beyond revue to make his debut in musical plays as the lyricist of *Caprice* (1950), an adaptation of a pre-war play with music by his friend Geoffrey Wright, although the production never went beyond Birmingham on its try out tour. The Watergate Theatre was another 'tiny' independent theatre, very close to the Players' Theatre in Charing Cross,

Wilson's Oxford friends Wildeblood and Tynan were both involved with the Watergate, with Tynan as a director. The Watergate staged late-night revues, and Wilson wrote his first revue as a sole author for them, *See You Later* in 1951, which had another Oxford contemporary, Donald Swann, as accompanist and featured Dulcie Gray as a gardening Kate Greenaway character tending her lethally poisonous plants, in the song 'Garden Girl'. The show was well reviewed and Wilson now felt his career to be less precarious: 'In a small way, I appeared to have arrived, and for the first time I could believe that my future in the theatre might be assured' (Wilson 1975a, p. 156). *See You Later* was followed by a sequel, *See You Again* in 1952. It was at the Watergate that Wilson first encountered the work of Ronald Firbank, with the production of *The Princess Zoubaroff* in 1951; Wilson would go on to adapt Firbank's *Valmouth* as a musical in 1958. It was also during the run of *See You Later* that a woman friend who had appeared in a sketch styled on the 1920s first floated the idea of an entire show set in the period and suggested it to the Players' Theatre. That show would become *The Boy Friend*, the production which was to secure Wilson's reputation and status in musical theatre.

The programme for the Wyndham's Theatre production of *The Boy Friend*, the West End theatre to which it transferred from the Players' in 1954, carried a biography of Sandy Wilson which pointed to his youthful successes:

> Sandy Wilson: 33-year-old author composer and lyricist who emerged as an outstanding theatre personality with 'The Boy Friend'. Educated at Harrow and Oxford, he has written many sketches and numbers which have been performed in revues in the West End and out of London his own shows for which he has written music, book and lyrics are 'See You Later', 1953 (at the Edinburgh Festival and at the Watergate Theatre, London); the second edition, 'See You Again' and 'The Buccaneer' at the Lyric Hammersmith. 'The Boy Friend' was a smash hit at the Players' Theatre, Embassy and Wyndham's and revealed its creator as one of the most versatile newcomers to the London stage for many a long year. (Wyndham's programme, 1954)

Wilson may have been versatile, but he was never to repeat the success of *The Boy Friend*. *The Boy Friend* seemed to herald a future for Wilson as a West End success and to be the culmination of his boyhood dream of emulating Noël Coward as a writer and composer. Wilson was celebrated as 'Personality of the Month' in *Plays and Players* in 1954, the year of *The Boy Friend*'s transfer; he was acclaimed at the time as a boy wonder, the rightful successor to Noël Coward, as a contemporary review made clear: 'Wilson may well be the Coward of the present generation, for he not only composes music and writes his own scripts, but acts, produces, has his own cabaret act. . . . At the moment there are no writers of musicals of Wilson's age (29) to compete with him' (quoted in Wright, 2010, p. 73). However, as Wright points out: 'the British audience was in no mood to welcome a new Coward, having grown a little tired of the old one' (Wright, 2010, p. 73). Coward was no longer in the ascendancy of West End theatre, by 1955 he was performing cabaret in Las Vegas, a parody of the sophisticated playwright and songwriter he had once been.

Wilson's 'cabaret act' was performed with the Australian singer Jon Rose who was his partner throughout the period of *The Boy Friend*. Rose first makes an appearance in Wilson's autobiography in 1952, in which he is described as a friend and flat mate, although a more significant (and tempestuous) relationship is hinted at:

> I decided that I would have to find someone to share the flat with me, partly because I needed help with the expenses, but mostly because I hated living alone . . . in the end I asked a friend of mine, Jon Rose, who was living in a minute bed-sitter in Bayswater to move in. Jon was Australian and a singer. . . . He was volatile and articulate – at times excessively so – and possessed of a personality with [*sic*] either charmed people into the ground or sent them screaming out of the room. We had a close and stormy friendship which lasted for several years, and no account of the following events would be complete or honest if Jon's part in them were omitted. (Wilson, 1975a, p. 181)

Wilson is not entirely 'complete or honest' in his account of their relationship; although by 1975 homosexuality was no longer criminal for men over the age of twenty-one, he was not prepared to acknowledge his sexuality in print. An unpublished chapter of the autobiography is (very slightly) less circumspect about the relationship with Rose, only in that Rose is regularly woven into accounts of domestic and travel arrangements. There is however no reference at all in either the published autobiography or in the unpublished chapter to the significant relationship that Wilson was in at the time of writing, with Chak Yui, whom Wilson had met in Hong Kong in 1970 and which would last until the end of Wilson's life.

The relationship with Rose was clearly unbalanced from its beginning; Wilson already had written for the West End theatre and the production of *The Boy Friend* was lined up with the Players' Theatre, while Rose's singing career was failing to ignite; as Wilson describes it:

At the time of his moving in Jon's singing career seemed to have come temporarily to a halt and he was making a precarious living at other occupations such as modelling for art students and working on the night shift in Walls' Ice Cream factory, a useful, if unpleasant, job, for out-of-work actors at the time. (Wilson, 1975a, p. 181)

Once *The Boy Friend* had transferred to the Wyndham's Theatre, Wilson set up a limited company with Rose and he was, according to Wilson's unpublished chapter, instrumental in discussions about several projects with Wilson. In 1957, they jointly published *Who's Who for Beginners*, a parodic collection of 'twenty-six Notable People with accompanying photographs' (Wilson and Rose, p. 5), with words by Wilson and photographs by Rose. *Who's Who for Beginners* campily displays their cultural capital and theatrical knowledge. The featured characters are drawn from fashionable contemporary culture: 'they represent, we feel, the topnotch in practically every sphere of life today: literature, art, religion, theatre, cinema, politics, interior decorating' (Wilson and Rose, p. 5). While ostensibly puncturing pretension and pomposity, the choice of figures does demonstrate a distinct unease with the contemporary culture of the 1950s. There is a clear anxiety about modernity, the earnest realism of contemporary film and theatre comes in for particular scorn. The entry for the 'Vaunts' expresses a nostalgia for a golden age of celebrity actors (the Vaunts are recognizably a composite of Laurence Olivier and Vivien Leigh and of Michael Redgrave and Rachel Kempson): 'a married theatrical dynasty . . . they do at least bring to the London stage the leavening of grace and gentility which such American imports as *A View from the Bridge* and *A Hatful of Rain*[14] have made us tend to ignore or even forget' (Wilson and Rose, p. 5). 'Dame Winifred Dynasty' is a Shakespearean actor (posed by a man in drag, possibly Rose himself) who is a combination of Peggy Ashcroft and Dame Edith Evans. There is a 'Herbert Hodson', a clear reference to Harold Hobson, then the *Sunday Times* critic, who was notorious for reviewing plays in Paris rather than in London.

Published one year after *Look Back in Anger*, *Who's Who for Beginners* demonstrates a particularly sharp disdain for the actors, writers, critics and producers who belonged to the new generation of angry young men. The character of 'Reg Glupton' is an amalgam of any number of angry young men as both a playwright and novelist, but he bears most resemblance to Colin Wilson: 'a new and original talent' who 'confidently outlines the pattern of self-destruction which is in store for our civilization' (Wilson and Rose, p. 23). Despite a disingenuous disclaimer in the form of an erratum at the end of the book, every one of the characters is similarly identifiable as a composite figure of the 1950s cultural world: 'We have discovered at the last moment that none of the characters portrayed in this book actually exists, and therefore any resemblance between them and anybody living or dead is, of course, purely coincidental' (Wilson and Rose, p. 34). Although itself wilfully apolitical, the vignettes do show traces of the contemporary political issues with which writers such as Cyril Connolly (who makes an appearance as Cecil Donnelly) were concerned; the Suez crisis, nuclear war, Middle Eastern corruption and international finance. Agamemnon Xenophobiakis is a thinly disguised Aristotle Onassis: 'the diminutive financial magician from Macedonia . . . he is now probably the richest man in the world . . . looking for fresh worlds to conquer, and yet more ways of making money' (Wilson and Rose, p. 56). Despite the professed sophistication of *Who's Who for Beginners* its racial and gender politics are distinctly dubious; there is an uneasy satirical portrait of an Indian freedom fighter, Madame Shoddi Rottaji (posed by a man in a sari), who stays at Claridges when in London but 'has not forgotten her humble upbringing among the masses of her beloved India' (Wilson and Rose, p. 4). Doctor Foggarty 'the Principal of St Ethelrea's College, Oxford', is lampooned as a masculine blue stocking, her picture posed by a man in drag (again, possibly Rose).

One entry, Nigel Paddock, is closely modelled on Wilson himself: 'a young Oxbridge graduate . . . he has given the West End theatre the wistful, nostalgic freshness of his long-running little masterpiece *The Friendly Days*' (Wilson and Rose, p. 37), a fair description of *The Boy Friend*, which was then still running in the West End. As a company director, Rose accompanied Wilson to New York for the American production and supported him through the experience of bullying American producers described in the autobiography, but he features largely as a travelling companion and loyal colleague. By 1955, newspaper reports of Wilson's projected plans did refer to Rose as Wilson's 'partner'. Rose was Wilson's business partner at the time, but newspaper reports in May of that year describe Wilson's stay in hospital with broken ribs and the attendance of his partner; in that context the term 'partner' does acquire a domestic edge. It is not clear how Wilson sustained his injuries (undated clippings, Sandy Wilson's scrapbook). An *Evening Standard* report of Wilson's recuperative holiday to Greece does not reference Rose in either the report or the accompanying photograph, showing Wilson instead with two women friends (*Evening Standard*, 16 May 1955, Sandy Wilson archive). By 1956, there were clear strains in the relationship, despite their joint publication of *Who's Who for Beginners*. As they prepare to move in to a house in Hampstead (a long cherished project), Wilson takes up an offer to direct *The Boy Friend* in South Africa and acknowledges: 'We had been closely involved over everything for quite a long time now, and there were obvious signs that a spell apart would do us no harm at all' (unpublished autobiographical chapter, p. 329, Sandy Wilson archive).

Wilson was equivocal about his relationship status in press interviews after the success of *The Boy Friend* (unsurprisingly, given that homosexual acts between men were criminalized at the time), but, to his credit, never claimed a female partner or fiancée (although he had many women friends who might well have been prepared to stand in as such). Newspaper interviews tended to be similarly coy in their reporting of Wilson's relationship status; a 1955 interview with the *Evening Standard* asks if Wilson is engaged to which he responds: '"Not officially". "unofficially?" Wilson smiles a mysterious smile and says he'd rather not say anything about that' (*Evening Standard*, 2 September 1955). A 1956 article in the *Daily Herald* (17 February 1956, Sandy Wilson archive) was headlined 'The Boy Friend's girl friend is called Sylvia' – only to reveal that Sylvia is the name of Wilson's cat. In the unpublished chapter of his autobiography Wilson grumpily, but with some justification, refers to press intrusion into his relationships:

> The Press, by and large, were kind to me, and I only jibbed at their insistent curiosity about my finances and my private life; I considered that the public should judge me only by my work, and what I was earning and who I went to bed with was my own affair. This sometimes led reporters to describe me as 'sullen' or 'uncommunicative'; in return I would now describe them as 'nosy' and 'impertinent'. (unpublished autobiographical chapter, p. 327, Sandy Wilson archive)

Many of Wilson's friends were disapproving of the relationship with Jon Rose, not because it was a same-sex relationship, but because they found Rose difficult. Christopher Isherwood recalls in his diaries: 'The Australian boyfriend of Sandy Wilson . . . I must admit he was hard to take' (Isherwood, 1996, p. 824). A 1975 letter to Wilson from 'Lis' (Elisabeth Harris, a friend from Oxford) suggests that many of Wilson's closest friends shared that opinion of Jon Rose, and goes on to explain that Rose ruined one of her parties by chasing a (married) male guest: 'Specifically, what led to <u>me</u> making less effort to see <u>you</u> – was Jon Rose. . . . I didn't invite you home because of Jon. The Godley's (Michael and Heather)[15], bless them, put up with Jon for your sake' (letter from Elisabeth Harris to Sandy Wilson, 11 November 1975, Sandy Wilson archive). By 1975, the relationship with Chak Yui was clearly settled; friends and family appear to have been very comfortable with his final partner, almost always including 'Chak' in their greetings and best wishes and in invitations (which was not the case in letters dating from the relationship with Rose). An undated interview with Wilson refers to a 'friend': 'He [Wilson] doesn't do a great deal of cooking. The friend who shares the house excels at that' (undated clipping, Sandy Wilson archive).

This 'friend' must have been Chak, who, from the testimony of the letters, was a wonderful cook.

By 1956, although *The Boy Friend* was still going strong in its West End production, there was a marked shift in theatre away from the gentle camp aesthetic of *Salad Days* and *The Boy Friend* towards a new seriousness in drama, as Wilson and Rose had so scathingly noted in *Who's Who for Beginners*. As Snelson puts it: 'The inoffensive styles of Slade and Wilson in their first big successes contrasted with the increasingly serious intent of other contemporary theatre works' (Snelson, p. 143). Of course, 1956 marks the date of *Look Back in Anger* at the Royal Court, one of those works 'with serious intent'. In its use of regional accents, working-class characters and gritty sets, *Look Back in Anger* was a stark contrast with the escapism, privileged settings and characters of *Salad Days* and *The Boy Friend*. Osborne's writing offered a foregrounding not only of class but also of an assertive masculinity; it represented a rejection of camp and of perceived effeminacy. Dan Rebellato has rightly argued that there is in theatre history a false opposition between the Royal Court as a new avant-garde and the glamorous appeal of West End productions such as those of Binkie Beaumont, the producer for Coward and Novello. Sandy Wilson's connections and career demonstrate quite how false that opposition is. While a great admirer of Coward and Novello, and a relish for Beaumont's West End productions, Wilson also had strong connections with the Royal Court, and with the new wave of theatre. He knew many of the key figures at the English Stage Company from his time at Oxford, and it was the Royal Court who invited him to write for them after the success of *The Boy Friend*. He had been close to Kenneth Tynan, Tony Richardson and John Schlesinger at Oxford, George Devine, director of the English Stage Company, was a mentor at the Old Vic Theatre School. Wilson became friends with John Osborne, even suggesting that they collaborate on a musical together, as he recollected in 1975:

> One evening at a party I met John Osborne who was then living with his leading lady from LOOK BACK IN ANGER, Mary Ure, whom he later married. I took to them both at once and found John, surprisingly, a gentle and lovable character. I wrote to him the next day and suggested that we collaborate on a modern musical. He responded enthusiastically and we became good friends, although, when he did write a musical, it was on his own, and, for all sorts of reasons, a disaster. (unpublished autobiographical chapter, p. 328, Sandy Wilson archive)

Wilson also worked with those who would later be hailed as the vanguard of the 'satire boom'. Wilson contributed music to a revue, *Pieces of Eight*, in 1959, which was largely written by Peter Cook, with sketches by Harold Pinter and produced at the Apollo theatre in the West End. Kenneth Williams (who would later appear in *The Buccaneer*) and Fenella Fielding (who would later become a star in *Valmouth*) both performed in it. After *The Boy Friend* Wilson continued to contribute to West End revues and musical theatre, he wrote the musical numbers for Robert Tonitch's *Call It Love* in 1960, which only ran for five performances at the Wyndham's Theatre in 1960. In 1969 he wrote the score for *As Dorothy Parker Once Said*, based on her work, performed at the Palace Theatre Watford by Libby Morris, and wrote songs for television and radio; he contributed to the 1960 BBC *Voices in the Air* alongside his fellow ETC student Donald Swann (performing with Michael Flanders), a radio programme which included sketches written by Pinter and the absurdist playwright N. F. Simpson. Ned Sherrin recalls Wilson writing for *That Was the Week That Was* (Sherrin, 2005, p. 126); Wilson was actively engaged in new modes of cabaret and theatre. *Pieces of Eight* represented a bridge, in its writers and cast, between the 'intimate' revues of the early 1950s and the satire of *Beyond the Fringe* in 1960. Wilson is quietly scathing about *Beyond the Fringe* in his autobiography pointing out with some justification that it was yet another form of 'intimate review' (Wilson, 1975a, p. 129). Peter Cook, Jonathan Miller, Alan Bennett and Dudley Moore had all, like Sandy Wilson, learned their craft and were given the opportunity to perform at Oxford and Cambridge universities.

Wilson contacted many of his Oxford contemporaries and those from the casts of his revues and *The Boy Friend* in his research for his autobiography; his notebooks punctiliously mark not only that he contacted the key figures but also that he arranged meetings with them. The publication of the autobiography brought a rash of admiring letters, from fans, those who had been in or directed productions of *The Boy Friend* across the world, theatre friends, army friends and friends from Oxford. Wilson was a prolific letter writer, with a wide range of correspondents (all carefully kept and now housed in his archive at the Harry Ransom Center). His circle was wide and included contemporary writers, critics and intellectuals, as well as theatrical luminaries. His archives are full of thank-you letters and cards from actors and friends thanking him for his thoughtfulness and kind letters on the occasion of illness, bereavement or opening nights. He was clearly a good friend to his circle; a letter from Joan (there is no surname) in 1970 (to whom he had clearly lent money) is not atypical in its pleasure in Sandy Wilson's friendship:

> You know – you *always* give me such a boost. Just thru' being with you. I feel revitalised! You are *such* a mixture of gentleness and strength. Every time I see you I feel *human* and *better*. Your generosity moves me very deeply . . . my dear, funny, marvellous, human – Sandy! (letter from Joan? 1970, Sandy Wilson archive)

Wilson remained loyal to his friends throughout his life, keeping up with friends from school and university. Wilson's school friend Brian Stratton Ferrier is still writing to him in 1991, and speaks for many friends when he writes: 'you've always been a good and loyal friend to me, and I do appreciate it, Sandy' (letter from Brian Stratton Ferrier, 5 April 1988, Sandy Wilson archive). Dulcie Gray, who had sung Wilson's 'Garden Girl' in 1951, was still writing to him in 1996: 'What a long and happy (though we don't see each other often enough!) friendship we've had' (letter from Dulcie Gray, 1996, Sandy Wilson archive). He was generous to students asking about his work, to those mounting amateur and student productions of *The Boy Friend*, often sharing his address and contact details and replying to requests for appearances and signatures. As a friend wrote, thanking him for a party: 'Sandy is so generous with his friends' (letter from Annie W., May, 1989, Sandy Wilson archive).

If Wilson's musical tastes and aesthetic sensibilities remained conservative, his political sympathies were left wing, he subscribed to the *New* Statesman and was loyal to the Labour Party throughout his life. He contributed to Neil Kinnock's election fund in 1992 and was a sponsor for the Labour Party in 1990, 1992 and 2000. His instincts were liberal; he was a signatory to a letter sent in 1955 to the *Daily Express* which despaired of the official response to Princess Margaret's relationship with the divorced Group Captain Townsend and used the incident to mount an attack on 'Establishment' hypocrisy. Other eminent signatories included Lindsay Anderson, the dancer John Cranko, Gavin Lambert, Humphrey Lyttleton and Wolf Mankowitz. The writers argued that the refusal of the 'Establishment' to countenance a marriage between a princess and a divorced man

> brought to a head the unease which we and many members of the younger generation have been feeling about the administration of this country since the war. . . .
>
> First, it has revived the old issue of class distinctions in public life.
>
> Second, it has shown us 'The Establishment' in full cry, that pious group of potentates.
>
> Third, it has exposed the true extent of our national hypocrisy. . . .
>
> The alliance of a swollen bureaucracy and an elderly oligarchy seems to us, in fact, far more disagreeable than an alliance between a princess and a commoner. The events of the past week have come on top of much else that is needlessly inhibiting in our national life. (*Daily Express* clipping, 3 November 1955, Sandy Wilson archive)

Wilson was no admirer of the Conservative Party, although his upbringing had inclined him towards a conservative politics, and he was particularly withering about Margaret Thatcher. For the General Election of 1983, he wrote a song (based on a musical hall trope) which called for an end to Mrs Thatcher's premiership:

> She was only a grocer's daughter
> But she knows how to mind the shop. . . .
> But one fine June day
> The People will say
> 'Thanks, Dear, but you've gone far enough . . .
> So Goodbye, Maggie,
> We're saying Goodbye
> And we don't mean Au Revoir!'
>
> (General Election song, 1983, Sandy Wilson archive)

Jonathan Miller wrote to Wilson from the Old Vic in 1989 to share their despair at Thatcher's reign: 'As you say the atmosphere which she generates becomes more dismal by the moment and like you I hope that I live to see it dispersed' (Letter from Jonathan Miller, 14 March 1989, Sandy Wilson archive). In 1992 Wilson sent a cassette of *Valmouth* to the Labour MP Gerald Kaufman who thanks him for his good wishes and writes: 'We shall do our best, but it is hard work against this lot' (Letter from Gerald Kaufman, Sandy Wilson archive, 1992). Wilson's friendships did however extend across party lines, he was also friends with the Conservative MP and *Times* columnist Matthew Parris.

Wilson died on 27 August 2014, in the Somerset house he shared with Chak Yui and which he had named 'Valmouth', after the production of which he was most proud. He had seen *The Boy Friend* conquer the West End, Broadway and the world, and the stage production would long outlive Ken Russell's film, which he loathed. He collected the programmes from productions of *The Boy Friend* around the world, went to see many of them and never ceased to be proud of his creation of the 'Villa Caprice'.

The historian of musicals, Adrian Wright is brusque in his estimation of Sandy Wilson's career:

> On the face of it, the career seems slim. Contributions to intimate reviews, a number here and there, and one whole revue to himself. One completely original musical. Two pastiches, one of them a success that literally went, and is still going, around the world. Three esoterics. There is a great deal more of which the public knows little. (Wright, 2010, p. 71)

This appraisal underestimates the longevity of Wilson's career, and does not acknowledge the extent to which he was a transitional figure in theatre history and in musical theatre. He was also a significant figure as a homosexual man who lived through and survived brutal anti-homosexual legislation in Britain. In an account of lesbian and gay histories, Laura Gowing argues: 'Between persecution and resistance, and behind the myth of invisibility, lesbian and gay history can establish a story of social, cultural and political resistances, collusions, manipulations and transformations' (Gowing, p. 64). Sandy Wilson was not at all invisible; he may have avoided persecution, although many of his closest friends did not, he was not an active resister, but he was adept at collusion and manipulation, and he is very much part of that story.

Mapping theatreland

Soho, the West End and homosexual law reform

> You need to be careful when you go looking for queers. There are many questions
> to ponder. Where might you find them? Where are their haunts?
>
> (Medhurst, 2006, p. 21)

In his childhood, Sandy Wilson had mapped central London by tracking its
theatres and cinemas. His map was remarkably consistent with the survey of
'vice spots' outlined by the Metropolitan police. The Home Office Committee
on Sexual Offences, set up in 1954 to investigate homosexuality and
prostitution, focussed its attention particularly on London and specifically on
the West End and Soho. Sites identified as potential 'vice spots' were literally
mapped by the police and by the Home Office; Sir Lawrence Dunne, Chief
Metropolitan Magistrate at Bow Street, reported that many were adjacent to
or within near distance of London's theatres: 'the notorious sites at Victoria
Station, Piccadilly Circus underground station, Leicester Square, and the
urinals at Brydges Place, off the Strand, Rose Street, close by St Martin's Lane
in theatreland' (Mort, 2010, p. 154). Soho and the West End were central
stages on which the politics of homosexual law reform were played out
throughout the 1950s and 1960s.

The Boy Friend opened at the Players' Theatre, just off the Strand, at a
moment of febrile debate around homosexuality. In 1952, the *Sunday
Pictorial* had run a three-part series, 'Evil Men', in which the journalist
Douglas Warth characterized homosexual men as 'freaks and rarities' and
sternly warned against this 'unnatural sexual vice' which was all the more
alarming because the 'vice' was not clearly visible (see Curran and Seaton,
2018, p. 101). Under the guise of security in the Cold War context, ostensibly
in response to the defections of the 'Cambridge ring' spies Guy Burgess
and Donald Maclean to the Soviet Union in 1951, the Home Office and
Scotland Yard had announced a crackdown on 'male vice', which led to a
steep rise in arrests of homosexual men. In England and Wales in 1953, 2,166
men were tried for sexual offences with other men, and 1,257 were found

'guilty' (see Waters, 1999, p. 137). Churchill's cabinet had, according to Mort, 'nervously discussed homosexuality and prostitution three times during the winter of 1953' (Mort, 2010, p. 3).

Kinsey and his team had published *Sexual Behavior in the Human Male* in 1948,[1] a bestselling report which seemed to confirm the establishment's worst fears, that homosexuality was both prevalent and invisible. Kinsey reported that 37 per cent of his interviewees had had at least one same-sex relationship, and commented: 'This is more than one male in three of the persons that one may meet as he passes along a city street' (Kinsey et al. 1948, p. 623). According to Moe Meyer, Kinsey's report was central to a moral panic surrounding homosexuality in both Britain and America:

> Kinsey's refiguration of homosexuality unsettled and destabilized the social knowledge upon which rested both the techniques of homosexual identity construction and the public's ability to read that identity up until 1950. . . . For the public at large a panic ensued. (Meyer, 2010, p. 79)

In the British context, the association of the Communist spies Burgess and Maclean with Cambridge led to an establishment mistrust, if not demonization, of university, particularly Oxbridge, educated homosexual men. In 1954, the year that *The Boy Friend* transferred to the West End, a group within the Church of England went against the grain of police and press intolerance in producing an 'interim' report on 'The problem of homosexuality' for private circulation. The report was compiled by 'a group of Anglican clergy and doctors etc.' and advocated the legalization of sex between consenting adult men and recommended an equal age of consent. It was also the year in which the Montagu trial took place. Peter Wildeblood, a friend and contemporary of Wilson's at Oxford, and a fellow member of the Oxford Experimental Theatre, was a key figure in the trial; Wildeblood, with Lord Montagu of Beaulieu[2] and Montagu's cousin Michael Pitt-Rivers, was found guilty of 'homosexual offences' with two young airmen. The airmen were given immunity in return for naming names, in a case that became a tabloid sensation. The case was the lever for the Wolfenden Report, published by the Home Office in 1957. The report was officially titled 'The Report of the Departmental Committee on Homosexual Offences and Prostitution', but was widely known as the Wolfenden Report, after its chair Lord John Wolfenden. According to Mort, the impact of the Montagu trial and its coverage in the press 'provoked a national debate about fashionable society and its links with London's queer cultures' (Mort, 2010, p. 84).

The theatre was a significant link in the interface of fashionable London with 'queer cultures' and was widely recognized as such, in the popular press and among the general public. In Wildeblood's 1956 *A Way of Life*, he recalls an anecdote which demonstrates the widespread public association between gay men, the theatre, media and the arts:

> suddenly for no reason at all this aunt started talking about homosexuality and how everyone who was that way should be strangled at birth. So my mother looked her straight in the eye and said: 'Sybil, don't be so silly, If that was done, we should have no plays to go to, no books to read, no television to watch' (Wildeblood, 1956, p. 82)

In Rodney Garland's 1953 novel *The Heart in Exile*, the hero's first encounter with his lover, Julian, takes the form of a discussion about the theatre, in which a mutual love of the theatre is clearly a signifier of their shared homosexuality; the narrator comments: 'the stage is one field in which the invert has certain advantages' (Garland, 1953, p. 139). Even attending the theatre had connotations of effeminacy and 'vice', and was used against Lord Montagu in the trial: 'At Montagu's trial, aggressive prosecution questioning of the defendants threw the spotlight on champagne parties and theatre visits that the young aristocrat had supposedly arranged for his friends . . . with their suggestions of sinful glamour' (Mort, 2010, p. 86). Wildeblood's[3] own account of the trial and his incarceration in *Against the Law* published in 1955[4] identifies theatres as spaces where homosexual men gathered and recognized one another:

> The homosexual world, invisible to almost all who do not live in it . . . . In London there were still a great many men, outwardly 'respectable' . . . . I used to see them at theatrical first-nights and in the clubs which were patronised by homosexuals, discreetly dressed, careful in their behaviour – the last people ever to be suspected. (Wildeblood, 1955, p. 35)

Peter Wildeblood explains that his first meetings with openly gay men were with men associated with the theatre: 'Towards the end of my schooldays and during the first few months of my service in the RAF, I had met a number of people connected in various ways with the theatre and other arts, some of whom were frankly homosexual' (Wildeblood, 1955, p. 22).

Theatres themselves were widely recognized spaces for meeting gay men and for sexual encounters, as Gardiner explains:

> Several theatres and music halls . . . became known 'trolling grounds'. . . .
> The theatre bar would remain open all through the performance and

patrons making eye contact there could wander off to the conveniently dark area of the promenade where more intimate contact might be made. As the promenade was often extremely crowded, and theatre staff frequently gay themselves, this was a less risky business than it sounds. (Gardiner, 1992, p. 17)

In Jeffrey Weeks and Kevin Porter's collection of oral histories of homosexual men born between the late nineteenth century and the 1920s, who were adults in the 1950s, theatre features large as a site where it was possible to meet other men and to identify as gay. One man remembered:

I took my aunt out one night to the theatre and we went to the gallery of the old Prince of Wales theatre. . . . We were in the gallery and I realised then, by instinct. Nobody told me. I kept on looking at the back and it was jet black, and crowded, crowded full of people standing although there were a lot of empty seats. And that was, I think, my first realisation that this was a scene which I wanted to join in, I went two or three days afterwards . . . and stood at the back and what was going on there was nobody's business!

They were big meeting places. . . . I went round those theatres quite a lot. (quoted in Weeks and Porter, p. 94)

The West End of London, and especially the theatre, was central to the currency of Polari among homosexual men. According to Paul Baker:

It was London, with its numerous entertainment venues, that became the base for Polari. As well as its theatres and music halls, London, like many big cities, became home to gay men, who moved there for numerous reasons: anonymity, greater tolerance, a more cosmopolitan lifestyle, work opportunities, access to other men etc. . . . Dancers, known as *wallopers,* and singers, known as *voches* (voices), delighted in the language derived from Parlaree which they claimed for themselves. While many of these performers were gay, there were plenty who weren't, and for them Polari, or *Parlary* as it was more commonly known in the first half of the twentieth century, was simply the language of the theatre, with words associated with the stage. . . . This form of theatre-speak could also be classed as 'West End' Polari. (Baker, P. 2006, pp. 32–4)

'West End' Polari was distinct from 'East End' Polari because it was 'fundamentally based on theatre' (Baker P., 2006, p. 71). That 'theatre-speak' was particularly widely spoken in the bars, theatres and clubs of Soho, where the 'wallopers' and 'voches' regularly gathered. Mort describes theatre people (from strip clubs and from theatres) as integral to the bohemianism and sexual transgressions that Soho offered: 'On-stage and off-stage, dancers and showgirls projected sexual personalities and bodily idioms that disrupted traditional dichotomies of vice and virtue' (Mort, 2010, p. 23).

The guide book *The Good Time Guide to London* outlines the pleasures to be found in the West End of London, and, while it can, in 1951, only be implicit about the potential for homosexual encounters, it does point to the diversity of the communities that frequented Soho and the West End:

> most people find it convenient to regard the West End – that part of town which surrounds Piccadilly Circus – as the centre. This is playland. It keeps brighter lights, later hours than the rest of the town.
>
> Most of the finest shops and the biggest hotels are to be found here, besides the more attractive theatres, cinemas and night clubs. Mayfair, to the west of Piccadilly, is one of the best residential districts in the city – but a few hundred yards away towards Soho you will find dark alleys and cul-de-sacs, third-rate night clubs and dingy cafés – all the traditional settings for a lurid detective story. (Aldor, 1951, p. 94)

Mort finds in this abuttal of a louche bohemia with bourgeois respectability a metaphor for the competing discourses on sexual mores in the 1950s; he describes Soho as an environment in which 'Excessive drinking bouts, public displays of bad behaviour and chance sexual encounters (whether heterosexual or between men) were the rules of the game' (Mort, 1996, p. 153). Soho thus represented a counter-site in which transgressive behaviours (as homosexuality would have been until the 1967 Sexual Offences Act) were possible. The very architecture and layout of Soho streets facilitated illicit encounters; as Mort explains: 'Soho's pre-eminence as a place for social and sexual encounters was made possible by the narrow courts and alleys that enabled urban cruising, spectating and loitering of all kinds. . . . Soho's urban landscape was and still is porous and multi-layered.' (Mort, 2010, p. 13).

Soho as an area had developed from a royal hunting ground[5] in the late eighteenth century to become a fashionable bourgeois suburb mixed with artisanal workshops;[6] that mix of elegance and shabby bohemianism has characterized Soho ever since. The aristocracy and upper classes fled after an outbreak of cholera in 1854, while music hall, coffee houses, bars and brothels moved in. It has been at the centre of the entertainment industry since the nineteenth century, and is still closely packed with offices for publishing, film, music and film production, and for agents of all kinds.

Soho had a particular resonance and glamour in the post-war austerity of the 1950s; as Barker puts it: 'This was an uptight, grey little decade' (Barker, 2019, p. 117), and the lights of the West End and the bars of Soho provided some welcome respite. Soho alleviated that greyness, as Nigel Richardson puts it: 'Miraculously, while the rest of Britain, indeed the rest of Europe nursed a monochrome post-war hangover, Soho had colour' (Richardson, 2000, p. 61). There is a recurrent trope in the writings of gay men in the 1950s of Soho as an area of London that was exciting, bohemian and glamorous, a welcoming space that was particularly important as a counter to the overriding conventionality of the decade. Richardson's memoir of 2000 gives some flavour of the glamour that the nightlife of Soho represented for post-war Londoners: 'The prevailing hues of the post-war years were greys and browns; austerity throbbed like a hangover; people mended and made do. But here was colour and daring' (Richardson, 2000, p. 3).

The first chapter of Daniel Farson's *Soho in the Fifties* is titled 'Hunting in Soho', which is less a reference to Soho's origins as a hunting ground than it is to its potential for cruising. Farson similarly recalls the allure of Soho in the post-war gloom: 'When I arrived there in 1951, London was suffering from post-war depression and it was a revelation to discover people who behaved outrageously without a twinge of guilt' (Farson, 1987, p. 7). In his introduction to Farson's memoir, George Melly writes of his own Soho in the period and echoes many writers in his memory of Soho as an exception to the conformist 1950s:

> within that that village there roamed an exceptional collection of diverse creatures who stood at least for the right to pursue their own dreams and nightmares. The fifties were a time of austerity, of punitive conventions. . . . Soho was perhaps the only area in London where the rules didn't apply. It was a Bohemian no-go area, tolerance its password, where bad behaviour was cherished – at any rate in retrospect. Only bores were made unwelcome. (Melly, 1987, p. xiii)

Wildeblood's 1958 novel is titled *West End People*, and begins with the central protagonist, Cherry, escaping the confinements of suburban Surrey and immediately making her way to Piccadilly Circus and then to Soho, a narrative similar to that of Wilson's 1950 musical *Caprice*. 'Dilly' is, according to the linguist Paul Baker, one of the very few proper nouns to be found in Polari (Baker, P., 2006, p. 41). Piccadilly Circus was a central focus both for homosexual men and for the Metropolitan police in search of arrests. As Richard Hornsey explains:

Piccadilly Circus, with its cosmopolitan street culture and gaudy commercial illuminations, had long been imagined to be the epicentre of London's queer street culture. As the meeting point between Piccadilly, Regent Street and Leicester Square . . . it was already marked by its transient hordes and incessant bustle. (Hornsey, 2010, p. 103)

Piccadilly Circus is a hub, at which Shaftesbury Avenue and the Haymarket also meet, and it is within close walking distance of the Strand and St Martin's Lane, all lined with theatres and cinemas, as Sandy Wilson had recognized as a child. The theatre historian W. J. Macqueen Pope identified the fringes of Soho as 'Poverty Corner', a place where theatre people gathered, in his *An Indiscreet Guide to Theatreland* (which is nonetheless, as it had to be in 1947, very discreet on the subject of sexuality):

> It is a little world of its own, a city within a city, a state within a state, peopled entirely by the smaller and less fortunate fry of the Theatrical profession. . . . They stand on the corner of Charing Cross Road, just outside the Tube station, and outside Wyndham's Theatre, opposite the London Hippodrome. . . . They are all sorts of shapes and size, but the unmistakeable mark of the entertainment world is on them. . . . they are the showfolk, the dwellers in the land of make-believe, which, so often, also leads to Poverty Corner. . . . Outwardly the faces were brave, the appearance beyond reproach. A little flamboyant perhaps, but clean and spotless. . . . They would stay there all day . . . so long as there was a chance of a job. (Macqueen Pope, 1947, p. 90)

This 'little world of its own' was then, as it still is, dominated by the theatre. Soho was the centre of this world, the heart of theatreland and of homosexual culture; in Peter Ackroyd's 2017 history of Queer London, Soho has more entries than any other London location. The 2017 exhibition *Queer British Art* at the Tate Gallery (held to mark the fiftieth anniversary of the 1967 Sexual Offences Act) included an entire section devoted to Soho, 'Arcadia and Soho'. Soho as a setting for the 'man-about-town' is confirmed by the advertisements in the 1946 *Indiscreet Guide to Soho* which offer 'casual clothes for men who demand the ultimate in apparel', shaving accessories, Bay Rum hair darkening, Chinese and Kosher restaurants. The Soho visitor was clearly assumed to care about appearance and to be cosmopolitan in their culinary tastes. Mort explains that Soho had long been a centre for the cultural and theatrical world:

> In the years before 1914, Soho had become an established centre for sections of the cultural and artistic avant-garde. . . . In the inter-war years

> Soho's population was augmented by sexual as well as cultural dissidence. Homosexual men began to patronise the Golden Lion pub in Dean Street in the 1920s as the district became part of a network of homosexuality adjacent to the theatre world of Leicester Square. A decade late the arrival of the film industry in Soho Square, added to the hybridity of Soho. (Mort, 1996, p. 153)

Soho has a long history of raffishness and of offering a welcome to gay men; as Mort and Fryer both point out, Aubrey Beardsley and Oscar Wilde were regular visitors at the Café Royale, situated at the point that Soho meets Regent Street, and Oscar Wilde entertained at Kettners in Romilly Street. Soho had also been an important site for gay encounters during the Second World War, as Fryer explains:

> During the height of the Second World War, central London was awash with British and Allied servicemen, enjoying precious hours of leave, never knowing whether these would be their last. There was an urgency about the need for entertainment and companionship. Brief encounters, straight and gay, occurred in the blackouts. In the early 1950s some of that febrile atmosphere persisted. Soho was an ideal place to escape the aura of austerity that still pervaded the rest of the country. (Fryer, p. 5)

What made many of these illicit encounters possible was that the private drinking clubs of Soho could evade the licensing laws which restricted the hours of drinking, and, with their membership lists, a known clientele and discreet entrances, they also offered a degree of protection from the police. As Gardiner describes these clubs:

> one could repair to one of the numerous private drinking clubs that dotted the Soho area. These were open from the afternoon till 11.00 and run strictly on a membership basis, usually a single room behind locked doors: intimate, friendly places presided over by a genial and sympathetic host or hostess who knew all the customers by name, and provided them with soft lighting and over-priced, after hours gin. (Gardiner, 1992, p. 17)

Among the most well known of the bars was (and still is) the French House in Dean Street,[7] immortalized in *The Pink Room*, the 1952 play by Rodney Ackland (who was himself an actor), first produced at the Lyric Hammersmith (largely financed by Terence Rattigan; the play was later rewritten as *Absolute Hell*,[8] with the homosexual subtext of the original play made explicit). Other such clubs were the Rockingham in Archer Street, just off Shaftesbury Avenue, and the Gargoyle Club, in Dean Street, which had been opened in 1925 by David Tennent, once married to Hermione Baddeley, Wilson's friend and patron. Noël Coward, Somerset Maugham and the Cambridge spies Guy Burgess and Donald Maclean were all members. As Mort explains, many such clubs were 'Largely queer-run and enforcing a strict door policy as well as high membership fees, they advertised as private clubs in order to evade police surveillance, exclude rough trade and deter the straight public' (Mort, 2010, p. 235); consequently they were relatively safe spaces. Farson (who was a regular drinker at the French House) remembered that, in the 1950s, the owners of such 'queer' clubs were often ex-servicemen and themselves homosexual:

> Far from being a furtive sort of person he was usually an upright gentleman, middle-aged and enthusiastic, neatly dressed . . . Frequently the owner *had* been a major or a naval commander and sported a tie to that effect. . . . The war had given him the happiest years of his life, for he had responded with bravery leading his men across the lines . . . his homosexuality was a fact of life, something to be neither proud of nor ashamed of, just the throw of the dice to be accepted with the brightest of smiles. In different circumstances he would have been reputable; as the owner of a 'queer' club he was beyond the pale because such practices were criminal. (Farson, 1987, pp. 71–2)

There were also a number of pubs in Soho and Fitzrovia which were relaxed in their attitudes towards homosexuality; Gardiner cites The Golden Lion in Dean Street, The Salisbury in St Martin's Lane, The Lamb and Flag in Covent Garden and The Fitzroy Tavern in Charlotte Street, Fitzrovia, all within close distance of the theatres and theatrical offices of Shaftesbury Avenue, St Martin's Lane and the Strand. Farson quotes a police report which described the Fitzroy Tavern as a 'den of vice':

> for the most part its occupants were quite obvious male homosexuals who dyed their hair and rouged their cheeks and behaved in an effeminate manner with effeminate voices. . . . These perverts were simply overrunning the place, behaving in a scandalous manner and attempting to seduce members of the forces. (quoted in Farson, 1987, p. 81)

In 1956 the brewery closed the Fitzroy after a series of police raids and the prosecution of the landlord for 'keeping a disorderly house' (Mort, 2010, p. 236).

Theatre clubs with bars, among them the Players' Theatre Club where Wilson regularly met friends, were more discreet spaces in which men could evade surveillance; these theatre bars also kept late hours in order to allow theatre people to drink after working, and offered another level of protection in being restricted to members. Farson also identifies the Golden Lion as a 'queer friendly' pub, describing it as 'hysterically camp' and a site where homosexuals required to act straight in their working lives could be 'themselves': 'Homosexuals who needed to live a lie during office hours could relax in the company of strangers in the Lion and be themselves, using the bar as a stage for their extravagance' (Farson, 1987, p. 78). Wilson's friend Peter Wildeblood was among those men leading a double life, working as a journalist on Fleet Street and living a homosexual life, he writes of a constant sense of anxiety in the period before his arrest:

> I was forced to be deceitful, living one life during my working hours and another when I was free. I had two sets of friends; almost, one might say, two faces. At the back of my mind there was always a nagging fear that my two worlds might suddenly collide; that somebody who knew about me would meet somebody who did not know, and that disaster would ensue. (Wildeblood, 1955, p. 32)

Peter Wildeblood came out of the experience of the trial and his imprisonment as an active campaigner for homosexual rights and made a passionate case for legal and prison reform in *Against the Law*. A copy of *Against the Law* was sent, at the suggestion of Allen Lane the founder of Penguin books, to every sitting MP in Westminster; the cover for the first edition carries the rallying strap line: 'The moving inside story of the "Montagu Case" by the young journalist who was one of its victims.' The trial and conviction forced an unsought public coming out for Wildeblood, but also some sort of liberation. In *Against the Law*, he describes the shuttling between the world of respectability and the shadowy 'underworld' which was required of gay men in the 1950s: 'I have been on both sides of the fence which separates Society from its misfits, the world from the underworld, and the no-man's-land which surrounds it is a territory which I have crossed and re-crossed many times' (Wildeblood, 1956, p. 10). Wildeblood was one of those 'young men who come down from Oxford and write gossip', in the title of Ryan Linkof's account of society gossip and homosexuality in the interwar years. Linkof points to the fact that many of the gossip columnists in Fleet Street were then homosexual, as remained the case in the post-war period[9] and into the 1950s. Linkof associates homosexual secrecy with the image of a mask and argues that

Gossip was fundamentally about identifying what kinds of behaviours and 'poses' were required to be a successful social actor. Queer gossip writers seemed particularly preoccupied with these questions, revealing a marked interest in the lies that people tell themselves in the pursuit of public approval.

A common theme among several homosexual gossip writers was the question of the 'masks' that people affected when interacting at social functions. (Linkof, 2015, p. 121)

The 'mask' is repeatedly evoked in Wildeblood's writing, both fictional and autobiographical; in *A Way of Life* he states that the Montagu trial meant that 'I was able, at last, to move out of a false position and take up a true one. There was no further need for pretence; I could discard the mask which had been such a burden to me all my life' (Wildeblood, 1956, p. 189). *The Boy Friend* literally presents its characters as masked in the final ball scene; Sandy Wilson, however, never quite did 'discard the mask', avoiding any direct reference to his sexuality in his writing, even long after the decriminalization of homosexuality. While he never denied his sexuality, he kept it discreet in the tradition of Beaumont, Coward, Rattigan and Novello, only able to be open in the accepting world of the theatre and among his close circle of friends.

Wildeblood was imprisoned for eighteen months; it is clear from letters in Wilson's archives that many of his Oxford friends were both frightened and concerned at his arrest, rallying to provide him with moral and financial support. Wildeblood was visited in prison by Lord Frank Pakenham, later Lord Longford,[10] who was a vocal supporter of Montagu and Wildeblood. Longford was then preparing a report for the Nuffield Foundation on the 'Causes of Crime' (see Wildeblood, 1955, p. 163). It was through Longford that Wildeblood was invited to give evidence to the House of Lords Committee on Homosexual Offences, the only acknowledged homosexual to do so. As he expressed it: 'The government was finally goaded into setting up a Committee to investigate the antique and savage laws under which we had been charged' (Wildeblood, 1955, p. 188). Kinsey, whose report had been so significant to the contemporary discourses on male sexuality, was another witness to the Wolfenden government inquiry. He had done research in Wormwood Scrubs male prison and was shocked at the number of men who had been imprisoned for same-sex offences. In a lecture given in 1955 at the Maudsley Hospital, he argued for 'the wholesale reform of the sex laws because they were archaic and inhumane' (see Mort, 2010, p. 1).

The most direct way in which sex laws impacted on theatre was through censorship; the Lord Chamberlain's Office was required to licence every commercial theatre production and had decreed that homosexuality was not a topic to be dealt with on stage. The character of Geoffrey in Shelagh Delaney's *A Taste of Honey* was the first representation (and a sympathetic one) of an acknowledged gay man on stage in the Theatre Workshop production of 1958 – but already legal attitudes were beginning to thaw. In 1958 the Lord Chamberlain permitted some reference to homosexuality in stage plays and pronounced: 'This subject is now so widely debated, written about and talked over that its complete exclusion from the stage can no longer be regarded as justifiable' (quoted in Sinfield, 1983, p. 181).

Wildeblood's *A Way of Life* includes a description of a dinner party which suggests the rumblings of changes in the law and a furious impatience with the constraints of the closet (again making use of the image of the mask). A lawyer and a doctor discuss the British Medical Association report on homosexuality and the House of Lords Committee; one guest remarks: 'If only people realised how many of us there were, perhaps they might leave us alone. I mean if everybody could suddenly unmask . . . Or if we all suddenly turned blue, overnight, so that there was no further possibility of disguise. Every shade from Saxe to Prussian' (Wildeblood, 1956, p. 82). The same dinner party is overshadowed by the persistent homophobia of the contemporary press, two of the men attending are journalists, one of whom remarks: 'we have to keep on printing these articles about how all the queers ought to be put up against a wall and shot. It's rather funny really, considering some of the people we have on our Features staff' (Wildeblood, 1956, p. 82).

The Wolfenden Report recommended a partial decriminalization of homosexual acts in private between consenting men over the age of twenty-one, but it would take a decade for this to become law. This was the spur for the Homosexual Law Reform Society, which emerged as a campaign to implement the recommendations of the report; in 1958 the literature academic A. E. Dyson[11] organized a letter to *The Times* and garnered signatures from leading figures in the arts, politics, the Church of England and academia; Clement Attlee, J. B. Priestley, Bertrand Russell, Baroness Barbara Wootton and Angus Wilson[12] were among the signatories. The eminence of these names was part of a concerted effort to demonstrate how respectable the cause for the decriminalization of homosexuality could be; Weeks describes the Homosexual Law Reform Society as 'maintaining an air of well-drilled respectability' (Weeks, 1977, p. 169). Peter Wildeblood's self-presentation at the Wolfenden committee was similarly one of unthreatening propriety. As Mort explains, Wildeblood deliberately distanced himself from any association with flamboyant homosexuality or any suggestion of camp:

> Men like Peter Wildeblood, who gave evidence to the inquiry as a speaking homosexual subject, drew on social medicine and psychiatry as

well as confessional declarations familiar from autobiographical writing to announce their identity and distinguish their respectable condition from the degraded perverts and effeminate queens who populated the West End. (Mort, 2010, p. 11)

However, Mort also points out that this was somewhat disingenuous of Wildeblood: 'London's queer commercial and entertainment spaces that he denounced so vigorously in front of the committee were a part of his own sexual lifestyle during the 1950s' (Mort, 2010, p. 182); Wildeblood had himself run a bar in Soho's Berwick Street after his release from prison (an experience which formed the basis for his book *A Way of Life*).

There is a clear tension in the memoirs and fiction of homosexual men in the 1950s between those who embraced the extravagance of camp and those who refuted it, like Wildeblood, who insisted on his respectability in every aspect of his life, apart from his sexuality. Those tensions between the respectable reformism of the Homosexual Law Reform Society and a more confrontational anger were both generational and political and would be played out in future campaigns for homosexual rights. The Gay Liberation Front (GLF) would later make use of camp theatricality in political strategies such as 'zap actions', a strategy imported from American Pride marches in which protests against homophobia were directly understood as performances. Among the first public actions of the British GLF was the 'zap' of a meeting of the Festival of Light chaired by Mary Whitehouse in 1971. The Festival of Light was an Evangelical Christian moral crusade set up by Malcolm Muggeridge, Mary Whitehouse and, surprisingly, Lord Longford. Their rally at Westminster Hall was disrupted by members of the GLF, many in drag, who set mice into the crowd, sounded horns and turned off all the lights.

The Campaign for Homosexual Equality (CHE) emerged from the North Western Homosexual Law Reform Committee (NWHLRC), set up by a member of the Homosexual Law Reform Society, Allan Horsfall, in 1964, prompted by what he perceived as the Londoncentric focus[13] of the Homosexual Law Reform Society. It would take another three years before the recommendations of the Wolfenden Report would become legislation with the Sexual Offences Act of 1967, which decriminalized homosexual acts between consenting adults, but imposed an age of consent of twenty-one for homosexual men.[14] In Mort's assessment, the enactment of the report, despite its limitations, did have long-term positive effects for homosexual lives in England and the world:

The maelstrom of 1950s sexual politics forged a new system of governance that was one of the most enduring legacies to come out of

Whitehall. The Wolfenden committee's moral philosophy, a mixture of high-minded principles and bureaucratic pragmatism, set the parameters for legal reforms supported by successive Conservative and Labour governments. (Mort, 2010, p. 354)

CHE continued to campaign for the equalization of the age of consent and from 1969 campaigned for a more assertive 'promotion of legal and social equality for lesbians and gay men and bisexuals in England and Wales'.[15] CHE supported and took part in the first London Gay Pride marches,[16] to protest against the discrepancy in the age of consent for homosexual men.[17] The GLF is usually dated as beginning from the 1969 Stonewall Riots in New York which were prompted by a police raid of a gay bar; the GLF was an umbrella term for a range of campaigning gay organizations. The British GLF was set up in 1970, according to Baker, 'Partly due to frustration at the half-measure effect of the Sexual Offences Act, but also because the Act enabled gay people to collectivize in a way that had been difficult before' (Baker, P., 2019, p. 211). That collectivization allowed for the first marches in London. Both CHE and the GLF eschewed the respectability of the Homosexual Law Reform Society; the performance protests and often cheerfully flamboyant demonstrations of Gay Pride were far removed from the discretion of the Homosexual Law Reform Society, as was the GLF's injunction for gay people to be 'out and proud'. The GLF and CHE were disdainful of the camp and Polari of a previous generation, as Baker explains:

> As a result of new gay rights movements, there was a backlash against a number of established notions of gay identity which had developed over the 1950s and 1960s. . . . Camp identities were seen by some activists as being about as far removed from politics as possible, and therefore useless in the struggle for equality. (Baker, 2006, pp. 115–16)

Ironically, although both Wildeblood and Wilson enjoyed, and could themselves display campness (and understood Polari), they too were concerned to publicly distance themselves from flamboyant camp behaviours. The Gay Liberation movement did not at the time recognize the extent to which both camp and Polari were strategies of identification, subterfuge and subversion, a response to the pillorying of homosexual communities in the repressive conformism of the 1950s and early 1960s. Richard Dyer wrote an essay at the height of these debates, 'It's being so camp that keeps us going', a defence of camp, which argued that it was a response to and emerged out of the experience of oppression:

we find it easy to appear to fit in, we are good at picking up the rules, conventions, forms and appearances of different social circles. And why? Because we've had to be good at it, we've had to be good at disguises, at appearing to be one of the crowd, the same as everyone else . . . the camp sensibility is very much a product of our oppression. And inevitably, it is scarred by that oppression. (Dyer, 1992, p. 144)

Sandy Wilson was good at 'picking up the rules', and adept at assuming disguises, but, despite the breezy cheerfulness of his autobiography, he cannot but have been scarred. He lived through the most draconian legislation against homosexuality in Britain, and as a successful man of the theatre, and as a friend of Peter Wildeblood, he was at the centre of what Mort terms 'The maelstrom of 1950s sexual politics'. He knew he had to be careful, and he chose to align himself with the tradition of respectable discretion. Sandy Wilson wrote an undated and unpublished[18] play in one of the only pieces of writing in which he directly addresses the politics of his sexuality. A middle-aged homosexual man wrestles with the decision as to whether or not to attend a meeting about homosexual rights, it is clear from his prevarication that it would take some courage to be seen attending a meeting (which suggests that this was written in the 1950s, and that the meeting must have been one of the Homosexual Law Reform Society). After considering the arguments for and against, he decides to go. Wilson may not have been comfortable with public displays of his sexuality, but he was unquestionably a supporter of equal rights.

In a section titled 'Queer Goings-on' in his book on the Soho of the 1950s, Daniel Farson describes gay clubs of the time as shadowy, secretive places:

> Some of the risqué lyrics which drifted down from an upstairs room in the early evening or permeated faintly from a shuttered basement came from clubs which were used by homosexuals . . . in London the 'queer' clubs were slightly shabby in the literal sense of the word and slightly glum. . . . True to Soho where people were constantly searching for something or someone, the young men who came to the 'queer' clubs were desperately in need of entertainment to alleviate the tedium of their lives. The queens provided the distraction. (Farson, 1987, p. 71)

This may have been true of some of the Soho 'queer clubs', and it is certainly the case that the version of the French House offered in Ackland's play *Absolute Hell* is shabby and more than 'slightly glum'. The characters are all in a state of quiet desperation (in its original version, *The Pink Room* was subtitled *The Escapists*), and the play ends with the landlady alone sobbing 'Hell, Hell,

Hell, Hell, Hell, Hell, Hell, Hell' (Ackland, 2017, p. 234) as the building and the bar collapse around her. However, it is important to remember that this is not the only version of the homosexual experience in the Soho of the 1950s. There were bars and clubs that were vibrant and exciting, there were elegant clubs, small clubs and theatre bars such as the Watergate and the Players' Theatre which were warm and welcoming and where Wilson and Wildeblood regularly met their friends.

Daniel Farson describes Soho as 'a state of mind rather than a boundary, adapting to those who came here from abroad, anxious to start a new life in a new home' (Farson, 1987, p. 3). Those 'anxious to start a new life' in Soho were not only the waves of migrants from the Huguenots onwards but also young men and women from outside London. Fryer's mapping of bohemian Soho in the 1950s and 1960s suggests how fluid its boundaries were both geographically and conceptually:

> Formally, there is no fixed boundary to Soho. It blends into Fitzrovia to the north, Chinatown to the south, Piccadilly to the west and Bloomsbury to the east, but the most commonly accepted delineation of Soho puts it within a rough rectangle marked out by Shaftesbury Avenue, Regent Street, Oxford Street and the Charing Cross Road. Its heart is the tight little grid of streets north and south of Old Compton Street. (Fryer, 1998, p. 5)

Old Compton Street is now known as a centre of gay pleasures and consumption, with most of its bars, clubs and restaurants displaying the rainbow flag, in sharp contrast to the discreet entrances and blacked out windows which were necessary until 1967. But it should not be forgotten that as recently as 2005 the Conservative Westminster City Council ordered all bars and businesses in Soho to remove their flags, on the flimsy grounds that this constituted advertising. The decision was only reversed through an active campaign and the support of the then mayor of London, Ken Livingstone. And, in 1999, the Admiral Duncan pub on Old Compton Street, where it had been since 1832, was blown up in a homophobic attack which killed three and injured seventy people. A plaque in the bar memorializes the event. In the spirit of a resilient Soho, the Admiral Duncan reopened as a cabaret bar, with the slogan: 'the Admiral Duncan, a triumph of brash fun. . . . Known locally and internationally as an accepting, fun and embracing venue'.[19] The Admiral Duncan stands in the proud tradition of a Soho which has witnessed numerous attacks on its bohemian peoples and places, but which continues, despite gentrification, to refuse conformity and to maintain a raffish air of 'colour and daring'.

The Ivy League

Binkie Beaumont, Noël Coward, Ivor Novello and Terence Rattigan

Personne d'ailleurs dans le café ou ils ont leur table ne sait quelle est cette reunion, si c'est celle d'une societé de pêche, des secretaires de redaction . . . tant leur tenue est correcte, leur air réservé et froid, et tant ils n'osent regarder qu'a la dérobée les jeunes gens à la mode . . .

(Marcel Proust, *Sodome et Gomorrhe*[1])

The Ivy restaurant in West Street in central London was from its opening, and remains still, a centre for theatrical meetings. In the post-war period, the centre of gravity at the Ivy was the theatrical triumvirate of Noël Coward, Ivor Novello and 'Binkie' (Hugh) Beaumont, the theatrical impresario. All had been extremely powerful figures before the war and remained prominent men of the theatre in its aftermath. They were aspirational figures for Sandy Wilson, as successful men of the theatre and as homosexuals. Productions by Coward and Novello are cited meticulously and enthusiastically throughout Wilson's autobiography. Like Wilson, both men had footholds in cabaret and revue, and had made their names in musical theatre, they offered a model for the star lyricist and composer that Sandy Wilson had aspired to become since childhood. Coward was a defining figure for Wilson: 'the man who I had admired above all others and whom I had once so fervently hoped to emulate' (Wilson, 1975a, p. 207).

Novello was also an iconic celebrity for Wilson, who wrote a deferential study of him in 1975. Wilson's archive holds a photograph (which he had kept throughout his life) of a young and very handsome Novello robed in a toga and wearing a floral coronet. Wilson's book *Ivor* includes another photograph taken of Novello in drag at the age of twelve, which is simply captioned: '. . . in the style of the postcard beauties of the day. . . . The photograph was printed on postcards and Ivor tinted them himself and distributed them to his friends' (Wilson, 1975b, p. 108). Novello's operettas offered an introduction to the glamour and spectacle of the stage and to the possibilities of what a musical could be. Wilson remembered going as a schoolboy to 'the theatrical sensation of 1935 . . . *Glamorous Nights* . . . It was a gigantic Ruritanian spectacle, which included the shipwreck of a cruise liner in full view of the audience' (Wilson, 1975a, p. 46).

Novello, Coward and Beaumont regularly dined at the Ivy together. In his autobiography, Coward introduces Beaumont as 'Hugh (Binkie) Beaumont, one of my closest friends and my business associate for many years' (Coward, 1954, p. 234). The first entry in Coward's published diary refers to Binkie, and subsequent entries indicate that they regularly ate lunches and dinner together, at least twice a week, most often at the Ivy (other restaurants they favoured included the Savoy and Scotts, but the Ivy features more than any other). There was clearly both friendship and professional respect on both sides, and a close working relationship, as Coward writes of Binkie's advice: 'Binkie has been a dear and immensely helpful. At least he knows what he is talking about' (Payn and Morley, eds., p. 134). According to Beaumont's secretary, Kitty Black: 'at the Ivy, the theatrical restaurant . . . all the tables were allocated strictly in order of precedence. Ivor Novello and Noël Coward automatically rated the tables nearest the entrance and less important luminaries were graded down the room' (Black, 1984, p. 63).

The Ivy is located in the heart of Theatreland, close to Shaftesbury Avenue and at one end of St Martin's Lane, both lined with theatres, but it is off the main streets, in a corner opposite the small Ambassadors' Theatre. It occupies a space that is both in the centre of the West End and discreetly detached from it. Macqueen-Pope[2] describes the restaurant in *An Indiscreet Guide to Theatreland*:

> the Ivy Restaurant, the lunching, dining and supper place of the stars of today. It is almost a club, where certain members of the profession have the same table, and where at meal times you will be sure to find them. . . . It is the great artistic rendezvous of the day . . . (MacQueen-Pope, 1947, p. 78)

Sandy Wilson was introduced to the Ivy as a child by his theatrical Aunt Virginia, and was struck then by its importance as a venue for theatre people:

> we went to a play or a film and had dinner afterwards at the Ivy, which was then the favourite rendezvous of theatre people. Virginia had known the proprietor, Monsieur Abel, since the days when the Ivy was a small corner café with saw-dust on the floor, and he always kissed her hand and sat down with us for a chat. (Wilson, 1975a, p. 71)

'Monsieur Abel' (who was not French, but an Italian, Abele Giandolini) had opened the Ivy as a café on the same site as the later restaurant in 1917. From its beginnings, the restaurant kept late hours appropriate to those working in the theatre, and it drew a crowd of actors, directors, writers and impresarios. If Novello and Coward were the most celebrated among them, Beaumont was the most theatrically powerful. Novello and Coward had been the reigning princes of the West End throughout the 1930s and 1940s, as Snelson puts it: 'Both occupied the roles of playwright, film and stage actor, composer and . . . lyricist. They were both icons of their time with Coward as the urbane sophisticate and Novello as the male romantic ideal' (Snelson, p. 103). Coward makes frequent appearances in Wilson's autobiography and offers one of the very few moments in it which is explicitly camp; Wilson describes a backstage meeting at which 'wearing just his underpants, he [Coward] surveyed himself in the mirror and remarked: "Looking even more like an ageing Chinese madam than usual"' (Wilson, 1975a, p. 211). Just as Coward and Novello were musical and theatrical role models for Wilson, they also demonstrated that it was possible to be a celebrity and (discreetly) homosexual.

Coward had first met Ivor Novello at the age of seventeen (see Coward, 1954, p. 47), while Beaumont had known him since childhood. Novello had lived in the same street as Beaumont in Cardiff as Beaumont was growing up; twelve years older than Binkie, Novello was already working in the professional theatre, and, according to Beaumont's biographer, Richard Huggett, embodied the glamour of the stage for Beaumont: 'this beautiful, sparkling bird of paradise glowing with wealth, success and glamour. . . . In a strange, undefinable way, Ivor Novello epitomised everything that Binkie wanted' (Huggett, p. 38). Novello had been a great star on the London stage as a writer, composer and performer, both before and throughout the war, and continued to hold the public imagination in the early post-war period, as Morley explains: 'As the West End began to emerge from the effects of a long and debilitating war, Novello seemed professionally sure of what he was doing' (Morley, 1987, p. 107). Novello was admired by both Beaumont and Coward, if not entirely respected. In 1950 Coward writes of Novello's last production in terms which are both complimentary and slightly condescending: 'Went to *King's Rhapsody*. Really enjoyed it very much. It is highly sugary, romantic and extremely well done. Supper at Ivor's flat afterwards' (Payn and Morley eds., p. 160). There is however more than a hint of personal and professional jealousy in Coward's account of Novello's charm:

> I envied thoroughly everything about him. His looks, his personality, his assured position, his dinner clothes, his bedroom and bath, and above

all the supper party. I pictured him sipping champagne and laughing gaily, warm in the conviction that he was adored by everyone at the table. (Coward, 1984, p. 48)

Novello's friends were known for their campness, the theatre critic Sheridan Morley refers to the alternative titles 'that he and his circle gave these lavish romantic spectacles: "The Prancing Queers", "Careless Rupture", "Perchance to Scream" . . ' (Morley, 1987, p. 82). Wilson's study of Novello is discreet in its use of the memories of Novello's friends and colleagues, although there is a coded suggestion that women 'fans' could never know the 'real' Novello. There is also an acknowledgement of the significance of Novello's group of male friends who acted as both testament to his fame and as camouflage:

> Like Noël, Ivor moved with an entourage . . . . 'He went around in a gang' is how Sybil Thorndike describes it – and while a few of the courtiers of these two reigning monarchs moved between their territories, those closest to the throne remained the same year after year. For Ivor, it seemed, the company of his friends was not only a comfort and a protection but an emotional necessity. (Wilson, 1975b, p. 9)

Wilson did considerable research on his biography of Novello, contacting Ivor's friends and colleagues from far back, including the actress Beryl Samson who was briefly engaged to Novello.[3] His tribute begins with a paean to Novello's beauty that draws on the words of the homosexual writer Beverley Nichols:[4]

> He was beautiful. And he was a darling. . . . The good looks were almost, in the words of Beverly Nichols, 'too good to be true . . .' They embodied in one face, all the romantic ideals of his age: the Latin Lover, the Sheik of Araby and the Vagabond Gypsy. . . . A glance from those eyes, a glimpse of that profile was enough to excite the yearnings of a multitude of feminine hearts. (Wilson, 1975b, pp. 7–8)

It is clear from Wilson and Nichol's tributes that it was not only 'feminine hearts' who yearned. Sandy Wilson's book *Ivor* was published in the same year as his own autobiography and yet neither makes any direct reference to their subject's sexuality, even as late as 1975, almost a decade after the decriminalization of homosexuality. Novello was loved by both the public and his theatrical associates; Coward was so devastated by Novello's death in 1951 that he wrote a message to replace his planned foreword to Peter Noble's authorized biography:

I am too shattered by the news of Ivor Novello's death to write an estimate of his work or his personality that would do justice to either. We have been close friends for thirty-five years, and my feelings at the moment are too private and too unhappy to be put into words. (Coward, 1951, p. iii)

Coward and Novello entered the post-war period associated in the public mind with the Blitz spirit and patriotism of the war years, despite Novello's embarrassing prison sentence in Wormwood Scrubs for an offence over petrol-rationing. Ibell has suggested that Novello's two-month sentence was 'vindictive' when the offence was usually punishable by a £50 fine, but the 'presiding magistrate . . . was known for disliking the theatre in general and homosexuals in particular' (Ibell, p. 93). Sandy Wilson claimed that the sentence only 'enhanced, if that were possible, his already tremendous popularity' (Wilson, 1975b, p. 20), and this was borne out by the standing ovation that Novello received at his first stage appearance after his prison sentence (Ibell, 2009, p. 94).

Novello first became known as the composer of the 1914 patriotic song 'Keep the home fires burning', which became the defining song of the First World War, and the most popular song for pantomime. The lyrics had a renewed resonance in the Second World War; 'We'll gather lilacs in the Spring Again' was another of Novello's songs which captured the wistfulness of those separated by the Second World War; as Wilson put it in his autobiography, it was 'a sort of theme tune for the forces overseas who hoped soon to be homeward-bound' (Wilson, 1975b, p. 97). Novello had been something of a theatrical prodigy, with his first songs, including 'Fairy Laughter', performed in public when he was fifteen, and he was twenty-one when he wrote 'Keep the home fires burning'.

Both Novello and Coward had been responsible for successful theatre productions which continued throughout the war and were widely seen to have sustained British morale. An earlier generation than Wilson, they had established theatrical reputations which called on them to entertain the troops with concerts and plays, unlike the clerical filing of Wilson's wartime experience. Novello's *The Dancing Years* had first opened in the West End in 1939, it went on a national tour in 1940 when forced out of London because of the Blitz, and then returned to the Adelphi in 1942, where it played until 1944. A symbol of British resilience, *The Dancing Years* had also been on the right side during the war, the hero (played by Novello) is an Austrian Jew; this allowed Novello to make a direct critique of the Nazi régime. *Perchance to Dream*, which opened in 1945, ran successfully for 1,022 performances. While Novello's name may no longer have the currency it held in the 1940s and early 1950s, his songs remain familiar through film and television representations of the Second World War, when they are often used to connote British wartime spirit.

Noël Coward's ghostly comedy *Blithe Spirit* (produced by Beaumont) had opened in the West End during the war in 1941 and was still in production in 1946. Coward's patriotic paean to the British spirit, *This Happy Breed*, opened in 1942, and his celebration of British restraint, *Brief Encounter*,[5] which came out as a film (dir. David Lean) in November 1945, also served to confirm him as a patriot whose work embodied a British spirit of quiet fortitude. It is clear from his autobiography that Coward agonized considerably over the most appropriate role for him to play during the war and had taken advice from the 'highest quarters'. According to John Lahr, Churchill decided that Coward's skills lay in boosting morale: 'Go out and sing "Mad Dogs and Englishmen" while the guns are firing, that's your job' (Lahr, 1984, p. 23). Coward's short plays *Fumed Oak* and *Hands across the Sea* were performed at military bases, with John Gielgud starring (see Brandreth, p. 81). Coward also toured South Africa, Burma, India and Ceylon, giving concerts for troops in London and France; it was later revealed, with the publication of his letters in 1973, that he was simultaneously acting on behalf of the British Secret Service (see Day, 2014). Coward's reputation as a patriot and representative of the British stiff upper lip in the face of war was already confirmed by his performance in the 1942 film *In Which We Serve*. Coward played the captain of a battleship (loosely based on Louis Mountbatten as the commander of a ship sunk at the Battle of Cyprus in 1941); he wrote the script and the score, and directed the film (with the assistance of David Lean), which was both a commercial and critical success.

'Binkie' Beaumont was then the most powerful man in British theatre, as he was throughout the 1940s and 1950s, as the director of H. M. Tennent Ltd. H. M. Tennent, known as 'The Firm' in theatrical circles, had been founded in 1936; it is described by Kitty Black, who went to work there in 1937, as the 'most prestigious English impresario' (Black, 1984, p. 1). Beaumont had kept the West End theatre going throughout the war years; he was influential enough to persuade the government to keep theatres open after they went 'dark' in the week after the declaration of war, and he staged productions throughout the war, as Dorney and Gray explain: 'When the war ended in 1945, Tennent was responsible for twelve productions in eight of the thirty-six West End theatres. They had staged fifty-nine plays during the six years of war and would go on to stage many of the most influential plays of the next decade' (Dorney and Gray, 2014, p. 10).

Beaumont, Coward and Novello were, in the immediate post-war period, a triumvirate of successful men of the theatre who gathered a powerful circle around them and who dominated West End theatre; they shaped Wilson's earliest theatrical experiences and aspirations. Each had their own role and status: 'Ivor Novello was always "The Guv" and Noël Coward "The Master", Binkie was known to everyone in the firm as "The Boss"' (Black, p. 109). The actor John Gielgud and playwright Terence Rattigan were also regulars at the Ivy, often dining with Beaumont, Coward and Novello. They were often written about as a set, their shared sexuality implicit rather than stated; as in Kenneth Tynan's knowing 1953 description of Noël Coward:

> Forty years ago he was Slightly in *Peter Pan*, and you might say that he has been wholly in *Peter Pan* ever since. No private considerations have been allowed to deflect the drive of his career; like Gielgud and Rattigan, like the late Ivor Novello, he is a congenital bachelor. (quoted in Morley, 1999, p. 281)

Rattigan was the most successful British playwright of the time, his work regularly produced by H. M. Tennent. As Innes explains: 'throughout the decade . . . Rattigan dominated the West End. There was hardly a month without at least one of his plays on the stage' (Innes, p. 55). Binkie Beaumont had produced Rattigan's *Flare Path* in 1942 (when other managements had turned it down[6]), which was based on Rattigan's wartime service in the RAF. Churchill came to see the production and gave it his seal of approval; it was made into the patriotic film *The Way to the Stars* (dir. Anthony Asquith) six months before the end of the war in 1945.

Beaumont, Coward, Novello, with Rattigan, were thus extraordinarily powerful figures in the theatre of the post-war period, and popular public icons. They, and many of those who dined with them at the Ivy, were also prominent gay men in a period in which homosexual acts were illegal; they were eminent figures at a moment when the West End of London was a central focus for the press and the authorities, and they were particularly vulnerable. The Montagu trial meant that 'the full glare of hostile media attention was turned on the sexuality of the fashionable man-about-town . . . and provoked a national debate about fashionable society and its links with London's queer cultures' (Mort, 2010, p. 84); Beaumont, Novello and Coward were the embodiments of the 'fashionable man-about-town'. Famous theatrical men, as O'Connor has explained, were particularly vulnerable:

> Paranoia about homosexuality re-emerged with a vengeance after the second world war. . . . By 1955 convictions for gross indecency had

increased to 2,322, seven times the pre-war figure. Several infamous homosexual scandals characterised the mood of the early 1950s. The rich and famous became a particular target to hoist as examples to the general public. (O'Connor, 1998, p. 16)

Among those 'infamous' scandals was that surrounding John Gielgud. Gielgud, recently knighted, was arrested in a public lavatory in Chelsea. In Bengry's account:

> . . . Gielgud's case sparked a frenzy in the papers – the case appeared in every national and many local publications. . . . coverage moved from the Sunday scandal papers to even the respected national and daily papers. The *Daily Mail* gave the case front-page coverage, asking whether Gielgud would still appear at the opening *of A Day by the Sea* the following Monday in Liverpool. (Bengry, 2012, p. 171)

Gielgud did appear in the play, and was received with cheers, as he was when the play transferred to London. Theatre audiences were more liberal than the constabulary, law or the press.

For all their professional reputations and success, Beaumont, Coward and Novello were direct targets for the Metropolitan police. They may not have been born wealthy but they all maintained an upper-class persona; they not only performed a sexuality that was not their own, but also a class position. Their images (with the exception of Terence Rattigan[7]) as urbane upper-class men were creations, their origins not as high class as they appeared. All three had worked professionally in the theatre from a very early age and their earnings were necessary to the family income. Beaumont and Novello had both grown up in Cardiff, where Beaumont's divorced mother took in theatrical lodgers and Novello's mother was a singing teacher. Beaumont first worked in theatre as a box office assistant and then as an assistant stage manager in Cardiff; Novello had sold his first song at the age of seventeen (see Wilson, 1975b). In retrospect, writing the introduction for the publication of *This Happy Breed*, Coward could quite cheerfully acknowledge his relatively humble origins:

> They implied that in setting the play in a milieu so far removed from the cocktail and caviar stratum to which I so obviously belonged, I was over-reaching myself. . . . Having been born in Teddington, having lived respectively at Sutton, Battersea Park and Clapham Common during all my formative years, I can confidently assert that I know a great deal

about the hearts and minds of South Londoners. (quoted in Dorney and Gray, 2014, p. 96)

Huggett has described the multiple personas that Beaumont assumed: 'of all his reputations, the Man of Mystery was the one which Binkie enjoyed the most, the one he sought most earnestly to cultivate and maintain. He achieved this by silence and concealment, partly by deceit' (Huggett, p. 34). John Lahr's estimation of Coward was also true of many of the theatrical gay men who dined at the Ivy: 'A star is his own greatest invention. . . . In his clipped, bright, confident style Coward irresistibly combined reserve and high camp' (Lahr, 1984, p. 22).

This personal ambiguity was also to be found in their work. As Sinfield has suggested, like the respectability of their public personas, the plays of Coward, Novello and Rattigan could be read as entirely straight, but could also be understood as addressing a queer audience:

> The mid-century theatre of Coward and Rattigan was characterised by a sleight-of-hand whereby massaging the anxieties of conservative, middlebrow audiences secured the box office, while an in-the-know minority thrilled to dangerously dissident nuances. In those circumstances there were, in effect, *two (simultaneous) performances,* one for each audience. For the time, this was a necessary and cunning way of insinuating subcultural awareness. (Sinfield, 1998, p. 154)

If they were not quite the upper-class urbane sophisticates they appeared, all three men were celebrities, and, in the aftermath of the Montagu trial, well-known men associated with the theatre were of especial interest to the Metropolitan authorities, as Dan Rebellato points out: 'The theatre, although not single-sexed by any means, was habitually described as encouraging homosexuality, almost of itself' (Rebellato, p. 160). Wildeblood bitterly cites the tabloid newspaper *The People* to point to its malicious pleasure in the 'outing' of prominent men associated with the arts:

> The sentences in the Montagu Case have caused glee in ultra-respectable circles, consternation and fear among many celebrities in the world of the stage, art and letters and exposed the complete failure of our so-called 'civilisation' to find any remedy for sexual perversion to replace cruel and barbaric punishment. (quoted in Wildeblood, 1955, p. 110)

Shellard has pointed to the irony of the fact that this pillorying of gay men and the censorship by the Lord Chamberlain's Office of any mention of homosexuality in British theatre occurred at a time when the theatre in London and the provinces was largely controlled by homosexual men:

> the paradox . . . was [that] the theatre offered for many homosexuals a rare possibility of sanctuary and that the London theatre of the late 1940s was dominated by Binkie Beaumont, Terence Rattigan and John Gielgud – whose sexual inclinations were deemed unpalatable by the body that prided itself on being entrusted with maintaining the moral health of the nation's drama. (Shellard, 1999, p. 14)

Shellard does not include Noël Coward and Ivor Novello among these dominant figures in the London theatre of the late 1940s and early 1950s, but they were regular diners with Beaumont, Rattigan and Gielgud at the Ivy restaurant, which was, in its status as a theatrical haunt, another 'sanctuary' for gay men.

Beaumont's domestic space also provided a safe environment; he was a significant figure as a centre of what Matt Houlbrook has termed a 'queer domesticity', a private social circle for a coterie of men. Houlbrook describes the flat where Beaumont lived with his partner John Perry in Lord North Street in Westminster, which was remembered as a haven for one male couple in the 1950s:

> such spaces allowed them – and others like them – to sustain wider friendship circles. Such informal evenings were regular, as for the circle socializing in Binkie Beaumont and John Perry's Lord North Street apartment. Here, secure in their privacy and able to talk though everyday worries, men found a powerful site of affirmation and respectability. (Houlbrook, 2005, p. 129)

It was not just in such private domestic spaces that gay 'friendship circles' were able to find this affirmation; there were also the liminal spaces of London, largely centred in Soho and the West End, where, particularly for men of the theatre, there was a semi-public, but discreet, culture of backstage gatherings, first-night parties, supper clubs and meetings in bars and restaurants. As Michael Relph, the producer of the 1961 *Victim*[8] (dir. Basil Dearden), remembered:

In those days film directors like Asquith and Hurst, as well as Noël Coward and Ivor Novello, were protected by the theatrical world. There wasn't any harassment of gay people in our profession. . . . However, a cat-and-mouse game existed with the police if gays stepped outside their particular world. (quoted in Bourne, 1996, p. 156)

This 'cat-and-mouse game' expressed itself spatially and geographically. The 'theatrical world' was a literal space in London's West End, in which there were sites with varying degrees of privacy, from domestic environments to the relatively public exposure of dining out. The Ivy diners were among those that Weeks has described as 'cosmopolitan citizens':

He or she can potentially feel at home in all parts of the worlds where a similar repertoire of cafés, bars, clubs, saunas, cruising areas, local neighbourhoods, styles of dress, modes of behaviour and values systems provide the material basis for a 'queer cosmopolitanism'. (Weeks, 2011, p. 36)

The West End was one such neighbourhood, and provided a space in which the Ivy League could both work and socialize. The restaurant, like the theatre, is a liminal space that occupies both the public and private spheres; the theatre allows for personal encounters in a public space, and private assignations can also take place in a public arena of a restaurant.

The writer and dramatist Neil Bartlett puts Beaumont, Coward, Novello and Rattigan together as a group, together with Somerset Maugham and Joe Orton[9] (who was of a later generation), both were known to them and were on occasion part of their circle. Bartlett suggests quite how significant these men were as a group for twentieth-century theatre in Britain:

if you remove Wilde, Rattigan, Maugham, Coward, Orton and Novello from the post-1900 British theatre profession – from the money-earning profession of theatre – you're left with a pretty serious problem at the box office. And if you remove . . . Binkie Beaumont then you lost half of the actors you've ever heard of. (Neil Bartlett, quoted in Sinfield, 1998, pp. 152–3)

Binkie Beaumont, along with his friends and colleagues, especially Coward, Novello and Rattigan, can be understood as belonging to the group that Andrew Ross has termed 'camp intellectuals':

Hitherto associated with the high-culture milieu of the theatre, camp intellectuals become an institution in the twentieth century, within the popular entertainment industries, reviving their role there as the representative or stand-in for a class that is no longer in a position to exercise its power to define official culture. (Ross, 1999, p. 64)

This institution, although undeniably camp, was in fact no less of an old boys' network than the traditional public school and Oxbridge-educated arbiters of taste; it was founded on a shared long experience of theatre. Although genteel and middle class, rather than wealthy, they all knew one another. Rebellato has questioned the 'belief that a homosexual mafia with Beaumont as its Godfather ran British theatre' (Rebellato, p. 56); it may be the case that Binkie Beaumont and his friends at the Ivy were not a formal Mafia, and that Binkie was no Godfather, and it is true that they did not have a monopoly over contemporary theatre; Prince Littler was an impresario to rival Beaumont in the period. Like Beaumont, he had worked in theatre from a very young age, but, unlike Beaumont, he had spent time working on Broadway; he was the figure who was largely responsible for first bringing American musical productions to the West End: *Brigadoon* in 1950, *Carousel* in 1951 and *Guys and Dolls* in 1953. Nonetheless, it remains the case that Binkie Beaumont and his associates did represent a powerful network of homosexual men whose influence over actors, directors, writers and theatre managers could not but have a hold over the shape of London theatre.

There is a complex interconnective web between the men, their work and their personal lives. Kitty Black suggests that these men of the theatre borrowed one another's personal style:

Like Binkie, Terry was the personification of charm. Always immaculate, he wielded a long cigarette holder in the Coward manner, and used a gold Fabergé cigarette case with careless ease. (Later Binkie was to acquire one of these as the obligatory status symbol.) (Black, 1984, p. 67)

It was not only mannerisms and accessories that this coterie borrowed from one another but also professional connections and friendships. The members of the Ivy League invested in one another's plays, they regularly produced or directed them, they advised one another on scripts and casting, attended each other's first nights (bringing with them their associated reputations) and sometimes slept with one another's partners (as was the case with John Gielgud's partner, John Perry, who left Gielgud for Beaumont[10]). In just one instance of this interconnectivity of the personal and the professional, Rattigan wrote *Love in Idleness* as a vehicle for Gertrude Lawrence (who was

Coward's long-standing theatre partner and who had been a close friend since stage school). When she turned it down, Ivor Novello engineered a meeting between Lynn Fontanne and Alfred Lunt (with whom Coward had starred in *Design for Living*) and Rattigan. The production went ahead in 1944 with Fontanne and Lunt in the leads, and Binkie Beaumont produced the play with investment from Coward. Much of their business, as Coward's diaries demonstrate, was conducted over lunches and dinners in West End restaurants, particularly the Ivy. Rebellato has challenged a version of post-war history in which gay men were neatly closeted and contained, in terms which could evoke the meetings at the Ivy:

> The traditional image of homosexuality in the forties and fifties as closeted, hidden and silent fails to recognise that it was actually throwing into question the boundaries between secrecy and openness, knowable and unknowable, visible and invisible, private and public, lies and honesty, intention and expression, performance and reception, interpretation and misinterpretation.(Rebellato, 1999, p. 190)

The Ivy was a space in which those boundaries were played out; a public arena which 'dissolved the boundary between public and private' (Houlbrook, 2005, p. 129), an addition to the private apartments which were the informal spaces for gay men to congregate. At the Ivy men could meet with one another at their own tables in full view, their homosexuality recognized by many, but which could remain invisible to those who preferred not to know. Wilson describes a meeting in Brighton with Beaumont, John Perry and Gielgud in a hotel suite when *Slings and Arrows* was previewing at the Theatre Royal before its London opening; he refers to Perry as Beaumont's 'partner' (Wilson, 1975a, p. 138), a reference that would have been knowingly understood by theatre aficionados.

By the mid-1950s, the discreet charm of the Ivy League was fading, it was the beginning of the end for the glamour of Novello and Coward, and Binkie Beaumont no longer had the sure touch over London's theatre that he had displayed throughout the 1940s and early 1950s. Novello died suddenly in 1951, famously after completing a final performance of *King's Rhapsody*, aged fifty-eight. Coward's post-war plays could not match the success of his earlier work and his once firm hold on the theatre-going public was beginning to wane in the late 1940s; his musicals *Pacific 1860* (1946) and *Ace of Clubs* (1949) were both critical and commercial failures. The 1954 musical, *After the Ball* (an adaptation of Oscar Wilde's *Lady Windermere's Fan*) ran for only 188 performances in London and seemed to confirm Coward as an outmoded figure; *Plays and Players* scathingly described the production as a 'provincial mediocrity of a musical play, incredibly old-fashioned, of the type which died in the twenties' (quoted in Wright, 2017, p. 60). Coward reinvented himself as a cabaret star, with an act developed from the success of his wartime performances for the troops; this was established at the Café de Paris in London and then moved to Las Vegas, where it was recorded in 1955; cabaret would define his public persona until his death.

The triumph of a wave of American musicals in the West End in the late 1940s and early 1950s (with which Coward's post-war work was so unfavourably compared) challenged Beaumont's kind of theatre, with their ensemble casts and American energy, they were widely welcomed as distinctly different. Beaumont's star-studded dramas could not match the ebullience of the imported American productions, and his customary lavish sets and wardrobes sat uneasily in a post-war rationed Britain. Although Beaumont did produce *Oklahoma!*, he did not have Prince Littler's experience of America, and his dramas centred around established West End stars were beginning, like Coward's musicals, to look 'incredibly old fashioned'.

Rattigan's reputation was already beginning to suffer before the Royal Court's production of *Look Back in Anger* in 1956. Both Beaumont and Rattigan attended the first night, but Beaumont was reported as leaving at the interval. Rattigan saw Osborne's play as a direct affront to his kind of writing and remarked to the theatre critic of the *Daily Express* that Osborne's play was saying: 'Look ma, how unlike Terence Rattigan I'm being' (quoted in Roberts, 2001, p. 48). He wrote to George Devine to apologize, but the damage was done, Rattigan became a synonym for an old-fashioned form of theatre for a younger generation of playwrights and critics. Shelagh Delaney notoriously claimed that she wrote *A Taste of Honey* after she thought she could do better, following a school outing to see Rattigan's play *Variation on a Theme* in 1958. Joe Orton's explicitly queer – rather than camp – drama threw down a gauntlet to the disguised sexuality and plea for respectability found in Terence Rattigan's work. Orton mounted a vendetta against Rattigan which was played out in Orton's wicked letters to the press in the persona of 'Edna Welthorpe', a version of the 'Aunt Edna', that Rattigan had posited as his audience in the preface to the second volume of his *Collected Plays* (Rattigan, 1953, p. xii). Kitty Black considered that this new drama reduced the hold that H. M. Tennant and Beaumont had once held over West End theatre: 'With the advent of the new wave of dramatists . . . perhaps his control of the London theatre became less all-powerful – he wasn't interested in kitchen sink drama anyway' (Black, 1984, p. 60).

Rebellato, however, has rightly argued against a version of theatre history in which the Royal Court and its production of *Look Back in Anger* are seen as a direct and decisive challenge to

> the giant accumulation of bricks-and-mortar, capital and conservative loyalty that Hugh 'Binkie' Beaumont and 'the Group' had amassed. This is history as fairy-tale; the smooth villainy of 'Binkie' Beaumont, the self-evident wickedness of the West End, and the Court's fresh-faced triumph against all the odds are there in every history. In the final showdown integrity triumphs against glitter, artistry against decoration and passion against repression. (Rebellato, p. 38)

Look Back in Anger undoubtedly represented a shift in contemporary London theatre, and the Ivy League did see it as a challenge to the dominance of their kind of theatre, but, as Rebellato points out, it was not as decisive a shift as many theatre historians have suggested. Any simple opposition between the avant-garde of the Royal Court and the commercial conservatism of the West End does not allow for the interconnectedness of the impresarios, the West End and the Royal Court, and of their writers, audiences, actors and directors. It was Sandy Wilson's friend Kenneth Tynan who was the most enthusiastic champion of *Look Back in Anger*.

Despite the declining power of the Ivy League, they were generous in passing their knowledge, experience and investment on to a new generation, lending their support to younger writers and directors. Rattigan was an admirer of Orton's 1964 *Entertaining Mr Sloane* and invested £3000 pounds in the original production. Gielgud appeared in a production of *King Lear* at Stratford directed by George Devine in 1955. By the end of the 1950s, Beaumont had brought the Broadway musicals *West Side Story* and *My Fair Lady* to the West End in 1958, and he was a member of the board of the new National Theatre until his death in 1973 (the same year that Noël Coward died).

In her account of 'A Queer Geography', Affrica Taylor draws attention to urban centres as heterotopic sites: 'a site of illusion, a site of simultaneous concealment and exposure, where things may be revealed to be not as they appear, and thereby disrupt the order of our thinking' (Taylor, p. 9). The Ivy restaurant was not strictly a heterotopia in that it did serve a conventional function and its customers abided by the conventional codes of behaviour in a restaurant. However, within the urban centre of London, among the bars and theatres of the West End, it was a space which allowed for concealment and exposure, an environment in which gay men could develop their own projects and networks.

Richard Dyer has also argued that such spaces were crucial to a queer cultural production:

> Queer culture had to occur in the institutional spaces available and certain spaces were more propitious than others for queer cultural production. . . . Equally, some men . . . acquired a certain amount of cultural clout that allowed them to do queer things within the straight acquired inclined structures they perforce worked within. (Dyer, 2002, p. 9)

If Beaumont, Coward, Novello, Rattigan and Sandy Wilson could not at the time have expressed it in these terms, they all understood London's West End theatre in the 1950s to be one of those 'institutional spaces', the men who ran it, the impresarios and their associates, possessed a great deal of 'cultural clout'. Within the space of the theatrical West End was the quasi-private space of the Ivy restaurant, which 'allowed them to do queer things' and which proved a most propitious space for a queer cultural production of theatre.

By the early 1960s, the Ivy had lost its lustre as a venue for theatre people and had become a place for tourists and commercial deals, as Wilson witheringly describes in his unpublished novel:

> It was hard to believe . . . that the Ivy was once a favourite rendezvous of theatre people. Business-men in hard black suits, with over-polished shoes and faces, clapped each other's shoulders over dry martinis, while the last of the lady tourists from South Africa and Australia, fitting in a week of theatre-going in London before flying back to the sun, loosened their furs and patted lacquered hair wired down by sequinned fascinators. (*Oxford's Not What it Used to Be*, second version, unpublished, undated manuscript, p. 28, Sandy Wilson archive)

It would take until 2005 for Novello's name to be cemented in the West End with the renaming of the Strand Theatre (where he had lived in a flat until his death) as the Novello Theatre in 2005; Coward's name and status were similarly honoured in the renaming of the Albery theatre as the Noël Coward Theatre in 2006. The Ivy restaurant was bought up by the Caprice Holdings Group in 2005 and, from 2015, was rolled out as a franchise, a 'heritage' brand. It is important to remember, at a time when gay rights are once again under threat, that the Ivy restaurant represents more than a heritage site, and to recognize the role that it played as a space for gay men to meet. Binkie Beaumont, Noël Coward, Terence Rattiga and Ivor Novello may not have been political militants, but it took some courage to meet with other homosexual men in a public place, particularly after the Montagu trial. As Baker has said of the Polari speakers he interviewed for his research project: 'they weren't political. . . . But their very existence was a political act' (Baker, 2019, p. 284). While Beaumont, Coward and Novello were too discreet to be hailed as heroes of the Gay Liberation Front over a decade later, they offered, to Sandy Wilson and to many other homosexual men of the next generation, an image of how to be a successful man of the theatre, a popular icon and a 'camp intellectual', while hiding in plain sight.

PLAYERS' THEATRE

Directors: DON GEMMELL   REGINALD WOOLLEY   GERVASE FARJEON

1936-1940   COVENT GARDEN (formerly Evans's late Joy's)
1940-1945   ALBEMARLE STREET
1945——   VILLIERS STREET (formerly Gatti's—Under-the-Arches)

VILLIERS STREET   STRAND   WC2

EVERY NIGHT EXCEPT SUNDAY

RIDGEWAY'S LATE JOYS

PRODUCED BY DON GEMMELL

The ARTISTES include —

Jean Anderson	Geoffrey Dunn	Joanna Horder	John Moll
Daphne Anderson	Clive Dunn	Hattie Jacques	Barbara Mullen
Hedli Anderson	Robert Eddison	Ernest Jay	Robert Nichols
Alexander Archdale	Lyn Evans	Mags Jenkins	Ronan O'Casey
Sydney Arnold	Jonathan Field	James Justice	Peggy van Praagh
Rosalind Atkinson	Elsie French	John Justin	Bill Rowbotham
Frank Baker	Philip Godfrey	Lilly Kann	Leonard Sachs
Frith Banbury	John Glyn Jones	Irving Kaye	Bill Shine
Charlotte Bidmead	May Hallatt	Julia Lang	Joan Sterndale Bennett
Heather Boys	Archie Harradine	Thérèse Langfield	Fred Stone
Ian Carmichael	Elton Hayes	Lisa Lee	Eleanor Summerfield
Erik Chitty	John Heawood	Charles Leno	Tony Sympson
Alec Clunes	John Hewer	Harry Locke	Peter Ustinov
Edric Connor	Geoffrey Hibbert	Diana Maddox	Violetta
Joyce Cummings	Owen Holder	Denis Martin	Josephine Wilson
Colleen Clifford	Vida Hope	Bernard Miles	Dennis Wood
Nuna Davey			

Chairman: Don Gemmell   At the pianoforte: Betty Lawrence & Stan Edwards

Scenery designed and painted by REGINALD WOOLLEY
Stage Director: GERVASE FARJEON
Stage Manager: MARY BENNETT assisted by VERNON RUSSELL
Ballets arranged by JOHN HEAWOOD
Costumes by PLAYERS' THEATRE WARDROBE, L. & H. NATHAN, Ltd.
Nylon Stockings by KAYSER BONDOR
Stage Lighting by MAJOR EQUIPMENT Co., Ltd.
Master Carpenter: FREDERICK DRAPER
Secretary: ENID COLLETT
Box Office: EDNA HEWER

1952

Design by H. V. Stephenson

Figure 4.1 'Late Joys'; programme, The Players' Theatre Club.

'Oh! The Fairies'

The Players' Theatre Club

Oh, the fairies; whoa the fairies,
Nothing but splendour and feminine gender.
Oh, the fairies; whoa the fairies,
Oh for the wing of a fairy queen.

(T. S. Lonsdale and William G. Eaton, 1878,
the Players' Theatre anthem)

The Players' Theatre Club was the theatre which commissioned and nurtured Sandy Wilson's most successful and widely known work, *The Boy Friend*, and oversaw its development from a small club entertainment into a West End and Broadway hit musical. From 1946 until its closure as a theatre in 2002, the Players' Theatre was situated not in the West End itself but its address in Villiers Street, off the Strand, was within walking distance. Like the Ivy restaurant, it was a concealed space, positioned underneath the arches of Charing Cross station.[1] A 1970 listing of *London Theatres and Music Halls* describes the building:

> Music hall constructed in two of the arches formed by the Charing Cross station which was constructed in 1863, on the site of the old Hungerford Market. In 1910 it became a cinema, and was not used again for live entertainment until 14th Jan. 1946 when the Players' Theatre company (a theatre club) moved there from 30 Albermarle Street having previously been at 43, King Street (Evan's Song and Supper Rooms) and 6, New Compton Street (Howard, p. 179)

The Players' was first opened as a theatre and supper club in 1936, in King Street, Covent Garden by Peter Ridgeway and Leonard Sachs, who was to become its best-known chairman. It then offered a late programme of cabaret and music hall beginning at 11.30 at night, so that theatre people, both audiences and

performers, could come on from another West End show. In the early part of
the war, the Players' company moved to various sites across central London;
to Evan's (late Joy's) Song and Supper Rooms in Covent Garden, a location
which gave its name, 'Late Joys' to the Players' music-hall programme (and to
three books about the theatre). Mr Joy had been the original proprietor of the
supper club, before it was taken over by Mr W. C. Evans, a comedian at the
Covent Garden Theatre. The Players' Theatre relished the pun and reproduced
it on the nightly song sheets. The 'Late Joys' programme was celebrated in a
book, *Late Joys at the Players' Theatre*, published during the war in 1943, when
many of the members, audience, production crew and cast had been called up.
In her editor's note, the acting director of the theatre, Jean Anderson, speaks
of 'the atmosphere of the entertainment and the incongruities to be seen at the
Players' (in Harradine, p. 8). Performances kept going throughout the war, as
a 1952 souvenir book proudly recalls: 'The war was on and the theatres shut
down – but not the Players'; that went on merrily through blitz, fires and many
natural forms of intimidation' (Sheridan, 1952, p. 40).

The Villiers Street site had once been Gatti's music hall, founded in 1867;
it had been used as a centre for experimental theatre in the 1920s and 1930s,
as a cinema, and had been occupied by ENSA[2] during the war from 1939
(see Mander and Mitchenson (b) pp. 298–303). The lease for Gatti's Charing
Cross Music Hall was taken over in 1946 by the actors Leonard Sachs (who
would go on to become the chairman of the televised *The Good Old Days*,
broadcast on the BBC from 1953), and Jean Anderson (who ran the Players'
during the war while Sachs was doing army service).

The programme for the 1954 production of *The Boy Friend* on its
transfer from Villiers Street to the West End carries an advertisement for
the Players' Theatre which promises: 'Victorian Music Hall, Restaurant, Bars,
Dancing' (Wyndham's Theatre programme, 1954). Music hall was already a
nostalgic enterprise in the post-war period, according to Hopkins: 'In the
thirteen years after the end of the war over 100 music halls closed down in
Britain' (Hopkins, p. 107). The Players' was unapologetically nostalgic in
its celebratory version of music hall, 'the last theatre in the world offering a
modern representation of Victorian music hall' (Baker 2005, p. 115). In 1951,
it could boast a new programme of music hall turns every fortnight. Under
the management of Leonard Sachs, the theatre's policy was to combine music
hall with new plays and revues. Gänzl describes the Players' programming in
terms which remained the formula for the theatre well into the 1970s:

> The Players' Theatre Club had been formed in 1936 on the same lines
> as the other little theatres, presenting 'interesting plays' and their own
> speciality, programmes of Victorian music hall, in a series of small

premises. After the war . . . it became firmly established, playing principally its popular 'Late Joys' programmes: a string of music hall turns linked by the jocular patter of a chairman. This diet of easy entertainment was varied by a Christmas pantomime, usually an early Victorian burlesque adapted to the theatre's needs with a fine fidelity to the original. (Gänzl, 1986, p. 641)

The Players' annual Victorian Christmas pantomime was preceded by a Harlequinade, and throughout the year the theatre offered a programme of contemporary and Victorian drama. The company did not restrict itself to 'easy entertainment'; in 1937 the theatre hosted the Unity Theatre production of *Waiting for Lefty* by Clifford Odets, a year after its opening in New York at the Group Theatre. The Players' was never however a directly political theatre; among its regular productions were Robert Browning's 1855 *In a Balcony*, work by Pirandello, along with now forgotten original plays by the Players' stalwarts, Leonard Sachs and Peter Ridgeway (see Sheridan, 1943, p. 112). The pantomime scripts were drawn from manuscripts in the British Library, often originally written by the Victorian dramatist J. R. Planché, adapted by the Players' regular performer and archivist, Archie Harradine and one of the Players' club directors, Don Gemmell.

In the 1951 *Goodtime Guide to London* Aldor includes the Players' Theatre Club in a map of the West End; in his description: 'you may watch old-fashioned music-hall beautifully dressed and presented, while drinking beer and (at your peril) arguing with the Chairman of the revels' (Aldor, p. 82). The Players' was however more than an 'old-fashioned music hall', it had a repertory company and a management team who were prepared to experiment with uncommercial writers and plays. It was one of the 'tiny theatres' that Wilson describes in his autobiography: 'which existed in the first place to present plays that would otherwise, either because of censorship or their uncommercial nature, never have been seen' (Wilson, 1975a, p. 129).

Macqueen-Pope's 1947 *Indiscreet Guide to Theatreland* includes the Players' as among what he terms the 'back room boys of the theatre',[3] a space outside the commercial West End which could try out new productions:

those brave, ambitious, small, semi-private theatres . . . in these small laboratories of the drama they make experiments, experiments with plays, players and ideas. Here they try out plays which are said to be non-commercial and do most valuable work. . . . Back rooms . . . such as The Players, the Torch, The Unity and the Chanticleer are priceless. (Macqueen-Pope, 1947, p. 130)

In the same year Norman Marshall includes the Players' in a list of 'pioneer theatres' and here describes the particularity of the Players' ethos and the variety of its programming:

> A theatre club with a character entirely different from all the others. . . . On Friday nights there was an informal cabaret, in which the performers included Arthur Askey, Cyril Fletcher and Alec Clunes. These performances were so successful that towards the end of 1937 Ridgeway decided to revive, under the title of *Late Joys*, the Song-and-Supper-Room. . . . At first the performances burlesqued the Victorians, but gradually there was less guying and more honest reproduction. The characteristics of the performances were charm, humour and gusto, combined with good singing. Meanwhile plays were still given during the early part of the evening. (Marshall, p. 216)

Leonard Sachs left the Players' in 1947, and Reginald Woolley, the stage designer and illustrator, his partner, Don Gemmell, an actor-producer, and Gervase Farjeon, a director, became the new board of directors. They brought in a programme of 'present-day entertainment' (Sheridan, 1951, p. 3) and by 1952 the Players' Theatre Club could boast over 3,000 members (Sheridan, 1952, p. 83). Sandy Wilson described the Players' status in the early 1950s (with perhaps some overstatement as to its membership and international standing) and his first meeting with two of the directors:

> it now had a membership running into several thousands and a world-wide reputation. Attached to the theatre is a restaurant usually referred to as the Supper Room, and it was here that I met Gervase Farjeon and Reggie Woolley, who designs all the Players' shows. Gervase has a charmingly shy manner . . . while Reggie combines a faintly mandarin appearance with a misleadingly destructive sense of humour. (Wilson, 1975, p. 173)

A 1993 obituary of Woolley suggests quite how significant the three directors were to the successful running of the theatre:

> He was the last of a triumvirate (with Gervase Farjeon and Don Gemmell) who kept the Players' Theatre on the map from 1939 as one of the merriest underground playhouses in London during the Blitz and as an honest-to-God example of traditional theatre. (Benedick, 20 March, 1993)

According to Mander and Mitchenson, under the direction of this 'triumvirate', 'the theatre achieved world-wide fame . . . for its own particular style of entertainment' (Mander and Mitchenson (b), p. 303). That particular style of entertainment was one of nostalgia; by the 1950s, traditional music hall was well on the wane, Wilmut has described 'its virtual demise in the late 1950s . . . the years from the end of the War to 1960 are really a quite separate story from that of the old music-hall' (Wilmut, p. 13). The 'old music-hall' was not however a separate story for the Players' Theatre, which prided itself on its adherence to the traditions of Victorian music hall, as Wilmut describes them: '"Music-hall" conjures up the popular idea of the Victorian halls, with red plush seats and a somewhat rowdy working-class audience, a chairman to introduce the acts and lots of chorus songs' (Wilmut, p. 13). If the Players' audience was not exactly working class, the seats were red plush, the audience rowdy and the chairman (who invariably was a man) central to proceedings in leading the chorus songs.

The 1952 souvenir programme relishes this nostalgia for the music hall, and begins with a fulsome tribute to the Victorian period, presenting the Players' as sustaining a cherished theatrical tradition in an age of modernity:

> it is salutary that in the Players' Theatre we have preserved a genuine, unaffected, unpretentious but boisterous Victorian music-hall at its very best – a part of the London stage of yesterday that would long since have disappeared from the English theatrical scene. (Sheridan, 1952, p. 3)

The use of music hall was not only nostalgic for a previous age but also a celebration of a boisterous form of popular culture and a subversion of the social and sexual respectability that had re-emerged so forcibly in the post-war period. Dagmar Kift has argued that Victorian music hall (as did its revival) challenged any idea of the Victorians as entirely prudish and respectable:

> The values propagated in the halls were anything but the Victorian values of hard work, sobriety or respect for marriage and the family. And if such values were propagated they were interpreted in a different manner from that of the ruling classes. The popular figure in the halls was not the hard-working teetotaller but the dandy. The moral tone was not conducive to wholesome and sober recreation, for the stage was dominated by scantily-clad dancers and acrobats. Marriage was not presented as something to be strived after but a disaster. (Kift, p. 77)

If Victorian nostalgia was the main offering of the Players' programming, the theatre club was also a fashionable place to be in the decade of the 1950s. The Wyndham's programme for the West End transfer of *The Boy Friend* expresses this paradox of the Players' as a theatre that combined both the 'progressive' and traditional and which was both nostalgic and fashionable:

> an old established but progressive theatre club in Villiers Street, known mainly for a Victorian entertainment called *Late Joys* which it presents nightly to its members. The activities of the Players; however, are by no means confined to the *Late Joys*. It is a theatre of experiment and has produced in its time a wide variety of entertainment including straight plays . . . pantomime, revue and musical entertainments of all kinds. (Wyndham's Theatre programme, *The Boy Friend*, 1954, p. 2)

This mix of the contemporary and traditional chimed with the context of a post-war London and captured a particular 1950s sensibility; as Conekin, Mort and Waters have explained of the Coronation: 'the modern in this period was a hybrid affair, assembled out of tales about the past as well as narratives of the future' (Conekin et al., p. 3). That hybridity was also evident at the 1951 Festival of Britain, which harked back to the Victorian Great Exhibition of 1851 and simultaneously looked forward to a post-war future in a display that was marked by both nostalgia and optimism. A show modelled on the 'Late Joys' was performed at the Festival of Britain, with Leonard Sachs as the chair, and it was that production that brought the Players' music hall and performers to the attention of television[4] and a much wider audience. The Players' company was involved in the first week of broadcast television after the war, with a programme of Edwardian music hall.

The Players' Theatre shared the same spirit of modest hope found at the Festival of Britain; the theatre club had, like London, survived the war and now faced a future constrained by rationing. The spirit of 'making do and mending'[5] was central to the Players' ethos, as it would be to the sets and costumes of the original production of *The Boy Friend*.[6] Harradine remembered in 1943 that performers and directors were expected to turn their hands to anything that the theatre required: 'Reginald Woolley . . . spread a pretty sandwich in the snack bar, also painted the gas-brackets and decorated the "ante-saloon" . . . the young lady who served you your beer might also move you in a Tchaikovsky ballet, a programme seller as Principal Boy . . .' (Harradine, p. 17).

Reginald Woolley was both a director of the Players' and its in-house designer (and the first designer for *The Boy Friend*). He provided the illustrations for *Late Joys at the Players' Theatre* (and two later volumes) and was responsible for the ingenious sets for the annual pantomime, which managed to create at least two transformation scenes for each production, on the tiny stage at Villiers Street. An obituary noted Woolley's taste for the past and his comfortable fit with the ethos of the Players' Theatre:

> Woolley was a master of low-tech theatre. He may have used electricity to light his shows but you felt as you watched his evocations of palaces and forests, mountains and caves for the postage-stamp stage of the Players Theatre Club, in Villiers Street, London, that he might have been happier with gas or even candles.
>
> At any rate he loved to work in the past, and where better for a designer of such meticulous regard for a period before his own, than at that celebrated haven of Victorian conservation beneath Charing Cross station where the rumblings of the trains became so much a feature of the nightly variety bill, known as 'Late Joys'. (Benedick, 1993)

Woolley had also been involved in the design of the Festival's Pavilions at Battersea Park and brought back a Lion and Unicorn heraldic device to the Villiers Street theatre when the exhibition closed, where it remained until the Players' left Villiers Street in 2002. Edric Connor, who had brought the Trinidad All Steel Percussion Orchestra to the Festival of Britain, was a regular performer in the 'Joys' music hall from 1951.[7]

Frank Mort has described the significance of the Coronation's firework display in 1953, two years after the Festival of Britain and a year before the opening of *The Boy Friend*. The fireworks lit up London's West End which had been dark throughout the wartime blackout:

> The night-time spectacle was clearly visible from the windows of Pall Mall's clubland, preserve of the masculine political élite, and from gala balls organized by society hostesses in Mayfair and Belgravia, but it was also seen from popular rendezvous in the entertainment settings of the West End, where an unending crocodile of revellers snaked around Piccadilly Circus. Performers and audiences in theatreland, close by in Leicester Square, joined in the night-time festivities, with stars like Noël Coward appearing in late-night cabaret. (Mort, 2010, p. 26)

All these groups were members of the audience at the Players' throughout the 1950s; it was a club which attracted both high society[8] and theatre people; Noël Coward and Princess Margaret attended, as did theatrical luminaries Alfred Lunt, Lynne Fontanne and Marlene Dietrich (see Sheridan, 1952, p. 37). The 1952 souvenir programme makes much of the diversity of the members and the audience mix of aristocracy and bohemia: 'The man who tried to assign the Players' Theatre a place in the hierarchy of London Clubs would be extremely rash. It's common ground for all of them, Olympians of St. James's and Soho cellar-dwellers alike' (Dowling, p. 13).

A contemporary review in the *Manchester Guardian* also indicates the range of communities who attended the Players' Theatre: 'The audience is a mixture of the younger stage, a little of Mayfair and Bloomsbury and the Temple and a back-wash of the old bohemian world' (undated, quoted in Sheridan, 1943, p. 29). The Players' audience exemplified the emergent cultural landscape of London in the early 1950s as described by Mort:

> an eclectic mixture of worldly politicians and international visitors, along with socialites, photographers, actors, models and fashion designers were beginning to stimulate London's cultural atmosphere after the years of austerity. Many of these individuals congregated in fashionable pubs and clubs, which enterprising landlords had established as spaces for informal socializing and for relaxed displays of heterosocial and homosocial leisure. (Mort, 2010, p. 50)

Theatre clubs were among the fashionable spaces where this mixture congregated; it was not, however, only enterprise that motivated club owners, spaces such as the Players' Theatre Club provided a venue in which 'homosocial leisure' and pleasures were made possible outside the confines of a domestic space. Central to the ethos of the Players' was that it was a private members' club, largely run by homosexual men, and as such the theatre, its restaurant and bar provided a safe space for homosocial friendships at a time when homosexual acts between men were criminalized. It was one of the 'privileged sites' that Mort has identified: 'Such spaces functioned not only as a backdrop, they were active in the construction of men's identities. What took place in areas such as Soho, in London's West End, was the formation of particular taste communities, with divergent and often competing claims on social space' (Mort, 1996, p. 11).

The Players' had its own very particular 'taste community'. Wright refers to the Players' 'specific' audience which, he archly implies, had a distinctly camp sensibility: 'the taste of its members, used to a diet of highly stylised Victorian music hall pastiche, was known to be indulgent and even faintly esoteric' (Wright, 2010, p. 72). This 'highly stylized' pastiche, as Richard Dyer has suggested, in itself had the quality of camp (Dyer, 2007, p. 3). The double-entendres of music hall songs were a means of celebrating the vulgar and of positioning the theatre and its audience against the respectability of marriage and family. Kift has also argued that Victorian music hall offered audiences a 'somewhat dubious counter-culture' (Kift, p. 176):

Sex – in stark contrast to Victorian middle class notions was not taboo but a source of enjoyment. Furthermore, music hall songs took the subject to its logical end by dealing with marriage and family life. Here there is no more talk of bliss from either the male or female standpoint... when it came to singing the joys of married life, both sides were as a rule in agreement: it was a disaster. (Kift, p. 37)

That 'dubious counter-culture' takes on a particular edge in the context of a homosocial community; it is clear why a collective sharing of the miseries of conventional wedlock should be of appeal to a largely gay male audience in the morally conformist post-war era.[9] As Gordon explains, the two most successful theatre productions of 1953 and 1954 both had a distinctly camp edge: 'Both *The Boy Friend* and *Salad Days* treat their audience as privileged members of a clandestine club, gathering together in private to escape the privations of war, austerity and bureaucratically enforced conformism' (Gordon et al., p. 12). That conformism was not only 'bureaucratically enforced' in the late 1940s and early 1950s but carried with it the real threat of arrest and imprisonment for homosexual men.

Salad Days and *The Boy Friend* offered both escapism and a nostalgia for a less threatening time; as Gordon puts it, both productions

exploited a camp aesthetic, which deployed nostalgia together with the disorientating effects of pastiche and parody to project a coded 'gay' identity. The uninhibited cultivation of joy and pleasure in such shows was 'gay' in the innocent sense of the word, but to those in the know it was also 'gay' in a way that insiders recognized as potentially subversive'. (Gordon et al. p. 13)

The Players' Theatre Club was itself a 'clandestine club' and its audiences were certainly among 'those in the know'. For Susan Sontag, 'Camp is something of a private code, a badge of identity even, among small urban cliques' (Sontag, p. 105), and, she suggests, ritual is one of the defining features of camp. The audiences at the Players' regularly displayed that badge of identity as insiders who demonstrated their familiarity with the shared codes and conventions of the club; as Richard Dyer crisply puts it: 'to have a good camp together gives you a tremendous sense of identification and belonging' (Dyer, 1992, p. 135).

An evening at the theatre was marked by a series of shared rituals, referred to in the 1952 souvenir programme as the 'customs of the Players' (Sheridan, 1952, p. 13). Each performance began with a collective singing of 'Oh! the Fairies', known to the members and announced by the chairman (with firm emphasis) as 'the Players' Theatre anthem', the lyrics provided on the pink song sheet handed to every audience member. If, according to the Players' official historian, the anthem was ostensibly sung to the 'ladies in the audience' (Sheridan, 1952, p. 74), the homosexual connotations of the term 'fairies' would have been widely known in the post-war period.[10] 'Dear Old Pals' (G. W. Hunt, 1877[11]) was sung every night at the close of each performance and offered members a final expression of solidarity and communality.

The Players' official historian, Paul Sheridan, describes the regular attendance of audience members and their induction of newer members into the expected audience responses and into the codes of the club: 'they certainly came often, the valued compliment to the Players' as a club, and the old familiar faces one sees three and four times in the same week are the regulars who teach the younger and newer members the-long established retorts to the Chairman's bantering' (Sheridan, 1952, p. 75). The chairman's welcome and links to the music-hall acts were marked by a series of shared in-jokes, invariably pre-empted by the audience. Barry Cryer has described the role of the chairman in terms of a ritualized series of gestures:

> The chairman is the MC of the proceedings, resplendent in tailcoat, frilly shirt and white gloves, banging his gavel to announce the acts. This elegant creation was virtually invented at the Players' Theatre. . . . I was taken through the ritual: when to light and blow out candles, how to respond when a train roared overhead (the theatre was under the arches of Charing Cross Station), how to respond to hecklers . . . and other arcane activities. (Cryer, 1999, p. 68)

Cryer was taught these rituals by another chairman in a handing down of 'arcane activities' that continued across generations of chairmen until the end of the Players'. Many of these activities invoked a mythical Victorian past; 'Her Majesty, Queen Victoria' was offered a loyal toast every night, and the London, Chatham and Dover Railway Company (which had ceased trading in 1921) was roundly booed every time the rumble of trains from Charing Cross station above the theatre could be heard in the auditorium. Audience members from the former colonies were singled out and, in an expression of nostalgia for the British Empire and a reassertion of its erstwhile dominance, if found to be from Australia, were barracked with the question 'How does it feel to be the right way up?'.

Such rituals are referenced in the 1953 *London A to Z*, first published to celebrate the coronation of Queen Elizabeth:

> *The Players'* is a rule unto itself: a reconstruction of a nineteenth-century music hall, with ritual calls from a white-tied chairman to an audience

that always contains enough *habitués* to make the correct ritual responses. You can have a drink while you watch the diversions proffered for your entertainment, and join in the choruses of the old songs. (Metcalf, p. 128)

The 'white-tied' chairman dressed in a dinner jacket and white tails was integral to the proceedings, responsible for the conventions of the club and for the maintaining of its rituals; he[12] was crucial to the illusion of a Victorian past. *Picture Post* wrote in 1951:

> The Song and Supper Entertainment depends . . . on the personality of its Chairman. He is, and must be, a spiritual Victorian. Throned on the stage throughout the performance with the hammer and pint-pot before him, he is the compère, the jester, the arbiter of manners, just a little larger than life. (Dowling, p. 14)

In writing of the pleasures of the music hall in the 1950s MacQueen-Pope indicates his own familiarity with the rituals of the Players (one of the few theatres to offer music hall in London at the time and so likely to have been known to him). His language evokes the warm ambience, and escapism, of an evening at the Players' Theatre Club:

> It is a concourse of people, all drawn together for the purpose of enjoyment – communal enjoyment. . . . It is a co-operative effort with one idea in view, a happy evening. . . . True Music Hall is a place of light and laughter, a place of good cheer, of freedom, of do-as-you-please, go-as-you-please, where everyone is 'Jolly good company'; . . . It is a place where pals meet, where jokes are cracked, where, for a while, the outside world is forgotten. (Macqueen-Pope, 1950, pp. 437–8)

In his account of post-war British comedy, Andy Medhurst articulates the pleasures of sharing comedy in a communal setting, suggesting that the experience offers a sense of belonging and a means of identification with a group: 'Popular comedy is about achieving collective delight through communal recognition' (Medhust, p. 202). He goes on to write in terms which are not unlike MacQueen-Pope's 1950 evocation of the joys of the music hall:

> It is exactly because identities are so disputed, so slippery, so rocky and so anxious that the celebration of belonging offered by comedy is all the more welcome. Belonging may be a fiction, but it is a fiction from which solidarity and sustenance can be drawn. Comedy is a brief embrace in a threatening world, a moment of unity in a lifetime of

fissures, a haven against insecurity, a refuge from dissolution, a point of wholeness in a maelstrom of fragmentation, a chance to affirm that you exist and that you matter. Comedy's consoling fantasy is that however difficult life might be, however much forces beyond your control try to rip you to pieces, there can still be moments where – right here, right now – you can join those who are like you in a celebratory rite of communal recognition. Comedy says to us: you're among friends, relax, join in. (Medhurst, 2007, p. 19)

London in the late 1940s and 1950s was indeed a 'threatening world' for homosexual men, for whom 'the outside world' was then a place of anxiety. With its music-hall comic songs, pantomime and pastiche, the Players' Theatre Club offered that brief embrace. The repeated rituals, particularly the collective singing of the 'Players' theatre anthem', established codes for a 'celebratory rite of communal recognition' which the audience were not only invited to but required to join in. For Scott Long, camp offers a marginalized group an expression of hope: 'Camp – even at its most pessimistically conceived – still asseverates a kind of hope: it is a system of signs by which those who understand certain ironies will recognize each other and endure. It is a private language for some who intuit that public language has gone wrong' (Long, p. 90). As a private theatre club, the Players' provided both a celebration of belonging and a refuge. It was, as Barry Cryer has said, 'a sanctuary for gay men at an awful, awful time to be a gay man'.[13]

There is little in the souvenir programme and tribute books to suggest quite what a camp experience an evening at the Players' could be, beyond the florid extravagance of the language and the exaggerated poses in photographs of the company members. Nonetheless, in its rituals and performances, the Players' Theatre exemplified Sontag's 'the way of Camp': 'To camp is a mode of seduction – one which employs flamboyant mannerisms susceptible of a double interpretation, gestures full of duplicity, with a witty meaning for cognoscenti and another, more impersonal, for outsiders' (Sontag, p. 110).

In 1986 Benny Green could still write of the Players' Theatre as one of the last 'Empires' of music hall in Britain; while it is clear that the rituals remained in place, there is an elegiac recognition that the 'good old days' are now a nostalgic relic:

at the Players' Theatre in Villiers Street, just by Hungerford bridge at Charing Cross, may be discovered, or rediscovered, not merely the entertainment but the style of audience behaviour which was once the norm . . . any of the witnesses to music hall's cheerful confrontation with the real world, would see a bouquet of the old days, in the freedom of movement to and from the bars, the informality of the audience, the sharing of convention between the paying customer and the paid performer. But one TV show and one theatre, is after all, not very much. (Green, p. 313)

The 'TV show' was *The Good Old Days* which had already ceased broadcasting by the time Green was writing, in 1983. Although many of the performers for *The Good Old Days* were drawn from the Players' Theatre company, transported from its London venue, without its club atmosphere and with the 'anthem' no longer 'Oh! The Fairies' but the less ambiguous 'Down at the Old Bull and Bush', the televised version of the Players' music hall was shorn of its camp elements. As Kift has suggested, the television version offered 'a sentimentalised version of the halls' (Kift, p. 25), and cemented Victorian music hall as an entirely nostalgic exercise in the popular imagination.

The Players' Theatre Club remained in Villiers Street, a bastion of gentle and discreet camp until, in 2002, financial problems forced the Players' out from under their Charing Cross arch. They continue as a company, performing musical hall at the Museum of Comedy in Bloomsbury and other venues, but the arches, the bar, the regular audience and the club have gone. In the 1950s, however, the Players' Theatre Club was a successful and thriving venue which had the means and the flair to put on their own original productions, and, as Gänzl explains: 'In 1952 the Players' took the increasingly fashionable step of commissioning their own musical' (Gänzl, 2001, p. 641). That musical was *The Boy Friend* and it would cement the reputations of Sandy Wilson and of the Players'.

In a camp parody of his own celebrity status and in a spoof of contemporary theatre culture, Wilson described the origin of his musical, in terms which are not dissimilar from the description of the commission in his autobiography. Adopting the persona of Nigel Paddock, Wilson transposes the Players' Theatre into the even tinier 'Cryptogram Theatre', and Reginald Woolley into Alithea Ridley:

> he met Alithea Ridley, the enterprising and imaginative director of the tiny Cryptogram Theatre in Seven Dials. She asked him if he would care to write a small-scale musical which would fit into the miniature fifteen-seater playhouse, and Nigel obliged with the show that has now become a by-word in English theatrical history.
>
> As more than one critic has discovered, it is difficult to define the reasons for the success of this pocket-sized musical. If one asks Nigel himself, he will say, 'I wrote this show for fun, and I think that is what the audiences come for – for fun'. Its particular mélange of adolescent

gaiety and period pastiche has defied the items of professional purveyors
of entertainment. (Wilson and Rose, p. 41)

That 'mélange' belonged not just to *The Boy Friend*, but also to the Players'
Theatre Club which had been perfecting the art of period pastiche since
before the war. *The Boy Friend* did indeed become 'a by-word in theatrical
history', as Reginald Woolley's obituary noted:

> it grew from a filler of part of the variety programme to become one
> of the greatest international musical hits of the post-war era is now the
> stuff of legend: and it was not only Woolley's brilliant sets and costumes
> which helped it to triumph. It was also the tone of his decor, its small
> scale, modest but precise understanding of the 1920s. (Benedick, 1993)

Wilson kept in touch with Reginald Woolley and Don Gemmell throughout
his life; they wrote to him on the publication of his autobiography in 1975, and
Wilson's archives contain all their obituaries and the memorial service card for
Woolley's funeral. Sandy Wilson and the Players', Woolley and Gemmell were
important to one another both personally and professionally. The Players' was
a fitting home for Sandy Wilson, who had come from a background in small
theatre revues and cabaret; with its spirit of gentle pastiche and camp, the
theatre was the ideal location for *The Boy Friend* and a neat fit for the club
and its audience. Like the Joys music hall, *The Boy Friend* relied on charm, wit
and nostalgia and had a potential for a camp reading. As the Players' Theatre
was a welcoming and propitious venue for Sandy Wilson's musical, so too
was the social and political context auspicious for its opening in London. *The
Boy Friend* opened two months before the Coronation of Queen Elizabeth
II, and like the Coronation itself, rode a wave of post-war optimism that was
tempered with nostalgia. As Conekin, Mort and Waters explain:

> The Queen's Coronation in June 1953 was the occasion for the most
> extended display of official spectacle in Britain since the end of the
> Second World War. It was also a Janus faced event. Orchestrated
> against a background of elaborate tradition, it simultaneously strove to
> project a vision of the future. . . . This amalgamation of the traditional and
> the self-consciously modern – of the past with what was to come – was
> captured in the idea of the Coronation as making a *return to the future*.
> (Conekin et al. p. 1)

The Players' Theatre Club was similarly 'Janus faced' and shared that amalgam
of tradition and modernity; it prided itself on its adherence to 'authentic'

Victorian music hall, but it was also a self-consciously contemporary venue, and its production of *The Boy Friend* shared that spirit in its pastiche of the 1920s. The Players', *The Boy Friend* and the Coronation all managed, in 1953, to be simultaneously both fashionable and nostalgic, looking backwards to the past and forwards to the New Elizabethan age. Harold Hobson captured that spirit of the Players' in a 1954 article on the occasion of *The Boy Friend*'s transfer to New York:

> the Players' Theater, where many of our more sophisticated men and women in and around the theater meet to choruses from Victorian melodies and to stand respectfully at the mention of 'the Queen, God bless her' (the Queen being, of course, the Queen of the two Jubilees). (clipping, 1954, Wilson's scrapbook, Sandy Wilson archive)

'That certain thing called The Boy Friend'

The 1953 production of *The Boy Friend*

We're blue without
Can't do without
Our dreams just can't come true without
That certain thing called the boy friend.

(Sandy Wilson, 1953)

The Boy Friend was to be the defining theatrical production for the Players' Theatre club, as it was for Sandy Wilson's reputation. It was the most successful production that either would ever have and established both the Players' and Wilson as serious theatrical players. The first line of Wilson's 1975 autobiography opens with a reference to *The Boy Friend*, as if to acknowledge that it was to be his lifetime's achievement. *The Boy Friend* and Julian Slade's *Salad Days* (which followed at the Bristol Old Vic in 1954) were seen by the press and the public as something fresh and new, and specifically British; in Wright's estimation *The Boy Friend* was 'a musical that would share with *Salad Days* the reputation of being the flagship British show of the mid-1950s' (Wright, 2010, p. 72). Both had originated in small-scale productions from independent theatres outside the West End and were understood at the time to be a British riposte to the bombast of the American shows produced in large theatres; *Salad Days* required only two pianos and *The Boy Friend* just a small band. The excitement that *The Boy Friend* generated in London is evident from the cover of the paperback version of the script which appeared a year after its move to the West End: 'Have you seen *The Boy Friend?* That has certainly been London's most-asked question since December 1953' (*The Boy Friend*, Penguin edition, 1955).

The 1958 souvenir programme from the West End transfer tells the story of the 'romantic beginnings of "The Boy Friend"', which acknowledges its origins at the Players' Theatre[1] and points out that the production was by no means a guaranteed commercial success: 'It was not a commercial proposition in the ordinary sense. There was no star part. There was no chorus as such. Everything depended on a general high level of acting, and actors who were able to sing and dance, which is no longer usual' (Wyndham's souvenir programme, 1958, p. 3).

The first production at the Players' Theatre was nonetheless a major hit both critically and commercially, as Wilson proudly recalled in his autobiography: 'the show was a sell-out for every night of its run at the Players'. People even sat on the concrete steps at the side of the stage'[2] (Wilson, 1975a. p. 206). There were two productions at the Players', the second with an added third act, and it was this expanded version that went on to the Embassy Theatre in Swiss Cottage[3] where its reviews and audiences propelled it into the West End. As Kitty Black remembered: 'Reggie (Woolley) persuaded Wilson to add half an hour to the original show, put it on at the Embassy Theatre . . . and the following morning every management in town was clamouring to buy it' (Black, p. 220). Finally, in a partnership between the Players' Theatre and the impresario Bronson Albery, *The Boy Friend* moved into the Wyndham's Theatre in 1954, with sets and costumes again designed by the Players' Reginald Woolley and largely performed by the same cast. There it 'proved to be the greatest success that Wyndham's Theatre has ever had' (Wyndham's programme, 1954, p. 2); it ran there for five years and then moved to Broadway for a year.

The West End production was heralded as a new departure in British theatre and for the musical; according to Sheridan Morley, it would 'show, at home and abroad, precisely what the British could still do quite superbly. . . . this was in fact to be one of those miracle shows' (Morley, p. 132). The first paperback edition of the play similarly declaimed: 'For *The Boy Friend* is a "miracle" play: one of those rare phenomena . . . which start their careers with modest expectations and suddenly take on a life of their own and sweep the world' (Penguin edition, 1955). Vida Hope, the original director of *The Boy Friend*, also referred to it as a 'miracle' show in her preface to the script, as she points to its worldwide success:

> *The Boy Friend*, gaily playing to capacity in London and New York as I write these words, and due to open shortly in most of the major cities in other continents as well. Why? What makes it so successful? As the person most closely associated with it apart from the author, I'm afraid the answer is I just don't know. (Hope, p. 11)

In retrospect, there were clear conditions for why it should have been such a success; it was a 'miracle show' both in terms of its timing and in its original site of production. The Boy Friend was one of those productions that McQueen Pope described in 1947 as emerging from the 'laboratories' of small theatres: 'Now and again they split the atom, and the little play they have produced is blown clean out of their laboratory into the spaces of the West End theatre, and with it some new players, who are so good that the public and management are surprised' (Macqueen Pope, 1947, p. 130). The Players' Theatre had been a particularly welcoming context for The Boy Friend, its ethos of gentle camp and unabashed nostalgia ideal for The Boy Friend's affectionate fantasy of the 1920s, and it was the Players' that shaped and designed the first production. The production team was drawn from the Players' company: Reginald Woolley was the designer, described in the Wyndham's programme as 'a designer with a considerable West End reputation. . . . The Boy Friend was exactly the sort of thing at which he excelled' (Wyndham's souvenir programme, 1958). Vida Hope, the original director, had been one of the Players' long-standing and regular performers.[4] Hope had a background in devising and producing revues; the Wyndham's programme pays fulsome tribute to her abilities as a director, crediting the production's success to 'Vida Hope's flair for this sort of entertainment, her tireless energy and her sense of comedy that never transgressed the bounds of good taste' (Wyndham's souvenir programme, 1958).

The casting was largely drawn from the Players' regular artistes, who, as music-hall performers, could both sing and dance. Hattie Jacques[5] was originally envisaged as Madame Dubonnet, the proprietor of the finishing school in which it is set, but the part was eventually played by the Players' Joan Sterndale Bennett, a regular performer in the music-hall Joys; Violetta, the wife of Players' director Gervaise Farjeon, played Hortense, the French maid.

If the Players' Theatre was a welcoming and propitious venue for Sandy Wilson's musical, so too was the social and political context auspicious for its opening in London. The Boy Friend was produced in the context of the British post-war reconstruction; as Wilson saw it, it was 'a Valentine from one post-war period to another' (Wilson quoted in Trewin, 1958, p. 101). The setting of a nostalgic imagined world of the 1920s offered charm and gaiety to a beleaguered London (rationing would only be withdrawn in 1954). The Boy Friend opened just as Britain and London were celebrating what seemed to promise a 'New Elizabethan' age, with the Coronation of a young Queen Elizabeth II in 1953. Ben Pimlott has read the Coronation as an articulation of the 'restoration of the status quo ante bellum together with an anxious optimism' (Pimlott, p. 202). The Boy Friend shared that 'anxious optimism' in assembling a celebration of the past together with a promise for the future, with its emphasis on romance and in the flurry of weddings that ends the show. It was recognized at the time that *The Boy Friend* echoed the spirit of the Coronation; a contemporary review suggested that excerpts from the production could be incorporated into a Coronation revue: 'One would like to see at least the first act of *The Boy Friend* incorporated in some Coronation revue' (quoted in Wilson, 1975a, p. 205). While the musical expresses optimism, it is a world in which ambitions are modest, appropriate to an age of austerity and rationing.

The modesty of the scale and ambition of the production was itself a counterpoint to the string of blockbuster American musicals which had filled London's largest theatres in the early 1950s. West End theatre managements were in search of an alternative to the domination of its theatres by extravagant American productions; *Oklahoma!* had arrived at the Theatre Royal, Drury Lane and *Annie Get Your Gun* at the Coliseum in 1947, to be followed by *South Pacific* at Drury Lane, *Kiss Me Kate* at the Coliseum in 1951, *Call Me Madam* at the Coliseum in 1952, *The King and I* at Drury Lane in 1953. In Whitehouse's estimation 'it was the new shows imported from America which really set the tone of the post-war era' (Whitehouse, 2005, p. 41). The dominance of Beaumont, Coward and Novello over West End musical theatre was under challenge[6] from these American imports (although it was Beaumont who produced *Oklahoma!* in the London production). A 1946 review of Coward's *Ace of Clubs* in *Theatre World* reported: 'After our recent experience of the modern type of American musical in the shape of *Oklahoma!, Annie get Your Gun, Carousel*, etc., Mr Coward's latest work seems to be very much dated' (quoted in Wright, 2010, p. 59).

Harry Hopkins writes of the allure of the American musicals for a post-war London, and their displacement of the dominance of the glamorous musicals of Coward, Novello and Jack Buchanan in the period:

> By 1949, it began to seem that in theatrical terms at least Britain was now on the way to becoming the 49th State. . . . By their freshness and gusto, by their air of being 'about' something, most of all by their unforced demotic expressiveness and lack of class inhibition, the American productions struck the British at this time with the force of revelation. They at last succeeded in showing up the standard English drawing-room drama and the English 'musical' of the Ivor Novello or Jack Buchanan tradition for what they were – something of a moribund world. (Hopkins, p. 107)

The Boy Friend and later *Salad Days* were both greeted at the time as fresh and new by the press and the public and as distinctively English. A 1956 programme articulates the paradoxical mix of modernity and nostalgia that *The Boy Friend* presented, admiring the music and setting precisely for their nostalgic quality and identifying them as a riposte to the 'realism' of the American musicals:

> In writing 'THE BOY FRIEND', the author has deliberately chosen to satirise the musical comedy technique of the 1920s – the heyday of the old type of musical entertainment. His brilliant satirical picture of the manners and styles of the period is in itself a new departure in the field of musical comedy, but he has still chosen to retain that essential component of the true musical – a feeling of nostalgia, which the more successful musicals of the post-war era are, in their reality, so in danger of losing. (*The Boy Friend* programme, Her Majesty's Theatre, 1956)

In a draft of a 1957 article on the British musical, Wilson rather wistfully (and sourly) acknowledges that *The Boy Friend* and *Salad Days* were once seen as the British answer to the American blockbuster but argues that that promise was not fulfilled by British theatrical managements. Writing in the year that *West Side Story* opened on Broadway, Wilson bewails the lack of support for British musicals:

> Ten years ago 'Oklahoma!' swept triumphantly into Drury Lane Theatre, and ever since people in this country have been asking, 'Where is the British Musical?'. About three years ago false hopes were raised when 'Salad Days' and my own show 'The Boy Friend' became smash hits, 'The Boy Friend' going on to repeat its success on Broadway, in a bowdlerized version. The Press seemed to think that this was the answer, that the British Musical had been reborn. It was very kind of them, but very misguided, because it encouraged theatrical managements to unearth all sorts of nasty and little bijou musicals and fling them on cheaply in the hope of making the same sort of quick buck Julian Slade and I made for our managements. (Notebook, 1957, Sandy Wilson archive)[7]

More recent critics have also understood *The Boy Friend* and *Salad Days* as inventive and original; for Gordon they were 'the first genuinely innovative West End musicals after the war' (Gordon et al., p. 11). According to Snelson, both were 'perceived as a strike back at the American repertory. . . . In their different ways they present a particular sense of archetypal Britishness' (Snelson, p. 141). Wright, however, in tracing influences in his study of the musical, asserts that '*The Boy Friend* has more of Uncle Sam than the British bulldog about it' (Wright, 2010, p. 75). Wright nonetheless later went on to suggest that 'there was something completely fresh in the voice that Wilson brought to the genre . . . wandering alone into fields of pastiche and esoteric in which, looking around, he would find himself the sole occupant' (Wright, 2012, pp. 70–1). Wilson's 2014 obituary stated that 'when it opened in the West End in January 1954, it was revolutionary, a totally new and different kind of musical' (Freedland, 2014).

In fact, *The Boy Friend* was not as 'totally new and different' as it was seen at the time, or later, and Wilson was by no means 'the sole occupant' of the genre of musical pastiche; Julian Slade (the other half of *Round the Horne*'s Julian and Sandy) was similarly pastiching the 1920s in *Salad Days* which followed *The Boy Friend* in 1954. The Players' Theatre itself was known for its pastiche of Victorian music hall and pantomime, and both Coward and Novello had written musical pastiches often set in a vaguely Belle-Epoque European setting, a period which was no more historically distant to their heyday in the 1920s than the 1920s were to Julian Slade and Sandy Wilson writing in the 1950s. Coward's 1938 *Operette* celebrated and parodied Edwardian musical comedy, while Novello's elaborate plots, Viennese Waltzes and 'mittel-European' operatic parodies owed much to the operettas of Lehar and Offenbach (who themselves made extensive use of parody). Sandy Wilson borrowed from Coward and Novello, both of whom he heroized as prominent theatrical men and as dramatists and composers. Like Coward and Novello, Wilson had a background in revue, a training ground for clever songs and a precedent for the light-hearted musical that *The Boy Friend* would become. As Snelson explains, the music of *The Boy Friend* is

> derivative, using – albeit most skilfully – older styles. This approach is a constant one in British musical theatre. Novello consciously borrowed from a range of sources including classical music, Viennese operetta and certain characteristics of Richard Rogers. . . . Coward relied strongly on Victorian parlour music and music-hall styles throughout his works. (Snelson, p. 143)

The lyrics and music of *The Boy Friend* constantly reference the wit of Noël Coward and the glamour of Ivor Novello's pastiche operettas, while the structure betrays Wilson's thorough knowledge of the form of the popular musical.[8] His autobiography meticulously catalogues every Novello musical he saw as a child and every encounter he had with Coward. In the Foreword to a survey of musical comedy, Coward neatly describes the predictable plot of musical theatre in terms which describe the structure of Novello's productions, and which also apply to *The Boy Friend*:

> In most of those entertainments there was nearly always a bitter misunderstanding between the hero and the heroine at the end of the first act (if it was in two acts) or the second act (if it was in three acts). Either he would insult her publicly on discovering that she was a princess in her own right rather than the simple commoner he had imagined her to be, or she would wrench his engagement ring from her finger, fling it at his feet and faint dead away on hearing that he was not the humble tutor she had loved for himself alone, but a multi-millionaire. The ultimate reconciliation was usually achieved seconds before the final curtain, after the leading comedian had sung a topical song and there was nothing to do but forgive and forget. (Coward, 1969, pp. 7–8)

This is close to a description of the plot of *The Boy Friend*; if the mistaken identities are less about aristocracy than wealth, the bitter misunderstanding between hero and heroine and the reconciliation just before the final curtain are firmly in place.

The Boy Friend takes place in a world in which transgressions are forgiven and characters revealed for what they are; however, the performativity of the characters is not at all about gender and sexuality (as it can be in other forms of popular entertainment such as pantomime), but it is about class. *The Boy Friend* offers a look back to an apparently golden age of pleasure and innocence in which class privilege and plenty seem unchallenged; it is set in the South of France in the privileged and monied world of a finishing school. Snelson has suggested that: 'although primarily a tribute to musical comedies of the 1920s, finishing schools, debutantes, aristocrats in disguise all played to notions of class, particularly upper-class behaviour' (Snelson. p. 142). This does not however acknowledge a context in which fixed 'notions of class' had been challenged by the experience of war and by the post-war reconstruction.

The plot of *The Boy Friend*, such as it is, centres around disguise, in which, while almost all the central characters are either aristocratic or wealthy, they present themselves as not. There are disguises of class, both upward and downward; Tony, the boyfriend of the title, and Polly, the soubrette heroine, assume the status of working people and both are under a misapprehension about the other. Tony is in disguise as a messenger boy delivering Polly's dress for the ball, 'just a messenger boy and you a rich young lady from the Villa Caprice' (Wilson, 1955, p. 62). Polly, a millionaire's daughter (she is described by Madame Dubonnet as a 'poor little rich girl'[9]) has been instructed to beware of fortune hunters, and claims 'Rich? Oh, I'm not rich. You see – I just work there as Madame Dubonnet's secretary' (Wilson, 1955, p. 62). Tony, it later transpires, is the son of Lord and Lady Brockhurst, the 'Honourable Tony', who, as his mother tearfully reports 'has disappeared from Oxford in the middle of Hilary Term, ruining a brilliant career' (Wilson, 1955, p. 59). Although both hero and heroine are of the wealthy classes, in a love duet their aspirations are modest as they proclaim: 'A life of wealth does not appeal to me at all' and dream only of a modest room in Bloomsbury. Meanwhile, Madame Dubonnet, who appears to be an impeccably socially assured headmistress, has a louche past and was once seduced by Polly's father in a Paris bar on Armistice night (in the only reference there is in *The Boy Friend* to the First World War).

The play begins at carnival time in Nice on the eve of the Carnival ball, and the beach, in particular, is a carnivalesque space, where wealth and social status are not immediately apparent. The young ladies of the finishing school sing:

> There's no knowing
> Who you are going
> To meet sur le Plage[10]
> You may run up against a rajah . . .
> Or maybe your man
> Will be a poor man
> . . .
> Sur le Plage,
> Sur le Plage,
> Everyone looks the same.
>
> (Wilson, 1955, pp. 56–7)

The final act is literally carnivalesque, set at the carnival ball, where Polly is dressed as Pierrette and Tony appears as a masked Pierrot, confirming their destiny as the central romantic couple of the piece. *The Boy Friend* relishes its fantasy world, and exploits all the potential of dressing up. The costumes and styling of the ball owe much to images of fancy dress balls from the 1920s, and, in particular, one that is included in Wilson's own elegy to the decade, *The Roaring Twenties*; his caption for one image reads 'The Arts Ball at Covent Garden in 1922. As usual, Harlequins, Orientals and Spanish Ladies predominate' (Wilson, 1976, Figure 134), as they predominated in Wilson's version of the carnival ball and in Woolley's designs for *The Boy Friend*.

It is ironic that *Salad Days* and *The Boy Friend* were welcomed as the 'new faces' of the British musical when both are so heavily reliant on the decade of the 1920s. The production team, the young cast and the writer of *The Boy Friend* were all of the generation to have been children in the 1920s and who had grown up into the war years. The 1920s seems to have represented for them and for their audiences the halcyon days of a pre-war era, now seen through the prism of wartime experience, which gave it a particular glow of safety. In the context of rationing in Britain, the Cold War and McCarthyism in America, a return to a 'sybaritic' 1920s was understandable. Nostalgia for the 1920s extended beyond the world of theatre; the *Sunday Express* credited *The Boy Friend* with the revival of 1920s fashions, and itself demonstrates a yearning for what seemed to be a less anxious time:

> We're giving a big welcome to deep hats and low waists, Louis heels and jumper suits, ropes of beads and floating chiffon scarves. I put it all down to 'The Boy Friend'. How we've relished the swingy, happy tunes. . . . How we've lapped up the blissfully un-neurotic sentiment. How we've beaten our heels on the floor in time with the jerky, kicky dances. (*Sunday Express*, 13 February 1955, clipping, Sandy Wilson archive)

The Boy Friend's carnivalesque setting in a ladies' finishing school in the South of France offered a 'swingy' and 'happy 'fantasy of luxury and extravagance, which Snelson has described as 'the over-refined, nostalgic atmosphere of a fictitious and glamorised 1920s' (Snelson, p. 142). The musical may indeed have offered a 'fictitious' version of the period, but Wilson was not alone in his glamorization. In his 1958 study of theatre in the 1920s, the theatre critic J. C. Trewin looks back at the decade in decidedly camp terms and in language which evokes the lyrics of *The Boy Friend*:

> The Twenties were at least as gay[11] as the Thirties would be overcast. Storms may have battered them, alarms deafened them, governments crumpled round them. But at this remove, the word must be gay. In the middle of the decade the song was 'I want to be happy'. . . . Elsewhere: well, when the man that you care for takes care of you, you'll be happy, and therefore – *he'll* be happy too. (Trewin, p. 9)

Ken Tynan described *The Boy Friend* as a 'sly affectionate tribute to the decade in which he [Wilson] learned to walk. It takes him back, you might say, to places he never knew' (undated clipping, Sandy Wilson archive). Wilson himself claims in his autobiography that, although he had no direct memory of the decade, his childhood was infused with the sounds and fashions of the period:

The truth is that, though only an infant at the time, I was surrounded by elder sisters and their friends who were constantly learning the Charleston and playing 'Tea for Two' and 'Lady be Good' on an old cabinet gramophone. . . .

The fact that so many other people seem to look upon the period of *The Boy Friend* with the same fondness as myself, regardless of their age, has given me enormous pleasure. . . . *The Boy Friend* is simply a loving salute to those far-off days of the cloche hat and the short skirt. (Wilson, 1975a, p. 16)

If Wilson acknowledges that he had very little memory of the 1920s, the period was clearly very significant for him, to the extent that he wrote a tribute to the decade of his early childhood in 1976. In the introduction to his compilation of pictures, *The Roaring Twenties*, he writes that the decade was bound by two catastrophes, the First World War and the Wall Street Crash, but that, for him, it represented a lost utopia:

a kind of lost Paradise, a Garden of Eden whose gates clanged shut for ever at the beginning of the Thirties. . . . despite the aura of sophistication that hangs around them the atmosphere of jazz, cocktails and promiscuity, the Twenties seem to me an Age of Innocence, a time when Youth could truthfully say, 'Here we are, fresh, eager and unafraid. The future is ours to play with.' (Wilson, 1976, p. 6)

The context for the first production of *The Boy Friend* was a post-war settlement in which the Welfare State was still in a process of formation; for some, it did seem that 'the future was ours to play with'. But by 1953 it was clear that that future would not accommodate the legalization of homosexuality. There were particularly good reasons for homosexual men to be nostalgic in the early 1950s, a period which saw 'a new climate of intolerance' towards homosexuality (Richardson, p. 190). For university-educated homosexual men who had not themselves lived as adults in the 1920s, the 1920s seemed to have been a less oppressive time than their current experience. In a context where homosexuality was demonized, the ever deferred past appeared to be a safer space. *The Boy Friend* had arrived in London at the moment of the Montagu trial (which was ongoing during the run of the production), and at a point when the attention of the Metropolitan police was focussed on the West End of London and men associated with the theatre.

Like Wilson, his Oxford contemporary Peter Wildeblood had grown up in a relatively privileged 1920s interwar world, and shared Wilson's nostalgia for the period, in similar terms, remembering the fashions (from photographs if not directly) and the music:

> the family album shows a procession of cloche hats and silk-stockinged knees. There were going to be no more wars; the night-clubs were crowded and everyone danced the Charleston. The first songs I remember were 'Ramona', 'Charmaine', and 'A Room with a View'. (Wildeblood, 1955, p. 8)

The 1920s signified, especially for homosexual men, an apparently Arcadian moment, a period before the Depression and before the brutal crackdown of gay 'vice spots' in London's West End. Alan Sinfield has pointed to the connection between a celebration of the leisured classes and homosexuality:

> Homosexuality was a further reason for commitment to the lifestyle of the leisure class, where its practice was most possible. There was more toleration than elsewhere, one might evade difficulties through the deployment of money or influence. . . . If you had enough money you could travel, for homosexual activity was not illegal in much of continental Europe; for many, abroad came to symbolize an open and fulfilling sexual and emotional life. (Sinfield, 1999, p. 65)

That 'life-style of the leisure class' is the world of *The Boy Friend*. The stage directions as the play opens describe a luxurious set: 'The Drawing Room of the Villa Caprice,[12] Madame Dubonnet's Finishing School, on the outskirts of Nice.[13] At the back, French windows opening on to the garden, with a view of the sea beyond' (Wilson, 1955, p. 23). The setting in France also gives licence to (mild) sexual innuendo, particularly associated with the French characters Hortense and Madame Dubonnet, who are given the most flirtatious songs and lines with double-entendres (as in the song 'You-Don't-Want-to-Play-with-Me-Blues'). The continental setting in Nice, the sets and costumes all offered an escape from the world of a grey London of rationing; at a time of austerity, the staging looked back to an apparently golden age of youthful pleasures. The American writer Elaine Dundy, who was once married to Kenneth Tynan, Wilson's friend and Oxford contemporary, also remembered her childhood in the 1920s in terms of luxury and glamour:

> My memories of the twenties are scented with the clouds of Shalimar and L'Heure Bleu that I sprayed on myself from crystal cut-glass atomizers when dressing up in my mother's beautiful Paris evening gowns, all embroidered beads and floating chiffon and so skilfully sewn, with little weights hidden in the skirts to make them hang just so. (Dundy, 2001, p. 4)

Such pleasures were hard to come by in a post-war Britain of rationing. Rationing also affected the practicalities of theatre production, as Kitty Black remembered:

> War-time restrictions were beginning to make themselves felt in the theatre and all materials were now rationed, some things becoming almost impossible to obtain. One of the stage managers proved to have a rare talent for painting utility china to look like priceless porcelain, and silk stockings had to be darned and darned again. (Black, p. 61)

That spirit of 'making do and mending' inflected the costuming and sets of the first production at the Players'; Sandy Wilson's autobiography recounts that members of the cast raided their grandparent's wardrobes for clothing from the period, a costuming which also served to underscore the authenticity of the designs. Both Wilson and Vida Hope were insistent on accuracy to the period, and Hope and Woolley were meticulous in their attention to detail. In her foreword to the published script Hope explains that she set out to create

> a serious reproduction of a period and not a burlesque. . . . I well remember telling a rather young company that we were to present a show that would be witty, elegant, charming and tender, and that in no circumstances would I tolerate any laughing at the Twenties. . . . We all did a tremendous amount of research. (Hope, p. 12)

Wilson is similarly insistent in his autobiography that this production would not tolerate a sending up of the period. Gänzl attributes the success of *The Boy Friend* to this authenticity and to the sincerity of its tribute to the 1920s:

> it was always affectionate, never broad or brash, and always appealing. Wilson, Miss (Vida) Hope and the Players' directors were all of the same opinion: The Boy Friend was to be played straight and sincerely. When the laughs came they were to be laughs of recognition, of affection, of nostalgia as well, of course, as laughs for the genuine, timeless humour in the book and lyrics: not laughs aroused by grotesquerie or campy parody. It was an approach which ensured success for almost without exception, both critics and public were enchanted by *The Boy Friend*. (Gänzl, 1986, p. 643)

Nonetheless, the seriousness with which Wilson, Hope and the Players undertook that homage has in itself 'campy' elements. In a 1954 novel,

Christopher Isherwood (whose novels Wilson would go on to adapt) put camp into two categories, 'High' and 'Low', and argued of 'High Camp' that

> true High Camp always has an underlying seriousness. You can't camp about something you don't take seriously. You're not making fun *of* it; you're making fun *out* of it. You're expressing what's basically serious to you in terms of fun and artifice and elegance. (Isherwood, 1966, p. 115)

Both Wilson and Hope are insistent in their accounts of the first production that they were not 'making fun *of* it', but paying homage to the music and fashions of an era that had preceded them, and making 'fun *out* of' the 1920s; their mutual horror at the New York production was precisely because they felt that it was making fun *of* the decade. It is quite clear from Wilson's tributes to the period, in his books *The Roaring Twenties* and *Ivor*, how 'basically serious' the era was to him. In his introduction to *The Roaring Twenties* Wilson explains that the pleasures of the decade had an illicit appeal for him:

> I hardly remember the Twenties at all. But I do remember the early Thirties very clearly, and what was remarkable was that, in general, nobody referred to the Twenties, or, if they did, it was in a tone of either dismissal, disapproval or ridicule. There seemed to be a sense of guilt about the whole decade, the same sense of guilt as one is induced to feel the Morning After. . . . Everyone felt a slight unease about the previous ten years: they had had a wonderful time, but it had all been rather too much of a good thing, and now they were paying for it. As a small boy, only dimly aware of what the Depression meant, I found this hard to understand, and as the years went by I was drawn irresistibly, as to the garden gate marked 'No Entry', towards what had become almost a Forbidden Decade. (Wilson, 1976, p. 2)

In his tribute to the 'forbidden' decade in *The Boy Friend* Wilson takes an unabashed pleasure in entering the forbidden gate and, refusing any sense of guilt, celebrates his characters 'having a wonderful time'.

Pastiche is in its very nature nostalgic, working as it must with a form and mode that belongs to the past. Wright's chapter on Sandy Wilson in his survey of the British musical is titled 'Pastiche and Esoteric' and suggests that the form of pastiche comes at the cost of an emotional distance

> to whatever category The Boy Friend is consigned, it remains above all pastiche, with all the emotional restrictions that genre places on those who write it. Is it inevitable that The Boy Friend has always seemed a little

lacking in the heart department? – the price to be paid for pastiche. Heartstrings may be touched, but it is from afar. (Wright, 2010, p. 75)

It is that element of distance from the trials of heterosexual romance that renders the pastiche of *The Boy Friend* camp, and that same distance is to be found in the works of Novello and Coward. Richard Dyer has pointed to the alliance between pastiche and camp explaining that like camp 'Pastiche intends that it is understood as pastiche by those who read, see or hear it. For it to work, it needs to be "got" as a pastiche. . . . "You" need to get it, but . . . the concept of pastiche does not make a priori assumptions about who "you" is' (Dyer, 2007, p. 3).

Along with the audience of the Players' Theatre, the critic of the *Herald Tribune* did 'get it' at the time; a review of the New York production of *The Boy Friend* recognized, in coded terms, both the powerful pull of its nostalgia and the campness:

'The Boy Friend' is a highly specialized lark, lavishing all of its love on a slender jest. . . . There are those who will find it much too special, entirely too engaged with a vanished and vagrant time. But on its own terms, and in its own nostalgic niche, it's tremendous fun. (*Herald Tribune*, 10 October 1954, clipping, Sandy Wilson archive)

The 'tremendous fun' of *The Boy Friend* lies in part in the fact that while it can be read entirely straight as a heterosexual romance, it also offers the potential for a camp reading. As Wright puts it: '"The Boy Friend" had appealed to the sophisticate as well as proving eminently suitable for a night out with Aunt Edna, liable to be offended by any hint of vulgarity. Even the most subtle niceties might be missed by some of the audience' (Wright, 2010, p. 80). Among those 'subtle niceties' is the subtext suggested by the title,[14] while other camp elements include a chorus line of good-looking young men and the mischievous pleasure throughout in disguise and performance. According to Jack Babuscio, the 'incongruous contrast' of youth and old age is one of the characteristics of camp' (Babuscio, p 20); the unfailing show-stopping number[15] in *The Boy Friend* is a duet between the ageing Lord Brockhurst and the young flapper Maisie, 'It's never too late to have a fling', in which much is made of the age difference.[16] In 1973 there was a production in San Francisco which presented an 'All singing, All Dancing, All Male *The Boy Friend*'. The reviewer noted what the critics of the 1950s could not, in explicitly acknowledging its campness:

Sandy Wilson's unfailingly winsome musical . . . has made a logical transition into the camp of an all-male theater company. . . . No work I know is riper for impersonation than this delightfully batty spoof of a twenties musical. . . . 'The Boy Friend' lends itself so well to the shameless antics of drag. (undated clipping, scrap book, Sandy Wilson archive)

Looking back from the perspective of 1987, Sheridan Morley reflected on the afterlife of *The Boy Friend*, and attributed the success of the original production to its seriousness, a quality which Isherwood had identified as one of the features of 'High Camp':

> The brilliance of the original *Boy Friend* lay in its passion for historical accuracy and its understanding that small is beautiful: where the plot has worked less well over the last thirty years, as in the Broadway transfer and a 1983 Old Vic revival and a catastrophic Ken Russell movie, it has been because either that original passion or that original understanding has been somehow compromised. *The Boy Friend* is, like Rattigan's *French Without Tears* . . . a perfect miniature period piece. (Morley, 1987, p. 133)

This does not acknowledge the particular resonance of that 'passion for historical accuracy' in the post-war context, or that that nostalgia for an apparently carefree period was also picked up in the other great hit of the period, *Salad Days*. The nostalgia of *The Boy Friend* and *Salad Days* was intrinsic to their appeal to audiences at the time, and their pastiche was intimately bound up with a camp sensibility. Snelson rather unkindly argues, while recognizing their camp subtexts, that 'Both shows are . . . sexless, although sexuality through the codified language of a gay subculture casts a subtle shade' (Snelson, p. 141). Gordon has argued that both musicals

> exploited a camp aesthetic, which deployed nostalgia together with the disorientating effects of pastiche and parody to project a coded 'gay' identity. The uninhibited cultivation of joy and pleasure in such shows was 'gay' in the innocent sense of the word, but to those in the know it was also 'gay' in a way that insiders recognized as potentially subversive. (Gordon et al., p. 13)

While audiences at the Players' Theatre had long recognized the potential subversion, that 'cultivation of joy and pleasure' meant that *The Boy Friend* went on to become a major critical and commercial success across the world. It was to have multiple lives in the West End and on Broadway; after its success in the West End, *The Boy Friend* was picked up by Feuer and Martin productions for New York, where it opened at the Royale Theatre in 1954 (and made a star of Julie Andrews in the role of Polly). The New York programme credited the original production team: Vida Hope with the direction, sets and costumes by Reginald Woolley and choreography by John Heawood. Wilson and Hope however despaired over what they saw as the 'vulgarity' of the American production and there were ructions over casting even before they arrived in New York. A letter from Cy Feuer to Vida Hope and Wilson expresses 'intense disappointment, disappointment generally in your lack of confidence in us and specifically in your lack of flexibility regarding our *sole* casting reservation' (letter, 12 May 1954, Sandy Wilson archive). Both Wilson and Hope were, as the *New York Times* reported, barred from rehearsals at the theatre: 'A private detective . . . was stationed in the lobby of the Royale to bar Mr Wilson and Miss Hope from attending last week's rehearsals or previews' (undated clipping, Sandy Wilson archive).

Notwithstanding Vida Hope's and Wilson's despair at the New York production, it was a resounding success. An American friend recalled the first night in a letter to Wilson, which Wilson and Hope had refused to attend: 'six bars into the overture the audience – including me – started to applaud! Nothing like it, I can tell you, had ever been seen on Broadway – an audience on its feet and cheering in the middle of the overture' (letter from Ed Crimmons, 27 April 1954, Sandy Wilson archive). The American reviews, despite Wilson's and Hope's reservations, were overwhelmingly positive. The New York correspondent of the London *Times* reported that it was

> received with applause and cheers by the audience and with hardly less enthusiasm by critics. Critics described Mr Sandy Wilson's composition variously as a delightful burlesque, a pastiche and as a parody . . . but though differing about how to classify it, they were of one mind in liking it. (undated clipping, scrapbook, Sandy Wilson archive)

Despite Wilson's professed dislike of the New York production, he collected all the reviews and articles and kept them for the rest of his life. It is notable that the most frequently employed word in the headlines and descriptions of the American show is 'gay', often accompanied by the terms 'sparkling', 'charming' and 'delightful'.

Wilson's bitterness at the New York production and the producers' treatment of himself and Vida Hope is extensively discussed in his autobiography. In a talk at Oxford a year after the events, the memory still clearly rankled as he advised students:

> If you are rash enough to take your show to New York, you run the risk of the management forcing you to make the show into a 'smash-hit', which

entails removing every vestige of subtlety or originality from your work. If you refuse, as I did, then they will probably bar you from rehearsals and station a William Bendix[17] type at the stage door to pounce you out if you try to get near your own show. (Talk to the Oxford Experimental Theatre Club, 5 May 1955, p. 16, Sandy Wilson archive)

Wilson continued to be protective of *The Boy Friend*; he went to see professional and amateur productions throughout his life,[18] and collected programmes from them all; a whole folder in Sandy Wilson's archive is devoted to 'The Boy Friend, Commonwealth and Foreign programmes'. *The Boy Friend* clearly found an audience in the former British colonies; it saw productions in Hong Kong, Johannesburg, Christchurch, New Zealand, Zimbabwe (then Rhodesia) and in Canada. Its appeal however extended beyond the British colonies; it was also produced in Moscow, Turkey and in Belgrade, in the former Yugoslavia. Wilson received and collected fan letters from across the world; a 1987 letter from a member of the D'Oyly Carte Company is not untypical in its forthright enthusiasm: 'then I discovered your "Boy Friend" which I still say was the most uniquely wonderful work of this century, if you knew what the Boy Friend meant to me!' (letter from George Keates, 13 December 1987, Sandy Wilson archive). Not every eminent theatrical figure was as charmed by *The Boy Friend* – Richard Eyre, then director of the National Theatre in London, wrote in *The Observer* in 1993:

> There must be those in the remote corners of the English-speaking world who think that this pastiche of a pastiche of a Twenties musical is delightful, but I found its winsome melodies, its saccharine charm, its camp, smug, self-regarding milieu, as alien to me as an Aztec sacrifice, and at least as repulsive. (clipping, 1993, Sandy Wilson archive)

Although Wilson filed the letter for his archives, he was clearly stung by this, to the extent that he wrote a letter to *The Observer* the next week, pointing out:

> *The Boy Friend*, as I wrote it, so far from appealing only to 'those in the remote corners of the English-speaking world', is constantly performed both here and in America and has recently been revived with great success in Germany and Scandinavia.
>
> I am sorry that he looks back on it with such antipathy. But then I had to sit through his production of *High Society*. So perhaps we are quits? (Sandy Wilson, Letter to *The Observer*, 21 March 1993, Sandy Wilson archive).

Richard Eyre had the grace to reply with a personal letter to Wilson, in which he acknowledged that his production of *High Society* was 'ghastly', and went on to add 'Actually, it's not quite true to say we are quits; I saw VALMOUTH and enjoyed it immensely. So that puts you in credit' (Richard Eyre, letter to Sandy Wilson, 21 March 1993, Sandy Wilson archive). Wilson was clearly somewhat mollified by this, perhaps by the reference to *Valmouth*; he kept the letter.

By 1993, Eyre was not alone in seeing *The Boy Friend* as old hat, the artistic director of the Theatre Royal, Plymouth, wrote to Wilson's agent: 'I don't think "The Boy Friend" is on. I can't think of anyone who could reproduce the original. I really can't see the point in 1993!' (letter from Roger Redfarn to Sheila Lemon, 12 May 1993, Sandy Wilson archive). *The Boy Friend* however continued to 'mean a lot' to many, and particularly to the audiences and personnel at the Players' Theatre. It was brought into play to save the Players' at a time of financial crisis, in 1990 a charity gala with songs and players from *The Boy Friend* was staged in aid of the Players' Theatre and, in 1993, the original cast was brought together by Maria Charles[19] for another fund raiser for the Players.

Wilson's friend John Bedding[20] wrote to Wilson in 1984: 'THE BOY FRIEND really is a steel butterfly, is it not? . . . Fragile as it is, it has the most tremendous durability and strength and seems able to rise effortlessly above and beyond any odd production quirks which get thrust upon it' (letter from John W. Bedding, 2 August 1984, Sandy Wilson archive). *The Boy Friend* continued, and continues, to live on in revivals, repertory companies and amateur productions[21] across the world; as Gänzl puts it: 'There can scarcely be a regional repertory theatre in Britain which has not produced it' (Gänzl, 1986, p. 647). In 1929 Ivor Novello wrote of Noël Coward's musical *Bitter Sweet*, set in the late nineteenth century, that it was 'a *lovely,* lovely thing . . . so full of regret for a vanished, kindly silly darling age' (ed. Day, 2014, p. 156). Almost twenty-five years later, Sandy Wilson wrote another 'lovely, lovely thing', *The Boy Friend*, which looked back to the 1920s, and paid tribute to another 'vanished kindly silly darling age': the world of his childhood and the heyday of Novello and Coward, which was as distant to him as the late nineteenth century had been to them.

'What next?'

After *The Boy Friend*

Life is sweet,
But time is fleet
Beneath the magic of the moon.
Dancing time
May seem sublime,
But it ended all too soon.

('The Party's Over Now', Noël Coward, 1939)

A 'discarded'[1] chapter of Wilson's autobiography is titled 'What Next' and charts Wilson's career beyond the Broadway production of *The Boy Friend*. As he was by then well aware, *The Boy Friend* was the production that would always define his theatrical reputation; as he put it, this was 'a stricture I would obviously have to put up with for the rest of my life' (Wilson, unpublished autobiographical chapter, 1975, p. 319, Sandy Wilson archive). Wilson's obituaries all began with a focus on *The Boy Friend*, as in *The Guardian*: 'The composer and lyricist Sandy Wilson, who has died aged 90, achieved his greatest success while still in his 20s – and what a success it was' (Freedland, 2014). That success had cemented Wilson's status as an original voice in musical and theatre, and he seemed to be in a position where he could take anything to any theatre management in London. The propitious timing and venue that had worked so well for *The Boy Friend* were however to elude him in his next projects; a series of missteps and mistimings, some of them self-inflicted and some entirely unforeseeable, meant that Wilson would never achieve that same level of recognition again. Wilson's archives are full of notebooks and typescripts, which begin from 1940, for unproduced – and sometimes untitled – treatments for straight plays and musicals. There are lyrics, unpublished autobiographical chapters, stories and drafts of a novel; projects that came close to fruition, but which never saw the light of day.

After the success of *The Boy Friend*, Wilson seems to have been braver in dealing directly with explicitly camp and queer narratives; his work thereafter is largely based on writing by gay men. It is notable that, after the originality of the book and music of *The Boy Friend*, Wilson largely turned to adaptations of existing plays or novels rather than devise his own librettos, with the exception of the 1955 *The Buccaneer*. In a talk given to his own training ground, the Oxford Experimental Theatre Club, a year after the opening of *The Boy Friend* (while it was still running in the West End and on Broadway), he laid out the advantages of adapting an existing text:

> most of the American musical successes have been adaptations. . . . I think the idea of adapting something appeals for two reasons, one is starting with a firm story basis and one is using a plot that has already succeeded with the public in another form. The whole business of creating and launching a full-scale musical is so hazardous. (Wilson, talk to the Oxford Experimental Theatre Club, 5 May 1955, p. 8, Sandy Wilson archive)

The adaptation that Wilson was working on at the time was based on a story which had indeed been successful with the public; *Oh, Henry!* was a version of Alexander Korda's 1933 hit film starring Charles Laughton, which Wilson worked on between 1954 and 1955. Despite the success of Korda's film, it was to prove no less hazardous to launch than an original full-scale musical. *Oh, Henry!* was initially planned as a production helmed by Binkie Beaumont for the production company Tennents; it was posited as the follow up to the success of *The Boy Friend* in London and New York, touted in programmes and in press coverage as Wilson and Vida Hope's next project. Korda, according to newspaper reports, was not happy with Wilson's characterization of Henry (undated clippings, Sandy Wilson archive) and no management was prepared to put up the cost of production, which Wilson then estimated at £25,000.[2] *Oh, Henry!* does make attempts to address contemporary themes, taking on Britain's status in a post-war world, and making use of Anne of Cleves as an opportunity for jokes directed at the Germans. In a song of post-Imperial melancholy Henry sings:

> . . . look at the size of us!
> it's such a little place,
> This little island
> Just as little as a land can be . . .
>   (*Oh, Henry!* script, Act 1, p. 13, Sandy Wilson archive)

The historical nostalgia may have been too remote, and the melancholia too downbeat for audiences and investors, for no backer was forthcoming. The only appearance[3] of *Oh, Henry!* in the public realm was a 1958 excerpt, with Keith Michell[4] playing Henry on a television magazine programme. The *Daily Sketch* reported: 'Henry's been gathering dust . . . because nobody's taken that £25,000 risk to back it. Now TV has blown away the dust. Tonight brings a 15 minute excerpt. And Sandy will be in the studio, hoping . . .' (*Daily Sketch*, 13 May 1958). Despite a number of press reports on the television excerpt, all of which referred to Wilson's need for a backer, Wilson hoped in vain and *Oh, Henry!* was never produced.

The Buccaneer, rather than the aborted *Oh, Henry!*, was to be the show that Wilson described as that 'frightening obstacle in every writer's career, the Next Show after a Smash Hit' (Wilson, unpublished autobiographical chapter, 1975, p. 319, Sandy Wilson archive). Both the book and music of *The Buccaneer* were entirely original to Wilson; this time, Binkie Beaumont did take the production on, after it had first opened at the New Watergate theatre club, the scene of Wilson's earlier revue work.[5] Although it was not a great success at the Watergate, Beaumont backed a tour, taking it first to Brighton and Southsea, and then to London at the Lyric Hammersmith, in Kenneth Williams's words, an 'out of town' theatre (ed. Davies, 1994, p. 154), where it opened in 1955. Not one to forget a slight, Wilson was 'embarrassed' that John Perry, Beaumont's partner, who had sent Wilson 'a fairly rude letter' rejecting *The Buccaneer* (Wilson, unpublished autobiographical chapter, 1975, p. 308, Sandy Wilson archive) was put in charge of the production. He was also irked that it did not go straight into a West End theatre:

> I was a little hurt that he [Beaumont] did not have sufficient confidence to bring us into the West End straight away, but the Lyric had been established by Tennents as a successful and popular theatre and was certainly an ideal size for the show . . . although some critics compared it unfavourably to THE BOY FRIEND the notices were most excellent. All the cast did well, but Kenneth was obviously a major discovery and performed with brilliance. . . . It was satisfying to see THE BUCCANEER rescued from its ignominious débacle at the New Watergate. (Wilson, unpublished autobiographical chapter, 1975, p. 319, Sandy Wilson archive)

Notwithstanding this bumpy start, *The Buccaneer* was a modest success at the Lyric, and Wilson was interviewed for the BBC Television programme *Personality Parade* as 'the composer of *The Buccaneer* and *The Boy Friend*' (*Radio Times*, 30 September 1955, p. 38). *The Buccaneer* made a comic star of Williams,[6] nearly all the reviews of the Lyric production singled him out for praise. Wilson remembered Williams vividly and was proud of what he saw as providing a boost to his career:

> Our greatest find was the actor who played the prodigy, Montgomery . . . Kenneth Williams, who had lately attracted notice as the Dauphin opposite

Siobhan McKenna's St Joan. . . . he was also very funny and could sing. . . .
It was a master stroke of casting and a turning-point in Kenneth's career,
since he went on to become one of the best-known comedians in the
country. (unpublished autobiographical chapter, 1975, p. 308, Sandy
Wilson archive)

Kenneth Williams's own letters and diaries however demonstrate how much
he wanted to be a 'straight' actor, to continue on the trajectory of serious
dramatic roles such as the Dauphin, and how he despised being one 'of the
best-known comedians in the country'. Williams wrote a letter in 1972 about
going to see the film of *The Boy Friend*, which prompted a dismissive
reminiscence of performing in *The Buccaneer*:

> I was once in a Sandy Wilson musical on the stage – I played the boy-
> editor in his 'The Buccaneer' and it was an enormous success at the out
> of town theatre, which was the Lyric at Hammersmith, but when they
> transferred it to the West End it went to the Apollo Theatre and folded
> after about three weeks. (ed. Davies, 1994, p. 154)

Beaumont had promised that if it were successful at the Lyric, *The Buccaneer*
would move to the West End, but as Williams so sourly noted, it closed
early. The local press in Southsea and Brighton were largely kind: 'This
British musical sparkles with wit and good tunes' (*Southern Weekly News*,
26 August 1955). Comparisons with *The Boy Friend* were however inevitable,
at the London opening, the *Daily Mail*, *Evening News* and *Daily Mirror* all
carried the headline: 'Sandy Wilson does it again' (undated clippings, Sandy
Wilson archive), but a number of reviews saw *The Buccaneer* as inferior
to its predecessor (these are among the very few bad reviews that Wilson
catalogued in his archive). The *Evening Standard* critic reported 'I missed that
Boy Friend magic' (9 September 1955). *The Times* was, like *The Guardian*,
half-hearted about *The Buccaneer* and used its review as a means to berate
Wilson for not repeating that magic:

> Mr Sandy Wilson is evidently busily engaged in finding his feet,
> exploring every avenue, leaving no stone unturned, or whatever is the
> proper expression for a process of creative trial and error. Having first
> tried his hand, not unsuccessfully, at intimate revue, he next proceeded
> to prove to himself in *The Boy Friend* that he had mastered at least some
> of the difficulties of writing the kind of musical comedy that had amused
> us in the 1920s. His latest piece is also in the nature of an exercise. . . . *The
> Buccaneer* . . . we fear, is poor stuff. (undated, uncredited review, clipping
> *The Times*, Sandy Wilson archive)

Unlike *Oh, Henry! The Buccaneer* did deal directly with a topical issue. The title refers to a boys' magazine of the kind that Wilson would have remembered from childhood; *The Buccaneer* is clearly a version of the *Boy's Own Paper*, which was set up in 1879 by the Religious Tract Society to promote muscular Christian values and which continued publishing until 1967. Its advertising offered boy readers 'pure and entertaining reading . . . full of rousing patriotic stories' (Warner, p. 1). The conceit of the play is that the masculine Christian virtues and values of the magazine are no longer current in the mid-twentieth century, and that the very British *The Buccaneer* can only be rescued by a modernizing American publisher. *The Buccaneer* is at one level a rollicking celebration of traditional comic books for boys, but it is also a satire on the moral panic against 'the permissive society'.

The Buccaneer was first produced in London at a time when the comic book and its effects on young children were the subject of heated debate both in Britain and America; in 1955, the issue of boys' comics was very live. In 1954 the American Fredric Wertham had published *Seduction of the Innocent*[7] which articulated and focussed a moral panic around the American comic book. This led to an American Senate subcommittee on Juvenile Delinquency in the same year, which focussed on comic books; this in turn led to a restrictive code for publishers.[8] The Prologue to Wilson's play is set in 'Today'; the opening speech by a Member of Parliament, described in the script as 'a pompous old buffer', directly invokes the language of the contemporary debate around comic books: 'my primary concern is . . . the health – both in body and mind – of our younger generation. . . . I dared to deplore the shameful influx from America of what, in those days, were called "horror comics"' (*The Buccaneer* typescript, Act 1, p. 1, Sandy Wilson archive).

A contemporary review recognized the contemporaneity of *The Buccaneer's* concerns and recruited *The Buccaneer* into an argument against 'juvenile delinquency': 'Mr Wilson is nothing if not progressive. At the heart of this play is an up-to-the-minute issue, the increase in juvenile delinquency' (Geoffrey Tarran, undated review, Sandy Wilson archive). It is arguable, however, whether *The Buccaneer* is that 'progressive'; it is as nostalgic in its own way as *The Boy Friend*, as an elegy for a particularly British and Victorian form of popular culture threatened by American modernity. Wilson's stage directions set *The Buccaneer* magazine as a fondly remembered British bulwark against deplorable foreign imports and as representative of 'a small gallant band of British publishers who had kept alive just one of those fine, genuine magazines for boys which I remembered from my own youth . . . THE BUCCANEER . . .that upright, honest little magazine' (*The Buccaneer* typescript, Act 1, p. 1, Sandy Wilson archive).

The founding principles of the magazine are expressed in the first song of the musical; 'Good Clean Fun', which evokes a British morality that eschews anything effeminate or sexual and spoofs the moral and masculine certainties of journals such as the *Boy's Own Paper*:

> Nothing that's dirty and nothing that's bad
> Should ever take root in the mind of a lad . . .
> We must make perfectly certain and sure
> That what our boys read is unfailingly pure . . .
> And boys who are British should never be bored
> With good clean fun.

> ('Good Clean Fun', Act 1, *The Buccaneer*
> typescript, p. 4, Sandy Wilson archive)

In an opening flashback, the magazine is at the point of having to be sold to an American publisher; its office is shabby and neglected, its editor, the widow of the founder William Barraclough, is 'getting on in years' and circulation is dropping dramatically. The 'Good Clean Fun' of *The Buccaneer* is threatened by American comic books, as Mrs Barraclough laments: 'Boys don't seem to read anything else nowadays' (Act 1, *The Buccaneer* typescript, p. 2, Sandy Wilson archive).

The Buccaneer magazine promotes an unabashed celebration (as did the *Boy's Own Paper*) of British imperial power and manly heroes; the lead serial features the heroic 'Captain Fairbrother', an amalgamation of a range of colonial explorer heroes such as Rider Haggard's Allan Quatermain or Jack Harkaway of the *Boys of England* magazine,[9] who share an imperial belief in white supremacy:

> No task is too hard from him.
> No country is barred to him.
> In every latitude he shows the right man
> Is a White Man!

> ('Captain Fairbrother' song, Act 1, *The Buccaneer*
> typescript, p. 7, Sandy Wilson archive)

Captain Fairbrother is the embodiment of a Victorian ideal of imperial masculinity, and *The Buccaneer* magazine presents an entirely male world in which 'there is not a petticoat in the whole history', as in Rider Haggard's *King Solomon's Mines* (Haggard, p. 8). The elderly writer of the Captain Fairbrother serial entirely endorses Haggard: 'Our heroes have no time for the opposite . . . sex. That was a cardinal rule' (Act 1, *The Buccaneer* typescript, Sandy

Wilson archive, p. 8). The potential for a queer reading of this all-male realm is hinted at, in terms which would have been implicit at the first production in 1955 but widely recognized at the time of the revival of 1976. In an exchange with a potential investor, the wealthy divorcée Mrs Winterton asks her son, the precocious Montgomery (played by Kenneth Williams, who had yet to develop his reputation as a camp performer):

> Mrs W.: And is this magazine amusing?
> Montgomery: No. It's for boys.
> Mrs W.: 'THE BUCCANEER'. That's very gay, isn't it?
> (Act 1, *The Buccaneer* typescript, p. 22, Sandy Wilson archive)

The unabashedly commercial and vulgar American publisher (perhaps inflected by Wilson's own experiences with American producers over *The Boy Friend*), Mr Maximus, proposes to take over *The Buccaneer* and to retitle it as the 'Jumbo Jet', to introduce 'sex appeal' to the magazine and, to the horror of both the male and female staff, to bring a heroine into its all-male domain. 'Belinda Blast-Off, Space-Age Super-Girl' threatens the British imperial past with modern femininity, technology and American power. The struggle over *The Buccaneer* is not just about the future of the magazine but also about contemporary ideas of masculinity. Every character in the play has their own idea of what *The Buccaneer* should be and projects their own moral priorities into plans for its future. Mrs Barraclough, widow of the founder, sees it as a space for 'Healthy Adventure, where nothing disgraceful is done' (Act 1, *The Buccaneer* typescript, p. 4, Sandy Wilson archive). School boy Montgomery is a new generation of boyhood, and regards the magazine as resolutely old-fashioned; his plan breaks with another taboo, he wants to politicize *The Buccaneer* and to turn it into a political vehicle as the 'Children's New Statesman'. His tutor, Peter, is nostalgic for traditional childhood pleasures and sees the magazine as 'decent and wholesome. It represents something which is fast disappearing from modern life – the spirit of adventure' (Act 1, *The Buccaneer* typescript, p. 20, Sandy Wilson archive).

Montgomery is, like Wilson himself, emphatically not a sports enthusiast but a reader (he is first encountered reading his mother's copy of *Ulysses*); neither have any enthusiasm for the masculine sports which were so integral to muscular Christianity and the ethos of the *Boys' Own Papers*. In his autobiography Wilson writes cheerfully about his own lack of sporting prowess at Harrow:

> I had only been at Harrow for two weeks when I had a stroke of luck and broke my wrist playing Rugger. It was painful for a while, but it meant

that for the rest of the term I was excused all games and exercise. . . . So
while everyone else was rushing about on the Football fields, I used to
purchase a chocolate bar or two at the school tuck-shop and retire to my
room to read *Gone with the Wind*. (Wilson, 1975a, p. 53)

The play endorses this preference for reading over sportsmanship, in
rewarding Montgomery with a romantic interest, Marilyn, the American
daughter of the 'Tycoon', favours male intellect over brawny masculinity as
she sings:

> I don't go for beefcake now.
> I don't go for strong men. . . .
> He is no good at sports
> But he thinks lovely thoughts
> And, Oh! What a wonderful brain!
>
> ('Oh, What a Beautiful Brain', Act 1, *The Buccaneer*
> typescript, p. 31, Sandy Wilson archive)

While Wilson does challenge conventional masculinity to an extent, the
sexual politics of *The Buccaneer* are not in the end progressive. Marilyn is just
as precocious as Montgomery, but the script in no way challenges the way in
which he patronizes her: 'I think you're a bit superficial, but I suppose you
can't help that, being a woman' (*The Buccaneer* typescript Act 1, p. 29, Sandy
Wilson archive). None of the planned ideas for *The Buccaneer* come to fruition,
and English masculinity and the magazine remain unchanged. The play
ends with a magical resolution of tradition and modernity in which Captain
Fairbrother (Peter, the tutor in disguise, relishing his taste for adventure)
leads the children of England and America in a rally on Trafalgar Square: 'He
is leading the new generation to a better world . . . all these children want THE
BUCCANEER just as it is' (Act 11, *The Buccaneer* typescript, p. 77, Sandy
Wilson archive). *The Buccaneer* magazine remains 'just as it is', and quite what
Peter is leading the new generation towards remains unclear.

The Guardian's contemporary review was lukewarm, describing *The
Buccaneer* as: 'a lively little musical play . . . There is enough plot to string the
songs together, and some of the songs are pleasant . . . But the point of the piece
– if it exists at all – is very blunt and does not hurt. It is never quite clear whom
we are laughing at' (undated review, Sandy Wilson archive). This makes the
fair point that there is no clear object of satire in *The Buccaneer*; there are gibes
at American commercialism, at Victorian prudery and political pomposity,
but these are easy targets and it remains ambiguous as to whether the musical
is affectionately celebrating or lampooning the Victorian mores of muscular

Christianity. Captain Fairbrother's assertion that 'the right man is a white man' is never challenged and he remains a heroic figure. The ending demonstrates Wilson's own ambivalence and nostalgic conservatism; while he recognizes that the masculine values of the *Boys' Own Papers* are no longer sustainable in a post-war world, he nonetheless demonstrates an abiding affection for them. *The Buccaneer* was revived at the Apollo Theatre in London, but it never achieved the enduring affection that *The Boy Friend* enjoyed.

According to Wright: 'queerness was to be a component of his best work' (Wright, 2010, p. 72), but neither *The Boy Friend* or *The Buccaneer* made that 'queerness' evident, they both offered a potential for a camp reading but could be taken as entirely straight. Wilson went on to develop a number of projects based on the work of homosexual writers who would then have been widely recognized as gay (Cecil Beaton, Ronald Firbank, Compton Mackenzie and Christopher Isherwood), but none of them flew (with the exception of Ronald Firbank's *Valmouth*), for a range of reasons: casting, the producers flinching or, simply, bad timing.

Caprice (1950) pre-dated *The Boy Friend* as a script; Wilson wrote the lyrics to Geoffrey Wright's score. *Caprice* was based, like the later *Valmouth*, on a 1917 novel by Ronald Firbank, and in some ways prefigures it. Subtitled 'A Musical Tragedy', *Caprice* is concerned with the tension between the dull respectability of conventional middle-class life and the fantasy and glamour of the theatre; the scenes and characters of the theatre are not far removed from Wilson's account of his time with the Oxford Experimental Theatre Club in his autobiography and unpublished novel. The heroine is Sarah Sinquier, the daughter of a Cathedral Dean, who has theatrical aspirations. Sarah is first encountered in the Deanery of the Cathedral close, with church bells ringing around her, performing by herself and imagining herself in the role of actress. She is frustrated (as is Alice in Wilson's 1978 *The Clapham Wonder*) by small town respectable living and dreams of another life in London: 'London – City of Love – !' (*Caprice* typescript, Act 1, p. 6, Sandy Wilson archive). She sings a love song to a beautiful 'Congo' negress in a fantasy of exotic otherness (based on lyrics by Firbank and a precursor to the themes of *Valmouth*). In the second scene Sarah has made her escape to Shaftesbury Avenue where she is directed to the Café Royal. Here she is surrounded by louche characters engaged in theatrical gossip, among them are the camp Harold Weathercock and Noel Nice who 'share a studio' in Soho. In a song, a divorced 'adventuress' introduces Sarah to the exciting lives of creative and theatre people who refuse conventional morality :

They are singers and dancers and actors,
They are writers and makers of song.

They are tortured and talented, gifted and gay[10] . . .
And it's here that, my dear, you belong . . .

These are wonderful, wonderful people
Who lead wonderful, wonderful lives.
They indulge without end
In affairs that transcend
Those of mere humdrum husbands and wives
> (*Caprice* Typescript, Act 1, pp. 15–16, Sandy Wilson archive)

Sarah finds that she does indeed belong to this world, and, enthused by the theatre and the magic of performance, shares a kiss and declaration of love with May, another stage-struck young woman. It is not only her sexuality that is unlocked; the theatre opens up fantasy worlds of Egyptian pyramids, Indian pavilions, an aristocrat's garden in Nice; but neither the play nor the novel can allow her to enjoy these pleasures. Both end with Sarah's death in unexplained circumstances caused by an onstage accident for which May is responsible, whether this was inadvertent or deliberate remains unclear. *Caprice* did open at the Alhambra in Glasgow but closed in Birmingham a month later. According to Wright: 'This was musical making of the old school, even by 1950 standards' (Wright, 2010, p. 72); audiences were wearying of Coward and Novello, but were not yet prepared for Firbankian decadence.

After the New York success of *The Boy Friend*, the Broadway producer Gant Gaither approached Wilson to do an adaptation of *My Royal Past*, derived from a 1939 book of photographs and a scenario by Cecil Beaton which featured his male friends dressed in drag.[11] A musical version of *My Royal Past* had first been suggested to Gaither by Anita Loos (author of *Gentleman Prefer Blondes*, 1925) who initially wanted to write a version herself but later withdrew. She met with Wilson and Wilson's then partner, Jon Rose, in Paris, as Wilson describes it:

> The three of us sat in the sunshine, in the courtyard of her Paris hotel, over coffee, and completed the story line in an hour or so, an ideal method of collaboration. For various reasons, including the nature of the Broadway musical at that time and Jeannette MacDonald's susceptibilities, Cecil's original had to be broadened and bowdlerised. In the book the Grand Duchess Hedwig is, quite frankly, a nymphomaniac. (unpublished autobiographical chapter, 1975, p. 320, Sandy Wilson archive)

Beaton's original is a pastiche memoir apparently written by an European aristocrat, with the arch subtitle: 'as told to Cecil Beaton (or rather written by him).' Her preposterous title is the Baroness von Bülop *née* Princess Theodora Louise Alexina Ludmilla Sophie von Eckermann-Waldstein, a name that has echoes of Novello's mittel-European characters (Wilson acknowledged that Novello helped with the writing, see Wright, 2010, p. 72).

My Royal Past was originally planned as a vehicle for Hermione Gingold,[12] with an appearance by Jeanette MacDonald, and sets by Beaton. Vida Hope was again lined up to direct and the production was reported as such in *Vogue* (October, 1955, Sandy Wilson archive). Despite this line-up of star names, *My Royal Past* was never taken up; MacDonald withdrew and Gingold too lost patience with the casting process, the production was finally put, along with *Oh, Henry!*, on the shelf. The plot concerns Hedwig, the Grand Duchess of Hansburg and Hilda, Countess von Bulop, arriving impoverished in Brooklyn and in search of American husbands. As the title implies, Hedwig and Hilde are again creatures of nostalgia and their story is told in a flashback which revisits the tale of how they come to find themselves so impoverished. In their sexual appetites Hedwig and Hilda can be seen as precedents for the vamps of *Valmouth*, at their first appearance they are delighted to find that they have a view of the Brooklyn Navy Yard; as Hedwig comments 'It's full of men! Wonderful American men!' (*My Royal Past*, typescript, Act 1, p. 4, Sandy Wilson archive)

Two projects, which had the potential to be blockbusters and to confirm Wilson's reputation as a writer of the zeitgeist, were abandoned not because of the material or problems of casting, but because of bad timing. Wilson's musical version of Bernard Shaw's 1913 play *Pygmalion* was first mooted in 1955, while *The Boy Friend* was still drawing audiences in the West End and on Broadway, but the rights were not available; they had been sold to Alan Jay Lerner and Frederick Loewe who used them to produce *My Fair Lady* on Broadway. Wilson wryly noted: 'the rights to PYGMALION were disposed of elsewhere, and the result is now theatrical legend' (unpublished notebook, 1957, Sandy Wilson archive). Ironically, the American theatre production starred Julie Andrews,[13] who had made her name in the Broadway production of *The Boy Friend*, as Eliza Doolittle, and the costumes for the 1964 film version (dir. George Cukor) were designed by Cecil Beaton.

Wilson had good reason to feel bitter, in the aftermath of the failure of *Oh, Henry!* to find a producer and with the pre-empting of his own version of *Pygmalion*. In 1957, he wrote a notebook essay (his most vitriolic comments are directed at *My Fair Lady*) in which he blamed contemporary British theatre managements for their lack of ambition:

And where in the wastes of Shaftesbury Avenue or the deserts of Saint Martin's Lane does one find a Producer who really produces? . . . Where is the Management who will set in motion a big, bouncing, beautiful British Musical which will go bowling into the Coliseum or Drury Lane and then on to Broadway to prove to the world that We Can Do it Too . . .

It is really, I suppose, much less trouble to put an American ready-made and show it in front of the bedazzled British public. The poor suckers will take anything by now. (notebook, 1957, Sandy Wilson archive)

Wilson's musical version of Christopher Isherwood's *Berlin Stories* (*Goodbye to Berlin* and *Mr Norris Changes Trains*), which were first published in 1939,[14] was perhaps the most egregious case of inappropriate timing in his career. In this case, it was not the choice of material or problems of casting, but of being gazumped. *I Am a Camera*, a version of Isherwood's *Goodbye to Berlin*, had first been produced as a play in New York in 1951, written by John Van Druten, who had died in 1957. This was to become the basis for the Broadway production and later film of *Cabaret* (dir. Bob Fosse, 1972). David Black, a British producer, commissioned Wilson to write a score in 1963, but according to Wilson's agent, Joan Rees, was not to be trusted in securing the rights to Van Druten's script (letter from Joan Rees, 1964, Sandy Wilson archive). Wilson's American agent also tried to acquire the rights for Wilson's treatment (letter from Claire S. Degener, 7 July 1964, Sandy Wilson archive) but they were finally acquired by the American producer Hal Prince. Prince had a librettist in place, but as yet no composer and invited Wilson to play his songs to him. The librettist, Joe Masteroff, thought the songs too similar to those of *The Boy Friend* and lacking in the spirit of Weimar cabaret; in a symposium interview, Masteroff later recalled:

Sandy Wilson played us the score he had written for *I Am a Camera*. It was very nice, but it sounded exactly like *The Boy Friend*. It was set in the late 1920s, so I suppose he figured why not? When Hal and I left, we both agreed . . . that was not the way we wanted to hear it. What was interesting to us basically was the sound of Germany in that period. Obviously we had heard all the Kurt Weill music, all of the Lotte Lenya records, and somehow in the back of our heads that is how we wanted it to sound. Then, in some mysterious way, suddenly one day Hal Prince came to me and said 'You know, Sandy Wilson isn't going to do it after all. We are.' Just how all that happened, I don't know. (Landmark Symposium, undated report, Sandy Wilson archive)

This was disingenuous, it was Hal Prince's decision, not uninfluenced by Masteroff's response to Wilson's score, to commission John Kander as composer and with a libretto by Masteroff; even though Wilson had already completed the book and much of the score for his own version. Despite Julie Andrews' (then at the height of her star power after *Mary Poppins*, 1964, dir. Robert Stevenson) interest in playing Wilson's version of Sally Bowles,[15] Kander and Ebb's music and book for *Cabaret* became the defining version of Isherwood's novellas and Liza Minelli the definitive Sally Bowles.

Wilson was clearly bruised by the experience and was not slow in setting the record straight; he responded to Masteroff's account with a sarcastic letter to a friend:

> Joe Masteroff is of course entitled to say that my score for the Berlin Stories sounded 'exactly like *The Boy Friend*'– that's his opinion. . . . Mr Masteroff told me he had liked my work, but it did not fit in with his conception of Sally Bowles. And that was that. . . . I finally got to see Hal's brilliant production of CABARET in 1967, and I understood what Mr Masteroff had said about his conception of Sally Bowles. There was none.
> (undated letter to an unnamed editor, Sandy Wilson archive)

Wilson's unproduced script is closer to the original Isherwood texts than either Van Druten's *I am a Camera* or Kander and Ebb's *Cabaret*. Like *Cabaret*, the musical opens in a cabaret bar, but the first scene shows the young Isherwood arriving at his lodgings in Berlin where he meets his landlady Frau Schroeder and the other tenants, including a young prostitute, the couple Peter and Werner and where he first encounters Mr Norris (who features prominently in the novel and as a character in Wilson's version but who is absent from *Cabaret*). In Wilson's version, Sally Bowles does not appear until later scenes in the club, and, as in the novel, does not have the same prominence as in *Cabaret*. The Kit Kat Club of *Cabaret* is named the Lady Windermere Bar, as it is in *Goodbye to Berlin*; with its reference to Oscar Wilde it is more explicitly a gay bar and Christopher himself (renamed Brian Roberts in the film) is represented as clearly gay, rather than bisexual as the film suggests. Isherwood himself wrote to Wilson in 1966 to deplore the way in which Wilson had been treated and to explain the circumstances. He writes of

> the messed up situation which has gradually developed around the project of doing a musical based on I am a Camera and my own Berlin material. You have been the victim of this situation. You have been subject to a disappointment after all the work and enthusiasm you gave to the project, not to mention your great talent. . . . The Van Druten estate had the controlling voice in all negotiations, and that was that. It was decided that a Mr Hal Prince should put together a production in New York –

Mr Prince is currently one of the most successful producers on Broadway. Mr Prince got his own writers and composer and I understand that between them they already have all the music and songs and a rough draft of the book. (letter from Christopher Isherwood, 14 June 1966, Sandy Wilson archive)

Wilson's response to the disappointment was to return to the glory days of *The Boy Friend* and to write a sequel, *Divorce Me, Darling!* which returns the same characters to Nice a decade on. *Divorce Me, Darling!* was first produced by the Players' company and opened at the Players' Theatre as a Christmas show in 1964, before transferring to the Globe Theatre in the West End. The sets were again designed by Reginald Woolley, and in the initial Players' production many of the cast were the same as that of *The Boy Friend*: Violetta reprised her role as Hortense, Maria Charles as Dulcie, Joan Sterndale Bennett as Madame Dubonnet and Geoffrey Hibbert (from the Broadway production) as Lord Brockhurst.

As the title suggests, *Divorce Me, Darling!* departs from the light-hearted gaiety of *The Boy Friend* as the scenario moves the characters and setting from 1926 into 1936. While *The Boy Friend* had offered romance and optimism to a post-war world, *Divorce Me, Darling!* is sceptical in its treatment of marriage, and melancholy in the fact that the characters have aged, as Wilson had himself. The producer Peter Rawley remarked on the significance of the age difference of the cast and of the change of historical context in notes that were sent to Wilson before the opening: 'It is important . . . to remember that while the Boy Friend was concerned with adolescents, this play is concerned with young adults feeling their way towards maturity. And surely too, the generation of the thirties were reacting against the free and easy twenties' (undated notes from Peter Rawley, Sandy Wilson archive). This gets to the heart of why *Divorce Me, Darling!* could not capture hearts in the way that *The Boy Friend* had done; it was less youthful, less optimistic and more cynical; as Madame Dubonnet puts it 'The world today is rather triste' (Wilson, 1981, p. 11). Wright suggests: 'the characters are now older, more world-weary now . . . it is not young love in the air but divorce. Any hint of cynicism or serious doubt hardly obtrudes in *The Boy Friend*, but is essential to its sequel' (Wright, 2010, p. 83). There was, too, a political naivety in situating the plot in the decade immediately after the Wall Street Crash, which is alluded to but which does not seriously trouble the protagonists. The 1930s was not an appropriate period for a nostalgic celebration of privilege and wealth; the *Express* reviewer was not alone in pointing this out:

The thirties was the decade of post-Depression politics, when flirtation with Marxism was still considered respectable. . . . It was an inward-looking period, and Mr Wilson's attempt to superimpose a flamboyant identity on it is a misguided one, and accounts largely for the rather negative aura that adheres to his show. (*Express*, 2 February 1965, clipping, Sandy Wilson archive)

There is no 'flirtation with Marxism' in *Divorce Me, Darling*. The play opens with the multiple brides whose weddings were the celebratory ending of *The Boy Friend*; the 'young ladies' are now all married and have returned to Nice without their husbands. Together they mournfully sing: 'Where did romance disappear to? And why did it vanish away?' (Wilson, 1981, p. 6). Polly's millionaire father, Percival Brown, has lost his fortune in the Crash and is on the run in South America, while Madame Dubonnet, her former headmistress and now stepmother, has had to turn her hand to cabaret. As in *The Boy Friend*, the plot hinges on disguise and camouflage; the 'young ladies' are escaping their husbands in Nice, while claiming to be elsewhere. Lord Brocklehurst is escaping from his wife and her mission to bring 'Health and Beauty' to Nice. Madame Dubonnet is in disguise as Madame K, the cabaret artist, her husband as Mr Jones, who takes on a double disguise as he steps in to substitute for the President of Monomania. Hortense, the maid, disguises herself with a mask to become the cabaret artist Madame K, in order that Madame Dubonnet will not be recognized by her stepdaughter Polly. The disguises are not, as they in *The Boy Friend*, a means of levelling the playing field in the romantic stakes, but an evasion of spouses and of creditors. The finale in which the 'young ladies' declare their pregnancies shifts the ingenues of *The Boy Friend* into adulthood. The final resolution in which the (real) President of Monomania rewards Mr Browne for the impersonation which allowed the President to escape a bomb sits somewhat uneasily with the purportedly happy ending.

It is clear that the first production of *Divorce Me, Darling!* did not have the camaraderie of the Players' production of *The Boy Friend*. Wilson's autobiography makes no mention of *Divorce Me, Darling!* (despite the fact that it opened seven years before the Russell film which ends the autobiography). Letters in Wilson's archive suggest that the production process was more than a little bumpy. Joan Heal, who took over as Madame Dubonnet for the West End production, wrote an impassioned letter to Wilson which demonstrates that difficulties and bad feelings extended throughout the cast (although it is not clear what it is that Wilson has done):

I feel that I must WRITE to you and put a few facts to you that, in the general furore, you either do not KNOW, or have chosen to overlook. . . . That you should think that I would do ANYTHING to harm that show.

Or, worse, disrespect its author; is not only incredible . . . it is an insult . . . (letter from Joan Heal to Sandy Wilson, 20 January 1965, Sandy Wilson archive)

A letter signed by Reginald Woolley, Don Gemmell, then directors of Players' Ventures Limited and by Binkie Beaumont, who was responsible for the West End transfer from the Players' Theatre, thanks Wilson for bowing out of the production and for placing 'the conduct of the production of "Divorce Me, Darling!" unreservedly in the hands of the management':

> While we feel that this was a wise decision and perhaps the only one to give the musical a fair chance of success we know very well that it must have been a very difficult one to reach and that you placed the interest of the company and the investors before your own in a way which was quite admirable.
>
> We are truly sorry that the show has not so far turned out as you visualised it, but we hope very much that when it is finally presented at the Globe not only that it will be a great success but that it will be the sort of success you want. (letter from Reginald Woolley, Don Gemmell and Hugh Beaumont, 12 January 1965, Sandy Wilson archive)

Wilson's concerns were proved to be founded, although it is not clear whether a different production might have saved the musical. The production moved out of the comfort and camp sophistication of the Players' Theatre after a four-week run and went straight into the West End, where it closed after ninety-one performances at the Globe Theatre. The London reviews were almost uniformly unkind; the problem for many critics was what the *Evening News* referred to as the musical's 'rose-pink world of rich and frivolous allusion' (2 February 1965, Sandy Wilson archive). *Divorce Me, Darling!* could not confront the uneasy politics of the 1930s nor sustain the romance of *The Boy Friend*. *The Stage* also pointed to the inappropriate context, and compared *Divorce Me, Darling!* unfavourably with *The Boy Friend*: '(it) is not to be compared to the witty, deft, light-hearted show that ran for years and made Mr Wilson's name in the theatre. . . . Possibly the thirties do not so readily respond to parody and pastiche as the Twenties' (quoted in Wright, 2010, p. 84). The *Daily Sketch* was particularly scathing: 'The whole evening seems to be a catastrophical bore' (2 February 1965, Sandy Wilson archive). Harold Hobson was an exception, writing in *the Christian Science Monitor* 'it is as gay, as agreeable and as sophisticatedly naïve as its illustrious predecessor' (undated clipping, Sandy Wilson archive). In a later review for the *Sunday Times*, Hobson did acknowledge the limits of the 'rose-tinted' world of

Wilson's later musical: 'in the world which Mr Wilson in this instance chooses to inhabit such horrid things as adultery, desertion and co-respondents are as unknown as unemployment, strikes and Existentialism' (*Sunday Times*, 8 February 1965). This was somewhat unfair, while *Divorce Me, Darling!* attempted to studiously ignore the politics of the decade, it did hint at adultery, desertion and co-respondents. In a scene on adjoining balconies, which echoes Noël Coward's *Private Lives*, the romantic heroine Polly comes close to an affair with her friend Maisie's husband.

Divorce Me, Darling! garnered fan mail from Leslie Caron, Ian McKellen and many members of the audience (letters to Sandy Wilson, 1965, Sandy Wilson archive). Noël Coward was quoted positively in the *Daily Mirror*, perhaps pleased at the balcony scene tribute to him: 'I enjoyed the show very much, ... I thought the music was charming and some of the jokes very good' (*Daily Mirror*, 2 February 1965). The show however could not survive the 'bitchy notices,' as Wilson's friend Patrick Kinross described them (letter from Lord Kinross, 24 February 1965, Sandy Wilson archive). A scathing review from Clive Barnes (then the all-powerful theatre critic of the *New York Times*) scuppered plans to bring *Divorce Me, Darling!* to Broadway and the whim of a wealthy American investor finally put paid to any chance of an American transfer (letter from Harry Rigby, 14 January 1969, Sandy Wilson archive). Nonetheless, like *The Boy Friend, Divorce Me Darling!* went on to have a long afterlife in amateur and professional productions across the world, often produced together with *The Boy Friend* in a double bill. And Wilson kept programmes from all those productions, as he had for *The Boy Friend*. Wilson's archives are not however complete; while he subscribed to a clippings service, and he carefully filed reviews for every production of *The Boy Friend* and for his spoof biography, *This Is Sylvia*, bad reviews are very few and far between. And while he catalogued every version of his unproduced scripts and both versions of his unpublished novel, *Oxford Isn't What it Used to Be*, with the exception of letters relating to *Goodbye to Berlin*, there are no rejection letters or any indication as to why these remained unproduced and unpublished.

In an interview for the programme for a Chichester Festival Theatre revival of 1997, Wilson explains his own understanding of why it was that *Divorce Me, Darling!* failed to take flight: 'The Winter of 1965 really wasn't the moment for an affectionate look at the Thirties, it was the year of the Rolling Stones' worldwide hit *Satisfaction*, and Julie Christie in the film *Darling* . . . it was too soon' (*Divorce Me, Darling!* Programme, 1997, p. 10). It was not that it was too soon, it was rather that it was too late; audiences of the 1960s could not be expected to know the plot details of *The Boy Friend*, on which *Divorce Me, Darling!* relied, or to pick up references to the work of Noël Coward. As the *Daily Mirror* rather unkindly noted, many of the critics were no longer of a generation to remember the 1930s or to be familiar with *The Boy Friend*: 'It is unfortunate for Mr Wilson that several of the reviewers are too young to appreciate the accuracy of the pastiche' (*Daily Mirror*, 2 February 1965).

The nostalgic charm of *The Boy Friend* could not be carried over into the 1960s; according to Wright: 'the closure of *Divorce Me, Darling!* effectively ended Wilson's ongoing West End career, consigning him to the fringe of British musical theatre. This was a real injustice for a man who only ten years before was seen as the successor to Coward' (Wright, 2010, p. 88). Wilson was still looking back to the era of Coward and Novello at a time when a new generation of British and American musicals[16] were making nostalgia look distinctly old-fashioned. Coward's successor was not comfortable with the musical idioms of the 1960s; in an interview, Wilson was asked what he thought of contemporary popular music. "'I've hated it since 1950," he replied. "Since rock'n'roll I've turned a deaf ear'" (undated clipping, Sandy Wilson archive).

Queer utopianism

Valmouth

Safe are we from worldly ills
Time that kills
Passes us by
In Valmouth
Every care
Seems to fade in the air
Of Valmouth

(Valmouth typescript, Act 1, p. 5, Sandy Wilson archive)

The fraught and fractious circumstances of the production of *Divorce Me, Darling!* (whatever Sandy Wilson's involvement may have been, it is clear that he was not entirely innocent of the problems) would re-emerge forcefully with *Valmouth*. The troubles of the production of *Valmouth* were to be much greater and there were to be lasting and damaging consequences for the success of *Valmouth* and for Wilson's career and reputation. Wright sees *Valmouth* as the musical which relegated Wilson from the toast of the West End to the 'esoteric margins' of musical theatre (Wright, 2012, p. 146) and concludes that it was both a brave and reckless undertaking:

> *The Boy Friend* had appealed to the sophisticate as well as proving eminently suitable for a night-out with Aunt Edna.[1] . . . Booking a ticket for Aunt Edna to sit through Sandy Wilson's version of *Valmouth* might have resulted in a less comfortable evening. After the pastiche at the Villa Caprice [*The Boy Friend*] and the good clean fun of Mrs Barraclough and Co.[*The Buccaneer*], Wilson's lurch to the esoteric was daring, brilliant and perhaps fatal for his subsequent career. (Wright, 2010, p. 80)

It was an undertaking that was supported and initiated by the Royal Court Theatre. Tony Richardson of the English Stage Company, an

Oxford contemporary of Wilson's who had been a stage manager for the *Oxford Circus* revue for the Oxford University Experimental Theatre Club (programme, Oxford Playhouse, Sandy Wilson archive), wrote to Wilson in 1958 inviting him to write a musical of some kind for the English Stage Company, based at the Royal Court Theatre, then the heartland of cutting-edge theatre after the success of *Look Back in Anger* in 1956.[2] Wilson much later described his reaction to the invitation as 'flattered and rather surprised (typescript for a talk on *Valmouth*, Croydon Arts Centre, 1986, Sandy Wilson archive)'. Wilson had strong connections with people at the Royal Court; besides Tony Richardson, Kenneth Tynan (who had so championed *Look Back in Anger*) was an Oxford and Experimental Theatre Club contemporary of Wilson's, George Devine had taught Wilson at the Bristol Old Vic School (Wilson, 1975a, p. 134) and John Osborne had become a friend. Wilson later wrote 'an offer from the Royal Court was just the sort of thing I had been itching for' (unpublished autobiographical chapter, p. 330, Sandy Wilson archive). A revue was initially proposed but Wilson felt that 'revue as a theatrical medium was moribund' (unpublished autobiographical chapter, p. 330, Sandy Wilson archive), then a pantomime, 'and finally Jon[3] and I put forward the idea of "Valmouth" to which Tony reacted very enthusiastically' (letter to George Devine, 6 March 1958, Sandy Wilson archive). As Wilson later described the discussion:

> Tony's ears pricked up. Firbank was already persona grata among the cognoscenti and would obviously have cultural appeal for the Royal Court audiences. He said he would pass on the idea to George Devine, and a few days later the Royal Court gave me the go-ahead. I now read VALMOUTH again for the first time since 1950. My first reaction was that I must be out of my mind: the narrative was so slender, the relationships so complete, and the flavour of the whole so elusive – how could I ever capture it on the stage? But I was committed: George Devine had once said he hoped I would write a musical for him, and now he was expecting me to do it. ('What Next?', unpublished autobiographical chapter, p. 331, Sandy Wilson archive)

Wilson had first worked on Ronald Firbank's 1919 novel in 1953, and describes the genesis of *Valmouth*, the musical, as emerging from a late-night discussion among those involved in an out-of-town production of *The Buccaneer*:

> One night in Brighton we were all having dinner together after the performance, when the conversation somehow got onto the subject

of Ronald Fairbank. Billie Chappell[4] . . . turned to me and said, 'Have you ever thought of VALMOUTH as a musical? I think it would be marvellous'

In fact the thought had crossed my mind when I first read the novel in 1950, but at that time I had no reputation to justify my undertaking such an unusual subject . . . ('What Next?' unpublished autobiographical chapter, p. 319, Sandy Wilson archive)

A musical adaptation of Firbank's novella seems a strange choice for the English Stage Company; the culture of the English Stage Company at the time was an affirmation of working-class straight masculinity (as embodied in *Look Back in Anger*'s Jimmy Porter) and the camp sensibility of *Valmouth*, despite Richardson's approach to Wilson and Wilson's friendships with Osborne and Devine, was an odd fit for their repertoire.[5] In retrospect, it seems improbable that it should have been Tony Richardson, later to become a leading figure in the British New Wave film movement, who commissioned Wilson and that he and George Devine, the first Artistic Director of the Royal Court Theatre, should have been open to *Valmouth*, a novel of such high Catholic camp. Firbank has long been a signifier of camp; he is included by Sontag as a member of the camp canon (Sontag, p. 200), and is among Dyer's list of 'camp things' (Dyer, 1992, p. 138). According to Lane Clark:

> Ronald Firbank was a 'degenerate', a personality in pursuit of celebrity. He was also a serious writer who displaced subjective narrative and created what were among the first 'modern' novels of the twentieth century. A devotee of 'low' culture, Firbank adored the cinema and its stars and introduced cinematic techniques into his writing. . . . Cinema and jazz as degenerative forms of high culture perfectly matched the degenerate and 'dangerous' personality Firbank created as the core of his writing. (Lane Clark, p. 135)

Wilson shared with Firbank pleasures across the cultural spectrum, and 'adored' the cinema, but he was not a dangerous or degenerate personality, and his appreciation for jazz was rooted in the 1920s rather than the contemporary.

A review of *Valmouth*, peppered with euphemisms for camp, was written at the time of the brief New York production and offers a rather accurate description of Firbank's original novel: 'It is, imperfections and all, already perfect. A fey, elliptical, bawdy, arch, fantastical, always intellectual book, strewn with tightly sealed epigrams, neighing dialogue and jumpy, often inconclusive episodes, it emits a queer, oblique, sotto-voce music . . .' (undated clipping, *The New Yorker*, Sandy Wilson archive).

While *The Boy Friend* could be seen as 'fey' and 'arch', *Valmouth* is 'fantastical' and 'bawdy' where *The Boy Friend* was innocently gay. *Valmouth* includes flagellation, a black woman witch doctor, beautiful young men and an ageing vamp (who is not unlike the aristocratic ladies of *My Royal Past*). According to Wright, *Valmouth* 'recreates the artifice that is Firbank's unique voice, with all its queerness, its lack of moral delineation, its welcoming of the licentious and irreligious' (Wright, 2010, p. 82). Nonetheless, the Royal Court were prepared to take it on. Tony Richardson writes from the Royal Court that Beaumont and H. M. Tennent were not attracted to the project: 'Binki [*sic*][6] does not feel very interested, and was not very enthusiastic' (12 December 1957, Sandy Wilson archive), and the English Stage Company resolved to produce it themselves. In a 1955 talk at Oxford, Wilson reflected on the experience of acting as both composer and lyricist, and suggests too why he later would be so resistant to sharing the credits for *Valmouth*:

> if you are rash, like me, you may want to do the lot. It's very nice if you can get away with it, because you don't have to argue with collaborators, wait for the composer to set your lyric, wait for the lyricist to write words for you to set, or wait for the librettist to provide a story so that you can get started in the first place; you just do it all yourself between intervals of thinking you were a sensation-seeking megalomaniac even to attempt it. (Talk to the Oxford Experimental Theatre Club, 5 May 1955, p. 8, Sandy Wilson archive)

George Devine welcomed Wilson's treatment, with some reservations, which were, surprisingly, not about the subject matter or the script, but about the score. His verdict on Wilson's first draft of *Valmouth* was equivocal, while he admired the adaptation of Firbank's novel, he was less sure about the music:[7]

> I am really full of admiration for your treatment. . . . I think you have done a remarkable job on re-creating the essence of Firbank in theatrical terms. . . . While I am entirely enthusiastic about all I have outlined above, I must say that I am not so happy about the music. I find it delightful, charming and amusing, but lacking in the very satirical ambiguity, bite and astringency with which you have so successfully imbued the text. (Letter from George Devine, to Sandy Wilson, 9 September 1957, Sandy Wilson archive)

Devine suggests using another composer as a condition of the English Stage Company production of *Valmouth* (letter to Sandy Wilson, 4 March 1958). In 1958, in the wake of *Look Back in Anger*, a production at the Royal Court, with Devine as director, would have been very advantageous to Wilson's reputation as a contemporary writer, but this was a condition too far. Wilson was then at the height of his success as the writer of *The Boy Friend* and clearly felt possessive about his version of Firbank's *Valmouth*. His response to Devine demonstrates quite how deeply hurt he was:

> What you are now asking me to do is to jettison all that work, and allow not only another composer, but another lyric writer to interpret a work which was entirely my conception. I won't dwell on the fact that I have made my name as a composer and lyricist – that is unimportant in comparison to what I feel about 'Valmouth' itself. I will just say that I find your suggestion bordering on effrontery, and I would never countenance any other composer or lyric writer (and I would be interested to know who you have in mind) coming within a thousand miles of Firbank's work. The English Stage Company may have their own conception of how 'Valmouth' should be handled but 'Valmouth' is mine, and it will either materialise as I have written it, or not at all. (Letter to George Devine, 6 March 1958, Sandy Wilson archive)

The English Stage Company would not be moved and agreed to terminate their agreement with Wilson and Jon Rose's company. George Devine wrote emolliently: 'I quite understand that you should feel you want to get on with the thing yourselves, as it has turned out as it has, and I am sorry that it has come to nothing as far as we are concerned. It is just one of those things (letter from George Devine, 25 March 1958, Sandy Wilson archive). The producer Michael Codron stepped into the breach and *Valmouth* finally opened in Liverpool in 1958, directed by Vida Hope, the director of *The Boy Friend*. *Valmouth*, by any standards, was a challenge to produce, with a cast of twenty-two characters and thirteen scene changes, it was both an expensive and complicated production; Wilson himself acknowledged after opening night 'it is a very difficult show to stage' (*Daily Mail*, 17 September 1958, Sandy Wilson archive). Codron had connections with the Lyric Hammersmith,[8] *Valmouth* moved there and then went on to the Saville Theatre in the West End, but it would not come close to the success of *The Boy Friend*.

Valmouth is, like *The Boy Friend*, preoccupied with class, a concern that spoke to a post-war Britain in which the apparent certainties of the class system could no longer be taken for granted. Many of the character and set descriptions are lifted in large chunks from the novel, and the musical is set in an unspecified 'period of Ronald Firbank'. The past that is remembered by the ageing (but magically rejuvenated) Lady Parvula is, as is the setting of *The Boy Friend*, the era of the Bright Young Things, a world of wealthy aristocrats involved in 'mad cap' adventures. Friends are recalled with names such as 'Bimbo Stooks, Laura Van Hoof, Bushy Ames and Bungy Sussex. . . . They all of them had such expressive names' (*Valmouth* typescript, Act 1, p. 6, Sandy Wilson archive). Like the jungle of the later *His Monkey Wife*,[9] the play opens in an exoticized and utopian world where conventional mores, class and sexual relationships are suspended. Richard Dyer[10] has argued that the musical is in itself a utopian form; he suggests:

> The utopian musical makes explicit, in the social structure of the world it represents, the social model of utopia implicit in all entertainment. This is a model of a society of free (transparent, energetic) individuals, living life to the full (intensity) and in harmony with each other (community) without material want (abundance) but, crucially . . . not actually participating effectively in the control and organisation of society and accepting present hierarchies. (Dyer, 1973, p. 11)

'Valmouth' is a community in which the characters are indeed living life to the full, beyond their lifespan, and with real intensity and energy. In *Valmouth*, class positions are also complicated by questions of race (as is, implicitly, *His Monkey Wife*). As *The New Yorker* explained, the joke of both Firbank's novel and Wilson's musical play is

> the preposterously unlikely, barely bridling, carry-on-chaps reaction, or lack of reaction, that a group of embattled English aristocrats display when one of their sons marries beneath him – in this case, a dark-skinned savage in a pagan ceremony in the tropics and brings her home to an English resort . . . as lady of the manor. (undated clipping, *The New Yorker*, Sandy Wilson archive)

As the use of the words 'savage' and 'pagan' suggest here, the concern with race in both the novel and the play is less a serious investigation of racial identity than it is a stereotyping and exoticizing of ethnic difference. The witch doctor, Madame Vajnavalkya,[11] is accompanied on her entrance by 'mysterious strains of oriental music'. She and her niece, Niri-Esther, speak a mock Caribbean dialect together while invoking the gods of Islam and

Hinduism, Allah and Vishnu, along with Kismet, in a confused collage of Orientalist exoticism and Caribbean sensuality. The casual racism of the period is evident from the fact that the role of Niri-Esther was played in London by the white Pauline Shepherd, who had to black up for the part. In a pre-publicity interview, The *Daily Express* pointedly noted:

> Both parts are for coloured girls. For Cleo Laine this is simple enough. She is only half English.
>
> Suntanning her coffee complexion will be easy. . . . Turning colour will not be so easy for Pauline Shepherd . . . she has soft, very English colouring. (*Daily Express*, 5 January 1959, Sandy Wilson archive)

Madame Vajnavalkya's foreignness and exoticism are in themselves affronts to the sexual and moral conventions of Valmouth, although it is her access to magical powers that enables the youthfulness of the ladies of Valmouth. As she sings in a cod West Indian accent:

> I've got magic fingers
> Where I touch de magic lingers
> And dose ebil spirits fly . . .
> Let my magic fingers
> Work dair magic spell on you.
> > (*Valmouth* typescript, Act 1, p. 9, Sandy Wilson archive)

Valmouth is a place of rejuvenation, where the old flourish, thanks to the ministrations of Madame Vajnavalkya. It is a bucolic sanctuary, in which the inhabitants gather in the Market Square at the opening of the musical to sing (unironically):

> Safe are we from worldly ills
> Every care
> Seems to fade in the air
> Of Valmouth.
> > (*Valmouth* typescript, Act 1, p. 5, Sandy Wilson archive)

Valmouth is not however immune from class difference, and the different classes are firmly assigned their locations. The longest established inhabitants are the rural farming family, the Tookes, Grannie Tooke and her grandchildren, David and Thetis, who are youthful and apparently innocent in their 'natural' sexual allure. The 'Strangers' Hotel' is occupied by the aristocratic Lady Parvula de Panzoust, Sir Victor Vatt and Lady

Saunter. The Manor House, Hare Hatch, is inhabited by the upper-middle-class Mrs Hurstpierpoint and Mrs Thoroughfare. Also at Hare Hatch are a range of servants, a Catholic priest, Father Colley-Mahoney, and a nun, Sister Ecclesia, who, because of an imposed vow of silence, is only able to express herself through dancing. The play begins with Mrs Hurstpierpoint and Mrs Thoroughfare in a horse-drawn carriage on the road to Valmouth, accompanied by the Father Colley-Mahoney, when Madam Yajnavalkya appears in a motor car, a modern challenge to the old-fashioned carriage. Despite living in an English idyll, Lady Parvula and the ladies of Hare Hatch are, like the aristocrats of *My Royal Past*, consumed by nostalgia for a vanished age. They express their disappointment with the less glamorous present in a song:

> . . . we sometimes wonder what
> To do with the world we've got.
> It only seems like yesterday
> When life was like a song
> And all the girls were pretty
> And all the men were strong.
> The world appeared a better place
> Where nothing could go wrong.
>
>   (*Valmouth* typescript, Act 1, p. 24, Sandy Wilson archive)

Lady Parvula is an older, sexually rapacious woman who plans to 'sink with my libido high and flying' (*Valmouth* typescript, Act 1, p. 32, Sandy Wilson archive), but she is a figure of derision throughout the play rather than celebrated for this sexual energy. The shepherd boy, David Tooke, is an idealized object of desire for most of the characters. Although a declared and apparently devout Catholic, Lady Parvula is determined to seduce him: 'He must be mine . . . in my manner . . . in my way . .' (*Valmouth* typescript, Act 1, p. 11, Sandy Wilson archive). David Tooke is a man of nature, who eschews romance and the social in favour of the rural; he is repeatedly spoken of in images of fruit; Mrs Hurstpierpoint enquires 'But is he ripe?' (*Valmouth* typescript, Act 1, p. 2, Sandy Wilson archive), while he is described by Madame Yajnavalkya as 'awfully choice . .' (*Valmouth* typescript, Act 1, p. 30, Sandy Wilson archive). Lady Parvula's chief rival for the attentions of David is Niri-Esther, the niece of Madame Vajnavalkya, who is 'young and beautiful' with a 'dark face, framed in unbound hair' (*Valmouth* typescript, Act 1, p. 14, Sandy Wilson archive). Like David, she is a child of nature, but wilder and more threatening because of her 'exotic' origins; Niri-Esther is described by the ladies of Hare Hatch house as a 'savage' and an 'infidel' (*Valmouth* typescript, Act 1, p. 30, Sandy Wilson archive). Along with Thetis, the Tooke's granddaughter, she is an image of sexually vibrant, young womanhood counterpointed against Lady Parvula's age and fading beauty.

Captain Dick, who does not appear until the end of the first act, offers another idealized version of youthful beauty. He has echoes of Captain Fairbrother in *The Buccaneer*, as another iteration of the explorer hero; he is on an imperial adventure in what are described as 'those savage islands . . . Off the coast of Jamaica' (*Valmouth* typescript, Act 1, p. 2, Sandy Wilson archive). The son of Mrs Thoroughfare, Captain Dick is 'the heir presumptive' to Hare Hatch, and his choice of partner is widely understood to be significant to the future of Valmouth. Captain Dick is loved by both Thetis Tooke and Niri-Esther, both of whom believe themselves to be betrothed to him. Captain Dick declares his love for Niri-Esther in a song, while disclaiming her colour (a song that has distinct, and uneasy, similarities with Alfred Fatigay's love song in the later *His Monkey Wife*):

> She may be dark brown but Heaven blessed her
> With the sort of charm I never hoped to see
> And I found the shade of Niri-Esther
> Meant not a thing to me.
> > (*Valmouth* typescript, Act 1, p. 48, Sandy Wilson archive)

When Captain Dick, 'dark and handsome', finally appears, he is accompanied by his Midshipman Jack Whorwood who is 'young and fair', both are attired in naval uniform. Jack is clearly coded as effeminate; he declares himself as 'naturally vain' and camply asks Mrs Thoroughfare: 'why be dull and conventional? Why be banal?' (*Valmouth* typescript, Act II, p. 3, Sandy Wilson archive). Mrs Thoroughfare had earlier declared a penchant for the effeminate man: 'some men are ultra-womanly, and they're the kind I love', to which Lady Parvula responds 'I suppose that none but those whose courage is unquestionable can venture to be effeminate?' (*Valmouth* typescript, Act 1, p. 23, Sandy Wilson archive). The ladies of Valmouth are not naïve in their assessment of modes of masculinity.

Despite Captain Dick's avowed love for Niri-Esther, there are distinct homoerotic overtones in the relationship between him and Jack, as Dick declares to him: 'You have been a real chum – as Patroclus was to Achilles and even more' (*Valmouth* typescript, Act 1, p. 48, Sandy Wilson archive). Together they sing a song in celebration of male friendship:

> We were pals together on the ocean
> And on land we're comrades to the end

Though a sweetheart's sublime
There is always a time
When it's fine to have a friend.

> (*Valmouth* typescript, Act 1, p. 48, Sandy Wilson archive)

Niri-Esther nonetheless has expectations that she will become the Lady of the Manor on her anticipated marriage to Captain Dick. Her plans for the house are to change it from an (apparently) British bastion of upper-class respectability into a palace of sensual pleasures, importing exotic creatures and plants into the English air of Valmouth:

When I'm de lady of de manor,
I'll do exactly as I please . . .
I'll keep monkeys and parakeets
Plant de garden with oleander trees
I'll build pagodas in de paddock
And raise an idol on de lawn . . .
I shall ride around de park on a panther,
Wearing nothing but a great enormous hat.

> ('Lady of De Manor', *Valmouth* typescript,
> Act I, p. 34, Sandy Wilson archive)

Valmouth ends with a violent storm, in which Valmouth and all its inhabitants are swept away. Hare Hatch Manor is struck by lightning, the only survivors are Madame Yajanavalkya, Niri-Esther and Niri-Esther's child by Dick. It is that child who is set to take over the inheritance of Hare Hatch, and so it is that the exotic and foreign 'savages' finally take control over Valmouth. In notes for the 1960 New York production, Wilson explained that for him, these are the 'normal' characters:

> 'Valmouth' is a light-hearted parable of sinful Old Age in search of the innocent joys of Youth. Its protagonists are eventually overwhelmed by the torrents of Time – or 'the Wrath of the Almighty'. The only survivors are the 'normal' characters: Mrs Yajnavalkya, the bizarre Oriental masseuse, and her savage niece, Niri-Esther. But Valmouth lives on in their hearts. (Notes on *Valmouth*, 1960, Sandy Wilson archive)

Valmouth is self-consciously provocative and sets out to be shocking, but the musical (and arguably the novel, despite Lane Clark's claims for Firbank) ends up as irrepressibly arch. Its treatment of older women's sexuality, homosexuality and race is stereotypical rather than subversive. Madame Yajanavalkya and Niri-Esther, who inherit this world, are repeatedly described by the Catholic contingent as 'pagan' and 'savage'. While these characters might have offered a challenge and counterweight to the claimed respectability of the British upper classes, instead they are represented as bizarre and exoticized eccentrics. *Valmouth* is replete with gender inversions, transracial sexual relationships and perverse sexual practices, the excess contributing to the camp effect, as Pamela Robertson writes of Firbank's work: 'Ronald Firbank's novels . . . tie their camp effect to representations of transracial desire' (Robertson, p. 402). The dialogue of *Valmouth* (much taken directly from the novel) abounds in double-entendres; an arch discussion between the ladies of Hare Hatch concerning orchids ends with the exchange: 'We're very proud of a rose-lipped one, with a lilac beard' . . . 'A lilac what?' . . . 'Eulalia!' (*Valmouth* typescript, Act 1, p. 21, Sandy Wilson archive).

Catholicism in both the play and the novel (Firbank was a convert to Catholicism) is tinged throughout with perversity, most evidently in the eroticized sado-masochism of Mrs Hurstpierpoint who is, according to Lady Parvula, 'Still mortifying the flesh at her age . . . is it true she sometimes assumes spiked garters?' (*Valmouth* typescript, Act 1, p. 20, Sandy Wilson archive). The Hare Hatch Chapel holds a collection of fetishized relics of bodily parts from erstwhile saints; Lady Parvula's interest in these relics is greeted with the cry 'My dear, I believe you've latent proclivities!' (*Valmouth* typescript, Act 1, p. 47, Sandy Wilson archive). Among the 'Lives of the Saints' read by the ladies of Hare Hatch is that of 'S. Automona di Meris . . . boon companion of the blessed St. Elizabeth Bathilde, who, by dint of skipping changed her sex at the age of forty and became a man' (*Valmouth* typescript, Act 1, p. 37, Sandy Wilson archive). Cardinal Pirelli is reported to have attended a masquerade dressed as Sappho, and there are rumours among the ladies of his 'strange tendencies' (*Valmouth* typescript, Act 11, p. 14, Sandy Wilson archive). According to Dan Rebellato, these lines escaped the censor's cuts, because 'the barely comprehensible inversions . . . do not fall within the proscribed area, and so it has to stay in' (Rebellato, p. 177).

The English Stage Company, as it was required to do, had sent the script of *Valmouth* to the Lord Chamberlain's Office, which was, until 1968, the official British censor.[12] Rebellato has great fun identifying which references the Lord Chamberlain's Office missed and which were identified as 'obscene' (see Rebellato, pp. 176–7). The Office demanded twenty-two cuts to the script, including a number of religious references and the omission of the word 'bugger' (letter from the Lord Chamberlain's Office, 28 January 1958,

Sandy Wilson archive); their recommendation was that *Valmouth* should 'undergo extensive revision [and] deodorisation' (quoted in Rebellato, p. 177). The Lord Chamberlain's cuts however did not prevent the play from offending some Christian sensibilities. A Mrs King wrote personally to Wilson to explain that, much as she admired his work and had enjoyed *Valmouth*, she was

> not at all alone in having had many an unpleasant jolt at the amount of blasphemy. . . . I have been most interested to find out *how* many people whom I regarded as hard-boiled, irreligious, sophisticated or what not – have either been deeply upset by parts of the play – or else have refused to see it, simply because of its blasphemy. (undated letter from Mrs King, Sandy Wilson archive)

EMI refused to make a recording of *Valmouth* on similar grounds. The part of Madame Vajanavlyka was originally written for Bertice Reading,[13] but she was contracted to the play *Requiem for a Nun*. Cleo Laine took over for the West End transfer, and it was Laine who sang the role on the original cast recording, issued by Pye. This 1959 recording only served to deepen the rift between Wilson and those around the Royal Court; much to Wilson's chagrin this recording had different orchestrations. Wilson wrote a stinging letter on the release of the record to Cleo Laine, which also took aim at her husband, jazz musician John Dankworth:

> I find it hard to understand why you and Johnny found it necessary to disregard me, insult our orchestra and disappoint so many people who buy the record to hear the show as they heard it in the theatre and not a second-rate travesty of the composer's songs. . . . This letter is of course meant for Johnny as well as yourself, and I want you both to know that your display of selfishness and your lack of understanding and taste has almost ruined for me what will be my only souvenir of my own show. (letter to Cleo Laine, 3 March 1960, Sandy Wilson archive)

Cleo Laine's response is not on file in Wilson's archive. John Dankworth and Cleo Laine were then the most significant figures in contemporary British jazz. The Johnny Dankworth Orchestra, formed in 1953 with Laine as singer, was both a critical and popular success; in 1959, it played the Newport Jazz festival (the first British band to be invited to do so), Dankworth had played with Duke Ellington and Louis Armstrong in New York, and also worked with Sidney Bechet and Charlie Parker. This was a very different kind of jazz from the kind of music that Wilson espoused; his letter to Cleo Laine suggests an inability to change or to update a musical style that had worked so successfully for him in *The Boy Friend*. In being so inflexible there is a sense that he simply did not have any sensibility for contemporary jazz and no understanding of improvisation (Laine was then much admired for her scat singing). Wilson was stuck in the musical tradition of Coward and Novello rather than anything more contemporary and was intransigent in his own idea of how his music should be performed (also evident in his response to the New York production of *The Boy Friend*). He had successfully distanced himself from the Royal Court and its directors, all of whom were now significant figures in contemporary theatre and in the new wave of cinema. Cleo Laine had appeared as an actress at the Royal Court, and Dankworth wrote the scores for the 1958 *We are the Lambeth Boys* directed by Karel Reisz, and for *Saturday Night and Sunday Morning* (1960), also directed by Reisz and produced by Tony Richardson. Reisz, together with Tony Richardson and Lindsay Anderson (all key directors at the Royal Court) had formed the Free Cinema documentary movement, and later founded Woodfall Films (along with John Osborne).[14] In alienating Cleo Laine and John Dankworth, as well as the management of the English Stage Company, Wilson had made some powerful enemies.

The opening night of *Valmouth* at the Lyric Hammersmith, had technical problems, and the press reported mixed reactions from the audience; according to the *Daily Mail*: 'the audience sat stonily though some of the cracks' (17 September 1958, Sandy Wilson archive). Wilson would later remember: 'The truth is that the audience was divided: half of them loved every minute – and showed it – and the other half – including some of the critics, were either puzzled or shocked – or both' (typescript for a talk on *Valmouth* at the Croydon Arts Centre, 1986, Sandy Wilson archive). The reviews were very mixed, although, interestingly, they did not divide along the lines of sexuality. Angus Wilson (himself homosexual), writing in *The Observer*, was not enthusiastic. Harold Hobson however declared: 'Nothing like it has ever been done before, and nothing like it will ever be done again . . . . Mr Wilson's music is as fetching as his wit. Valmouth is caviar, enticing, but the best' (Harold Hobson, *Sunday Times*, undated clipping, Sandy Wilson archive). The impresario Donald Albery, of Donmar Productions, was another admirer of *Valmouth* and wrote to Wilson to say: 'personally I preferred it even to "The Boy Friend". It will be an absolute scandal if it doesn't come to the West End' (letter from Donald Albery, 9 October 1958, Sandy Wilson archive). *Valmouth* did go on to the West End at the Saville Theatre, where it again received mixed notices. *The Guardian* ruefully suggested that its esotericism would be beyond a popular audience, and not to the taste of a new generation:

Wilson doing a pastiche of Firbank doing a pastiche of Thomas Love Peacock or any other 'romantic' novelist of high intelligence, seems vulnerable material to fling into the jungle of West End musicals. The beat generation is likely to find itself beaten by the high intellectual content of this show. And ordinary people may easily find it much 'too clever' (perhaps this is the only nation in which it is possible to be 'too' clever). (*The Guardian*, 29 January 1959, Sandy Wilson archive)

Many reviews echoed this uneasiness, with terms such as 'sophisticated tastes', 'chic' and 'arty' employed as code words for camp. *Plays and Players* recognized that Firbank was a niche taste, and that *Valmouth* could not replicate the popular appeal of *The Boy Friend*:

It will be surprising if *Valmouth* has a run in any way comparable with Sandy Wilson's first musical, *The Boy Friend*. This is not because it is less good, but because its potential public is necessarily small.

Only fairly educated people have ever heard of Ronald Firbank, and not a large majority of those have actually read his books, nor would like them if they did, for the public for satirical fantasy was ever small. (*Plays and Players*, November, 1958)

The public for arch, camp Catholicism was even smaller; all the reviews pointed to its limited appeal. *The Times* identified *Valmouth* as a cult show which would not appeal to all tastes: '*Valmouth* . . . at the Lyric Theatre Hammersmith may not turn out a truly popular musical comedy; but so much valiant energy has gone to its making that it can be recommended as a good private joke which the sophisticated will chuckle over appreciatively' (3 October 1958, clipping, Sandy Wilson archive). The *Melody Maker* also saw it as an 'acquired taste': '*Valmouth* just misses . . . (it) brings with it a taste of most aspects of modern life, but it's something of an acquired taste' (31 January 1959, clipping, Sandy Wilson archive). The *Evening Standard* described it as 'an extravaganza, an immoral fairy tale for very chic grown ups' (3 October 1958, clipping, Sandy Wilson archive). The critic for *Vogue* (who was clearly familiar with Firbank and the original novel) was rather more explicit in acknowledging the sexual implications: 'Like the novel on which it is based, Sandy Wilson's musical of *Valmouth* is fuelled on innuendo. His book and lyrics lovingly reproduce the airless bi-sexual Firbank atmosphere and use quantities of the original bias-cut dialogue' (*Vogue*, November 1958, Sandy Wilson archive).

The popular press were generally scathing, their reviews primly disapproving, and with more than a whiff of homophobia, as in the *Sunday*

Dispatch review: '*Valmouth* tittered its way into the Saville last week – bringing its feeble score, wheezy orchestrations, sniggering sex eccentrics . . .' (1 February, 1959, clipping, Sandy Wilson archive). *The People* recommended it 'for the very arty only' (1 February 1959, clipping, Sandy Wilson archive), while *Reynolds News* commented: 'Sandy Wilson's unlikeable musical . . . . For minority tastes only' (1 February 1959, clipping, Sandy Wilson archive). The *Record Mirror* made it rather clearer (although still in coded language) that those 'minority' and 'arty' tastes were associated with homosexuality: 'there is a certain membership of a London club – another life who will derive enjoyment from some of the queer conversations and song couplets' (7 February, 1959 clipping, Sandy Wilson archive).

An appreciation of *Valmouth* did however extend beyond a single London club; it was a cult success among a range of sophisticated audiences. One letter to Sandy Wilson in 1960 describes Princess Margaret remarking that she had seen *Valmouth* three times (letter from Constance Carpenter, 7 April 1960, Sandy Wilson archive). Elaine Tynan (then Kenneth Tynan's[15] wife) wrote to say 'what a perfect delight – visual, aural, verbal (what's left!) – Valmouth was to me' (letter from Elaine Tynan, 6 October 1958, Sandy Wilson archive). Osbert Sitwell wrote a note of congratulations on the London production: 'I went to see *Valmouth* last night and enjoyed it tremendously. I am sure Ronald Firbank must be enjoying it wherever he may be. I never thought it would have been possible to present it in so masterly a fashion on the stage' (letter, 7 October 1958, Sandy Wilson archive). Vivien Leigh, the Scarlett O'Hara of Wilson's youthful fantasies (see Wilson, 1975a, p. 134), also wrote to congratulate Wilson:

> Please forgive an absolutely all-out, full-blown, forthright fan letter, but I can't help writing it because I thought 'Valmouth' was perfectly wonderful. It seemed to me to be an evening of total enjoyment and I feel downright distraught that it should have to end its run. . . . Yours gratefully and sincerely. (letter from Vivien Leigh, 10 September 1958, Sandy Wilson archive)

Valmouth is among the most admired of Wilson's scores; Julian Slade, the writer of *Salad Days*, wrote after it was broadcast on the BBC: 'your music for that show is so lovely' (letter, 30 April 1975, Sandy Wilson archive). The critic and writer Caryl Brahms enjoyed the music, but was sparing in her assessment overall, writing to Wilson:

> A wonderful way with a gay song that turns it suddenly to tears . . . the richness and fun and those tears – the incandescent imagination that

was in every part of the show – very nearly won me. I would say you did what you set out to do – It may not be entirely to my taste – but brilliant. (undated postcard from Caryl Brahms, Sandy Wilson archive)

Despite the mixed reception, *Valmouth* did transfer to New York in 1960, not to Broadway but to the York Playhouse, where it was then the most expensive show ever produced off-Broadway.[16] It ran for only fourteen performances and the *New York Times* reported the closure of a 'Tired Musical' (*New York Times*, 7 October 1960, Sandy Wilson archive). The notices were not enthusiastic, *The New Yorker* acerbically pointing out that in the American context, where segregation was still in operation, the 'astonishing ending will comfort the Deep South' (undated clipping from *The New Yorker*, Sandy Wilson archive).

Valmouth did have many fans in British theatrical circles who attempted to mount revivals. In 1966, ALS Management[17] proposed a new production as a joint Noel Gay/ALS production, with Bernard Delfont, but this never happened. In 1970 Michael Codron's company suggested a production, but by 1972, Codron regretfully concluded that 'Hampstead (Theatre Club) would have been squeezing whatever one does squeeze into a pint pot' (letter from Michael Codron, 2 May 1972, Sandy Wilson archive). This must have been disappointing to Wilson, because *The Boy Friend* had made the step to the West End from the Embassy Theatre, just up the road from the Hampstead Theatre Club. There was a proposed television production of *Valmouth* for Granada Television, and Wilson wrote the treatment for it, but this did not happen either. Extracts from *Valmouth* had been played on the BBC Light Programme *Show Time* in 1958 and on the Home Service in 1960, and it was broadcast in full as the BBC Radio 4 Monday Play in 1975. The reviewer for *The Guardian* could, in 1975, explicitly acknowledge the campness of the script as 'effective and gay (in both the old-fashioned and sometimes the modern, sense)' (undated clipping, Sandy Wilson archive).

Valmouth did see a revival at the Chichester Theatre in 1982, with Fenella Fielding, Doris Hare and Bertice Reading (but not Cleo Laine) among the original cast reprising their roles and with the dancer Robert Helpmann appearing as Cardinal Pirelli. John Bassett, a director at Thames Television, wrote an enthusiastic letter to Wilson in 1982 proposing a television version of the revival and suggesting the fantasy Welsh village Portmeirion[18] as a stand-in for Valmouth (letter from John Bassett, 23 February 1982, Sandy Wilson archive), but again, this did not happen. The theatre critic for the *Daily Mail*, Jack Tinkner (who was known for his flamboyance and embrace of camp) wrote a scathing review of the revival, which suggested that the time had passed for *Valmouth* and that Chichester was not the appropriate place to stage it. He recognized that Firbank's high camp of the 1920s and Wilson's nostalgia had been overtaken by the more explicit work of Joe Orton:

> If ever the time and place were inauspicious for a fragile venture of this nature, I have yet to hear of it. The world had forgotten how to relish sexual erotica, religious fervour, bisexual innuendo and mixed marriage. And Joe Orton had not yet come along to remind them of their pleasures. (Tinkner, *Daily Mail*, 20 May 1982)

Irving Wardle of *The Times* wrote of the revival: 'Sandy Wilson's musical has lingered on as a legend, a missing link, a victim of purblind managements' (*The Times*, 20 May 1982). Like Wardle, Richard Armitage of the Richard Armitage/Noel Gay Organisation saw *Valmouth* as a victim to a lack of understanding from an unappreciative public and described it as 'one of the world's great musical plays that suffered from the public's inability to comprehend it at the time' (letter to Sandy Wilson, 28 January 1982, Sandy Wilson archive). For Michael Billington, like Jack Tinkner, *Valmouth*'s interest lay in its status as a period piece:

> Ever since its first appearance in 1958 it has had the chic mystique of a cult show . . . it emerges in this . . . revival as a fascinating hot-house plant: a louche Brigadoon about a fantasy village rippling with myriad perversions . . . among the drab foothills of the post-war British musical it still represents a purple peak. (*The Guardian*, 20 May 1982, Sandy Wilson archive)

Wilson's *Valmouth* has retained that 'chic mystique' and remains admired by aficionados of camp. An Italian doctoral student[19] (later the author of a study of Firbank) wrote to Wilson in 1993: 'I was impressed by the Firbankian touch of your work, and I have been wondering how camp the *mise en scène* must have been' (letter from Fabio Cleto, 16 November 1993, Sandy Wilson archive). If it was a success among what Wilson termed the 'cognoscenti' ('What Next?', unpublished autobiographical chapter, p. 331, Sandy Wilson archive), *Valmouth* could not, as *The Boy Friend* had done, move into the mainstream but remained a cult success among a small but admiring audience. As one fan wrote: '"Valmouth" was creating its own public, who came again and again to see it, such a pity that it had to close' (letter to Sandy Wilson, 6 May 1959, Sandy Wilson archive).

Andrew Ross has suggested that camp (and *Valmouth* is perhaps the most camp of Wilson's works) can be a mode of subversion, and provide a utopian fantasy that the world could be different:

Whether as a pre-Stonewall, utopian, survivalist fantasy, or as a post-Stonewall return of the repressed, camp transforms, destabilizes, and subverts the existing balance of acceptance of sexual identity and sexual roles. It never proposes a *direct* relation between the conditions it speaks to – everyday life in the present – and the discourse it speaks with – usually a bricolage of features pilfered from conditions of the past. (Ross, 1993, p. 71)

Wilson's *Valmouth* predates Stonewall by over a decade and it refuses to address 'everyday life in the present'; instead, it offers a world of exoticism and romantic longing located in an imagined past, while speaking to a contemporary period dominated by sexual conformism. *Siren Song* was another musical concerned with sexual dissidence, this time centred on a community of women, and based on a 1928 novel by Compton Mackenzie, which fictionalised Mackenzie's memories of Capri. The musical was never produced.

In his 2009 study of 'Queer Futurity' José Esteban Muñoz identifies live theatre as 'a site for finding hope' (Muñoz, p. 4). Muñoz invokes the Frankfurt School in his account of utopianism, and although he is writing about the period of the 1950s and 1960s, he is more concerned with avant-garde poetry, dance and Andy Warhol's Factory than he is with the popular musical (however esoteric). It is unlikely that he was thinking of Firbank (who does not appear in his index) or of Sandy Wilson when he wrote: 'Astonishment helps one surpass the limitations of an alienating presentness and allows one to see a different time and place' (Muñoz, p. 5). Nonetheless, *Valmouth* is 'astonishing' in its pushing of the boundaries of 'an alienating presentness' and it does deliberately invoke a different time and place. Michael Billington is right to invoke *Brigadoon*;[20] Valmouth is, like *Brigadoon*, a fragile, fleeting and illusory place of the imagination. While Valmouth lasts, it is a utopia only for the handsome young man, and it cannot be sustained.

The charm and wit of Wilson's music, of his revues and of *The Boy Friend* were no longer current or fashionable by 1958. Having been greeted by the press as a fresh, new voice with *The Boy Friend*, only four years later Wilson was no longer part of the new wave and was relegated to the old guard. Nonetheless, *Valmouth* was so close to Sandy Wilson's heart that he named his house in Somerset after it. Wilson himself saw *Valmouth* as his best work; when asked in an interview as to which of his musicals was his favourite he responded:

Valmouth, I suppose. In theory a writer usually likes best what he has just written, and I was very proud of THE CLAPHAM WONDER, which the critics killed off at Canterbury last year. But VALMOUTH has a special place in my heart. It was *so* difficult to do, and so astonishingly good in the end, thanks to the Director, Vida Hope, to Tony Walton who designed it, and to that marvellous cast: Bertice Reading, Barbara Couper, Betty Hardy, Doris Hare – and of course Fenella Fielding! And I nearly forgot to mention Ronald Firbank. What characters and what dialogue! Yes, for me there will never be another show quite like VALMOUTH. (unattributed, undated interview,[21] Sandy Wilson archive)

Figure 8.1 *The Boy Friend*, directed by Ken Russell, 1971.

'A walpurgisnacht of self-indulgence'

The Ken Russell film of *The Boy Friend, His Monkey Wife, The Clapham Wonder* and *Aladdin*

Then I said to myself,
Well, At least you're different.

(*The Clapham Wonder*, typescript, Act 11,
p. 17, Sandy Wilson archive)

For the majority of audiences, familiarity with *The Boy Friend* is not through any stage production but rather through the 1972 Ken Russell film. As all of Wilson's obituaries pointed out, Wilson himself loathed the film; as *The Independent* put it: 'Wilson's distress was commensurate' (*The Independent*, 27 August 2014). Wilson refused to attend the premiere at the Empire Cinema, the site he remembered as the place 'where I had spent so many happy hours in my youth, enjoying the masterpieces of the old MGM' (Wilson, 1975a, p. 270). In a postscript which ends his autobiography he writes bitterly about the long process of the acquisition of the film rights, eventually held by MGM, and his distress at the final film.

The American producers of *The Boy Friend*, Feuer and Martin, had originally bought the film rights along with the Broadway rights in the first wave of *The Boy Friend*'s popular success. As *Variety* reported in 1955, while the stage production was running successfully both on Broadway and in the West End: 'Cy Feuer and Ernest H. Martin will probably produce their own film edition' (15 June, Sandy Wilson archive). In 1957 *The Boy Friend* was optioned by MGM from the Broadway producers after its critical and popular success in America, and Hedda Hopper reported that Debbie Reynolds and Bing Crosby had been approached to appear in the roles of Polly and her father (*Chicago Tribune*, 7 December 1957, clipping, Sandy Wilson archive).

Ross Hunter, the director of the 1967 *Thoroughly Modern Millie* (again, a pastiche of the 1920s), had wanted to direct it as another vehicle for Julie Andrews (who had made her name in the Broadway production of *The Boy Friend* and starred in *Thoroughly Modern Millie*), but MGM held on to the rights. The Hollywood musical was then fading as a genre, as Wilson put it: 'The days of buying up Broadway successes for astronomical sums were already drawing to a close' (Wilson, 1975a, p. 264). MGM had a long and proud history as a producer of musicals; throughout the 1950s they were responsible for some of the greatest American musical films, with innovative scores and choreography: *An American in Paris* and *Showboat* in 1951, *Singing in the Rain*, 1952, *Seven Brides for Seven Brothers*, 1957 and *South Pacific* in 1958. This run of critical and commercial hits could not however be sustained into the 1960s; MGM's later offerings were not well received by reviewers or by audiences. In 1960 *Bells are Ringing*, with Judy Holliday, had lost money at the box office, *The Unsinkable Molly Brown*, 1964, and *The Singing Nun*, 1966, both starring Debbie Reynolds, and *Goodbye Mr Chips* with Petula Clark in 1969, all had lukewarm critical receptions, and even a Doris Day vehicle, *Jumbo* in 1962, faded into obscurity. MGM were wary of investing in another big budget musical, but they still owned the rights to *The Boy Friend*.

By the 1960s, no Hollywood director had taken the project on. Justin de Villeneuve, the 'discoverer, mentor and romantic partner' of the model Twiggy (Wilson, 1975a, p. 267) approached Wilson for the rights to make a film as a vehicle for her. The rights were not in Wilson's power to grant but unknown to him, Twiggy and de Villeneuve had arrived at the meeting with Wilson already having sealed a deal with MGM. Without informing Wilson, Villeneuve and Ken Russell announced that they were making the film for MGM. Wilson was taken aback, but not outraged, as he put it in his autobiography: 'While deploring Twiggy's and Justin's lack of manners in not communicating with me, I could not help admiring their nerve and I sat back to wait with interest and curiosity the result of this rather bizarre alliance' (Wilson, 1975a, p. 268). Twiggy would later claim in a 1989 appearance on *Desert Island Discs* (BBC) that it was Ken Russell who had approached her to star in the film version of *The Boy Friend*, but it is clear from Sandy Wilson's autobiography and correspondence that it was Twiggy herself, with Justin de Villeneuve, who had approached Wilson's agent Joannie Rees to acquire the film rights well before Russell was brought in. Twiggy's star power and status as an emblem of contemporary fashion – she was then the face of the 1960s – and Russell's reputation were enough to persuade MGM to take a chance on another musical spectacular. But *The Boy Friend* was not a spectacular musical, it was not an appropriate vehicle for Twiggy, and Russell was not the right director.

Russell had come to the project garlanded with awards for the 1969 *Women in Love*, and also as a focus of controversy over *The Music Lovers* (1970) and *The Devils* (1971). While Wilson had admired *Women in Love*, especially its attention to period detail, he was not so impressed by *The Devils* and *The Music Lovers*, ominously commenting: 'Both were received with alarm and disgust by the more sensitive critics. . . . I began to wonder if this was, after all, the man best equipped to convey the delicate charm of *The Boy Friend* to the screen' (Wilson, 1975a, p. 269). If this response to Russell's oeuvre was more than a little prim, Wilson had good reason for his concerns; *The Boy Friend* was an odd project for Russell to choose, given his reputation as the enfant terrible of British cinema, and Russell was not noted for his 'delicate charm'. Nonetheless, having signed over the rights to the American producers of the Broadway version of *The Boy Friend*, Wilson had no control over his musical's afterlife, his agent, Joannie Rees reportedly wailed, 'I wish I could *do* something! . . . But I can't! I can't do anything!' (Wilson, 1975a, p. 269).

It is clear why Sandy Wilson did not care for Russell's film, far from preserving the loving pastiche of the 1920s, with all the authenticity that Vida Hope (the director), Reginald Woolley (the designer) and the cast were so proud of in the original production, Russell's film blew it up into a Hollywood spectacular with no respect for period detail. As Wilson had done himself with *Divorce Me, Darling!*, Russell relocates *The Boy Friend* from the 1920s to the 1930s. The camerawork and design repeatedly reference Busby Berkeley films of the 1930s and 1940s, with all their Hollywood spectacle. This period confusion is what so distressed Wilson, who recounts the careful attention to period detail in the first production in his autobiography; he described the film as 'a baffling experience' (Wilson, 1975a, p. 270). Sandy Wilson's music and lyrics were closer to the tradition of Noël Coward and Ivor Novello than they were to the Gershwin, Rodgers and Hammerstein, Cole Porter or Irving Berlin numbers which Peter Maxwell Davies's score pastiched.[1] The film does not acknowledge the pastiche of Wilson's original score; Wilson's songs are refracted through old recordings played on set on an ancient gramophone, while the film score transposes songs from the 1920s, 1930s and 1940s alongside Wilson's originals. There is no indication or recognition of the distinction between these and Wilson's own pastiches. The soundtrack for the film musical included two songs from the 1952 film *Singing in the Rain* (dir. Stanley Donen), while the final version of the film cut two of Wilson's original songs.

Despite a budget and cast beyond the dreams of the Players' Theatre, in losing any period grounding, the screen version lost the charm and the buoyancy of the original. For Sheridan Morley, Russell's screen version was 'catastrophic' and a betrayal of the original production: 'Precisely because

The Boy Friend was a tribute to that period (the 1920s) and not a burlesque, precisely because it was staged by a director with one eye on back numbers of the *Play Pictorials* of the era, it had a charm and confidence' (Morley, 1987, p. 132). Ken Russell did not have the eye for the period of either the 1920s or the 1950s to which *The Boy Friend* belonged, but rather for *Play Pictorials* from the 1930s and 1940s. His sets, costumes and score reference the Hollywood of that era, and particularly the films of Fred Astaire and Ginger Rogers and Busby Berkeley. If the film's setting is loosely the 1930s, the cinematic and musical references span across decades and at times evoke the psychedelia of the 1960s (which had already faded by 1971). A guide to camp and cult films describes *The Boy Friend* as a 'seemingly interminable compendium of backstage musical clichés . . . the period is sometime in the Art Deco "Twenties" or "Thirties"' (Roen, p. 26). The Art Deco of the film, however, owes more to the designs of Biba, then the most fashionable shop in London, than it does to any authentic 1930s costumes or sets. Russell did not get either the gentle and affectionate celebration of the 1920s or the modest aspirations of the 1950s that had been so important to the original production.

The film submerges Wilson's libretto under a welter of plot and subplots and fantasy sequences which have no historical specificity; Gänzl acerbically describes Russell's version as a 'little show drowned in gallons of "concept"' (Gänzl, 1986, p. 647). Russell's screen play turns *The Boy Friend* into a play within a play, in which a troupe of actors are performing the show in a shabby repertory theatre; the original show is thus immediately coded as tatty and old fashioned. Also grafted on to the original libretto is a subplot in which a Hollywood producer attends the performance to talent spot stars to take back to America, the original play is thus subjugated to a distinctly American and Hollywood glamour. A framing device is derived from the 1933 film musical *42nd Street* (dir. Lloyd Bacon), with choreography by Busby Berkeley, in which Twiggy, playing the understudy in the Ruby Keeler role, is required to take over from the injured leading lady (Glenda Jackson) and becomes a star. There was in fact some logic and a background to this scenario; at the dress rehearsal for the original Players' production of *The Boy Friend* the leading lady collapsed and was replaced by her understudy, Anne Rogers, who subsequently became a West End star (see Wilson, 1975a, pp. 196–7). It was also *The Boy Friend* which had turned Julie Andrews from an ingenue into a Broadway star, and it is clear that the same was expected for Twiggy, for whom this was her first starring role. Ken Russell was however less interested in the backstory of *The Boy Friend* than he was in Hollywood, as Richard Stirling describes:

> Set as a show-within-a-show, the film depicted a down-at-heel 1930s theatre company, touring a 1920s musical called *The Boy Friend*. The

musical is seen one desultory matinee, by a Hollywood director – in whose eye the tacky dances become phenomenal routines. It had nothing to do with *The Boy Friend* and everything to do with Ken Russell. (Stirling, p. 240)

The stage version of *The Boy Friend* is consistently represented as outdated, playing in a shabby repertory production trying hard to maintain an audience. The original *The Boy Friend* had offered an optimistic and romantic nostalgia for the period of the 1920s viewed through the prism of the rationed gloom of the 1950s. In Russell's version, the music, the stars (with the exception of Twiggy), the theatre, sets and costumes of the stage show are represented as down at heel and past their best, glamourized only in the vision of the Hollywood director. *The Boy Friend* has one guaranteed show-stopping number 'It's never too late (to fall in love)', which has never failed to rouse several encores in the stage production.[2] In Russell's film, the routine is overwhelmed by a narrative of competition between the performers, in which the joke of the song is overladen with professional rivalry. The poignant and modest duet 'All I want is a Room in Bloomsbury' between heroine Polly and hero Tony is literally blown up delivered as it is on an oversized set, in which the lovers are reduced to small mannequins. While the stage musical was modest and arch, the film version was flamboyant and ostentatious; Russell's overblown rendition did fall prey to campy parody, and neither critics nor the public were enchanted by the film.

Wilson did not spare his words in his own estimation of the film and damns Twiggy with faint praise:

> The film itself was a baffling experience. Knowing Russell's work and having seen so much advance publicity, I was prepared for it to be a travesty, but I did expect it to be an accomplished travesty, since, whatever one may think of his films, there is no denying Russell's technical expertise. But it turned out to be nothing but a mess: a wilful and at times incomprehensible confusion of Twenties and Thirties camp, through which poor Twiggy bravely twittered and pranced, almost suffocated by the welter of grotesquerie and surrounded by a cast whose unattractiveness was only rivalled by their incompetence. I could not help feeling sorry for the poor little thing . . . through Justin's folly and Russell's egotism, she was only a tiny beam of pathos in a walpurgisnacht of self-indulgence. (Wilson, 1975a, p. 270)

Wilson took some pleasure in the fact that the reaction of the American critics was 'almost unanimously bad' and in the fact that the stage version of *The Boy Friend* was now being advertised as 'The Real Thing. Accept no Substitutes' (Wilson, 1975a, p. 271). Despite a charismatic and feted director, Ken Russell, with stars including Christopher Gable, Twiggy and Glenda Jackson, and a budget of $3 million, the film version of *The Boy Friend* was not a success. In Russell's own autobiography *The Boy Friend* merits little discussion; he patronisingly suggests that 'Sandy Wilson's music, however tuneful, has diminishing returns as one pastiche Twenties number follows another' (Russell, p. 134). Russell goes on to blame MGM's cuts for the film's failure:

> Despite the big Busby Berkeley routines, the novelty value of the stage show, the great singing and dancing by the cast which included Twiggy and Tommy Tune, plus the brilliant designs of Shirley Kingdon and Tony Walton, the film was a flop. The acting was too broad, the gags too laboured and the pacing too slow. I should have cut it during the script stage, but, determined to be faithful to the original show, I kept in EVERYTHING! It was left to MGM, who financed the film, to do the job for me. A gorilla in boxing gloves could have done a better job. (Russell, p. 135)

Russell was not 'faithful to the original show', and in rating *The Boy Friend* only for its 'novelty value' he overrode everything that had contributed to its original success. The film was derided by critics at the time; Robert Ebert wrote in 1972 of the film's 'fundamental visual poverty . . . his camera is so joyless that it undermines every scene. . . . Russell doesn't seem to be having any fun. He doesn't want to draw out the magic of the wonderful Sandy Wilson songs, or the inner life of his performers' (Ebert, 1972)[3].

Martin Gottfried's estimation of the stage version is close to Sheridan Morley's assessment of *The Boy Friend* as 'a perfect miniature period piece' '(Morley, 1987, p. 133); both point to the 'underlying seriousness' that Isherwood identified as a feature of High Camp:

> Sandy Wilson's *The Boy Friend,* a rare British import on Broadway during the fifties is . . . true to itself. Its mimicry of twenties musical comedy is so straight faced that the show can almost be taken sincerely, and its mockery is affectionate rather than snide. Though verging perilously on the collegiate, it is close to being a perfect musical because its book and lyrics are written in such matched tones of voice. . . . *The Boy Friend* is virtually perfect in succeeding at what it intended. (Gottfried, pp. 20–1)

Ken Russell's film version is not straight-faced, and the music and libretto were not presented in 'matched tones of voice' (or in period); the film is neither true to nor fair to the original. Russell's film is, in retrospect, fun and camp, but it is not *The Boy Friend* and it does Sandy Wilson and the original production an injustice. Wilson may have been right that the fragile charm of *The Boy Friend* was a theatrical rather than a cinematic experience. By 1975, in his autobiography he could manage to be gracious towards Russell: 'To give Ken Russell his due, he had taken on what I already knew to be an impossible task. . . . *The Boy Friend* is essentially Theatre, relying for its effect on a style of production and performance that relates totally to a live audience (Wilson, 1975a, p. 271). Wilson was not however circumspect in his loathing of the Russell film and held a grudge against it for years, as late as 1984, in an interview he spoke in terms close to those he had expressed in 1975: 'I expected a violent travesty from Russell, but not an incomprehensible mess' (*Houston Chronicle*, 23 July 1984, Sandy Wilson archive). The film is now largely remembered as a camp classic and as an oddity in Ken Russell's filmography.

Wilson consoled himself at the time of the film's release with the fact that he was busy working on another musical: 'Luckily I was fully occupied with the writing and production of a new musical at the Hampstead Theatre Club' (Wilson, 1975a, p. 270). That musical was *His Monkey Wife*, 1971, which had been commissioned by the Hampstead Theatre Club. Based on a 1930 novel by John Collier, *His Monkey Wife or, Married to a Chimp*, it explores the relationship between a man and an ape and can be read as a plea for tolerance of different kinds of relationships.[4] Wilson described the origins of the show in the programme for a 1984 revival:

> At the end of 1970 Vivian Matalon asked me to write a new musical for the Hampstead Theatre Club[5]. He gave me carte blanche as to the choice of subject – and naturally my mind became a complete blank. But at a dinner party at which the playwright Rodney Ackland was a fellow guest I overheard him saying, 'Why doesn't someone make a musical of John Collier's His Monkey Wife' (programme for *His Monkey Wife*, Scarborough Theatre, 1984)

Although commissioned, the production was only made possible because Wilson invested his own money in it, against the advice of his solicitor who was not convinced that the show was commercially viable, as he wrote to Wilson:

> I spoke to Nigel Stannard at Hampstead Theatre Club . . . and he tells me that my assessment of the agreement was quite correct that you will not stand any real chance of the return of your investment. He went on to tell me, however, that you appreciated this and had, in fact, agreed (to put

it somewhat bluntly perhaps) to pay over £1300 (or £1500) for the sake of getting the show staged. (letter from Peter Stone, 24 December 1971, Sandy Wilson archive)

His Monkey Wife opens in a vaguely defined African jungle, 'Boboma, Central Africa', in some mythical time of British exploration, an indistinct historical and geographical setting that wilfully refuses any political context. As the Prologue has it:

Come with us, if you will, to another time and another place. Let our humble artifice transport you, if only in the imagination, to the jungle of Central Africa, or, to be more precise, to the Upper Congo. That is the place. The Time? Oh, just a while ago. Somewhat after Livingstone. . . . Shall we say: the Day before Yesterday. (*His Monkey Wife, A Musical Play*, typescript, 1971, Prologue, p. 1, Sandy Wilson archive)

Emily, the monkey wife of the title, first appears already anthropomorphized, dressed in a gingham apron with a flowered wreath on her head. She is reading; like the Creature in *Frankenstein* Emily has learned from her master, the English school teacher and hero of the play, Alfred Fatigay, who bears some resemblance to Captain Fairbrother of *The Buccaneer*. Fatigay is first seen in the standard uniform of the English Explorer hero: 'a solar topee, bush jacket and long shorts' (*His Monkey Wife, A Musical Play*, typescript, 1971, Prologue, p. 3, Sandy Wilson archive). Emily is clearly in love with him; she has (with the exception of one scene, in which she converses with a fellow chimpanzee) only two lines in the play; her declaration in the first scene: 'I LOVE ALFRED FATIGAY' and, in the final line of the play 'HONI SOIT QUI MAL Y PENSE' (*His Monkey Wife*, typescript, 1971, Act 2, p. 31, Sandy Wilson archive).

Emily is taken from her Central African jungle to Hampstead, England, by her master where she is intended as a domestic servant for his fiancée, Fern. Emily's silent, adoring and attentive femininity is juxtaposed with the brittle and sophisticated Fern Flint, Fatigay's intended fiancée, to Fern's disadvantage. While Emily is devoted to Fatigay, Fern is, with her friend Susan, cynical about marriage. Together Susan and Fern sing:

Marriage is a joy,
Marriage is a boon,
Marriage is the prelude to a happy honeymoon,
The final page in ev'ry fairy tale.
But the sting in the tale
Is the male . . .

Marriage is a sacrament, I heard the vicar say.
But he left out the important bit
That it means sacrifice
And you're it.

(*His Monkey Wife*, typescript, 1971, Act 1,
p. 2, Sandy Wilson archive)

Fern and Susan's close friend, Dennis Tickler, is another figure who disdains marriage; he is described in the stage directions as an 'effete – but not necessarily camp – young man' (*His Monkey Wife*, final script, 1971, Act 1, p. 8, Sandy Wilson archive). Despite this direction, Dennis's lines are distinctly camp; if his homosexuality is strongly implied rather than overt, the failure of the characters to recognize his sexuality is a recurring joke. The confidently heterosexual Alfred Fatigay dismisses him as 'a Wretched weed, a blighter of the first order' (*His Monkey Wife*, typescript, 1971, Act I, p. 26) while Fern mistakes Dennis's lack of sexual engagement with her as 'sublimation' of his desires. As Susan expresses her reluctance to marry 'I positively refuse to degenerate into humdrum domesticity', she turns to Dennis 'I'm sure *you* understand', to which he responds 'Oh I do, I do!' (*His Monkey Wife*, 1971, Act 1, pp. 9–10, Sandy Wilson archive). It is Dennis who is the first of the London set to see Emily's charm 'But my dear – she's divine!' (*His Monkey Wife*, typescript, Act 1, p. 11, Sandy Wilson archive).

Emily is characterized as an almost entirely silent, but thoroughly intellectual, chimpanzee; determined to educate herself, she progresses from reading *The Origin of the Species* in the Reading Room of the British Museum to the Huxleys, both Julian and Aldous. Escaping the confines of Hampstead, Emily takes up employment initially as an organ grinder's monkey where she is discovered by a theatrical agent and becomes a social success. In a suggestion that the theatrical profession is more tolerant than other elements of London society, the agent fails to recognize that Emily is a chimpanzee, on being informed that she is a monkey, his response is entirely positive (unlike the later horrified reaction of Alfred Fatigay): 'Why – why, this is *wonderful* ... I'd sooner have you than a human star any day.... I'm proud to have given her first break to a wonderful Chimp like you' (*His Monkey Wife*, typescript, Act II, pp. 17–18, Sandy Wilson archive). Emily flourishes in the theatre; her rapid rise through the ranks of the theatre is not unlike that in Wilson's 1954 spoof biography of a theatrical cat, *This Is Sylvia*.[6] She is eventually discovered by C. B. Cochran to become the star of his show, where she fronts a utopian number in which humans and apes dance together:

Monkeys all go on the spree
Now the Humans join in with 'em

Doing the Chimpanzee . . .
It's the latest dance sensation
Very soon we're going to see
Ev'ry creature in creation
Doing the Chimp,
Doing the Chimp,
Doing the Chimpanzee!!!

(*His Monkey Wife*, typescript, Act II,
pp. 18–19, Sandy Wilson archive)

Emily's new-found social status and confidence embolden her to trick Alfred Fatigay into marriage; she is motivated by her love for him, but he flees in horror. In the aftermath of the marriage their roles are reversed; she finds him destitute in Regent's Park, while she has become the toast of London. Giving up her theatrical ambitions, Emily devotes herself to Alfred and proves herself to be a worthy wife. Alfred finally dismisses Fern with the contemptuous comment: 'I understand one thing, and that is that a man would be better off with any chimp in the world, much less Emily, than with a woman like you' (*His Monkey Wife*, typescript, Act II, p. 26, Sandy Wilson archive). In a final song, that has distinct echoes of Captain Dick's love song to Niri-Esther in *Valmouth*, Alfred plays tribute to his monkey wife's qualities, in which her silence and simplicity feature large. In terms which are resonant of Coventry Patmore's 1854 poem 'The Angel in the House' Alfred recommends a monkey wife for all men:

It's true my wife is not a woman;
She's an angel come to earth. . .
I'm quite convinced that I
Will be better off with my Monkey Wife . . .
I'm happy with *my* mate,
For she shares my taste for the simple life. . . .
And her silence seems to be
Nothing less than golden.
So to all men I say:
You'd be better off today
If you settled down with a Monkey Wife . . .
They're splendid companions you know . . .

(*His Monkey Wife*, typescript, Act II,
p. 26, Sandy Wilson archive)

Albert and Emily end the play by returning to the jungle of Boboma; a relationship between a human and an animal cannot be sustained in a 'civilized' London, as a final voiceover explains: 'while in more civilised communities (t)his menage might have been considered – shall we say? Unusual, here in Boboma no one presumes to pass an opinion' (*His Monkey Wife*, typescript, Act II, p. 30, Sandy Wilson archive).

If the play is an attempt to make a plea for tolerance of different kinds of relationships, its sexual politics are far from progressive. It is consistently cruel in its attitude towards women and those who challenge gender stereotypes. Fern's desire to be admired for her intellect rather than her physical attributes is roundly satirized, while Emily's theatrical and intellectual success is much less important for both her and Alfred than is her solicitousness towards his needs. Fern, her friend Susan and the effeminate Dennis are brutally characterized as brittle, superficial and pretentious, while Emily's silent companionship and, it is strongly implied, 'natural' feminine domesticity is celebrated and rewarded. There is a suggestion in the play that a cross species relationship between a human and a chimpanzee could be read as analogous to a same-sex coupling (although by 1971, when *His Monkey Wife* first opened, after the 1967 Sexual Offences Act, sex in private between men over twenty-one was no longer illegal). When Alfred first recognizes that his bride is not the human Fern but the monkey Emily, he protests: 'There's a law – against – well – against chimps' (*His Monkey Wife*, typescript, Act II, p. 3, Sandy Wilson archive).

Milton Shulman recognized that the sexual politics of John Collier's 1930 novel were long out of date by 1971, commenting in his review: 'It seems to be an anti-feminist statement of particular virulence' (*Evening Standard*, 21 December 1971). Wilson was sufficiently stung by this to send a responding letter to the *Evening Standard*, but in claiming that Shulman had missed the point of the musical, he rather demonstrated that he himself had missed the point of Shulman's criticism:

> I . . . would have thought it obvious to any sensible male that Emily, the chimp, is an embodiment of all the pristine feminine virtues, such as gentleness, loyalty, perseverance and devotion, which have been bred out of some her 'civilised' human cousins. Accordingly, she triumphs in the end and wins her man, as a virtuous heroine should. (undated letter to the *Evening Standard*, Sandy Wilson's archive)

Wilson could not recognize that his version of the 'pristine feminine virtues' was Victorian rather than contemporary to the 1970s. As Wilson's accountant and the Hampstead Theatre management had anticipated, the reviews and audience response to *His Monkey Wife* were not positive enough to warrant a West End production. The leading players, June Ritchie and Robert Swann (who were themselves well reviewed), were both contracted to *Gone with the Wind* and so could not continue with the show. Despite a personal plea from Wilson to Michael Codron, then a director of the Hampstead Theatre Club (letter, 8 January 1972, Sandy Wilson archive), *His Monkey Wife* did not transfer. It was recorded by the original cast for President records; a review noted that the recording had rescued the show 'from undeserved oblivion' (*Gramophone* undated clipping, Sandy Wilson's archive).

It is clear from letters in Wilson's archive that he did his level best to rescue the musical from oblivion. An investor wrote to Wilson in 1971 to explain that he was unwilling to put in any money for a West End transfer: 'It's purely a subjective judgement; but it seemed to me – rather as with John Collier's novel – that once the situation had been sprung there was too little that you could do with it, however much wit and elegance you lavish on it' (letter from Freddie, 30 November 1971, Sandy Wilson archive). Freddie was not alone in his disinclination to support *His Monkey Wife*; the Off-Broadway Edison Theatre Corporation (letter from Norman Kean, 18 May 1972, Sandy Wilson archive) and 'small and experimental theatres in Germany' (letter from Peter Goldbaum Productions, 5 March 1972, Sandy Wilson archive) expressed mild interest, but nothing was to come from these approaches. Hal Prince wrote to Wilson with some encouragement, but distanced himself from promising any involvement from New York: 'I wish I had something tangible to say about HIS MONKEY WIFE. . . . I don't know how it would do here. . . . But who to present it? . . . I hope that someone occurs to me who could, and would, get involved' (letter from Hal Prince, 24 January 1972, Sandy Wilson archive). Finally, John Collier's agent firmly wrote to Wilson's agent in 1974 to say that John Collier, the author of the original novel, 'is not prepared to renew your option on HIS MONKEY WIFE any further . . . he does feel that the time has come to call a halt and concentrate on possible film enquiries' (letter from Anthony Jones to Sheila Lemon, 24 July 1974, Sandy Wilson archive). No film version of either the novel or the musical has been made.

In 1984 Alan Ayckbourn directed a revival of *His Monkey Wife* at the Stephen Joseph Theatre[7] in Scarborough. While most critics were enthusiastic about the revival and the play (clippings, Sandy Wilson archive), the (male) critic of *The Guardian* sounded a note of caution and, over a decade after Milton Shulman had made the same point, argued that the sexual politics of the text were not acceptable in 1984: 'I'm told it went down well in Hampstead. They must have liked the idea that a devoted, silent slave (who's cuddly in bed but doesn't demand too much) would prove to be an ideal wife for an English gentleman' (*The Guardian* 22 December 1984, Sandy Wilson archive). In fact, it had not gone down well in Hampstead, and neither audiences nor reviewers were comfortable with the idea of a wife as a 'devoted silent slave'. Like *The Buccaneer, His*

Monkey Wife was resolutely old-fashioned and nostalgic for a previous age of gender roles, and, as *Divorce Me, Darling!* had been in the 1960s, it was too late for the sexually sophisticated audiences of the 1970s. Sandy Wilson was deaf not just to shifts in contemporary music but also in gender politics.

Wright is more sympathetic than many critics to *His Monkey Wife*, praising the 'economy of lyric and simplicity of music' of the love songs (Wright, 2010, p. 91), but he later commented: 'Neatly put together, *His Monkey Wife* confirmed Wilson's integrity but placed him even further beyond the pale with London managements' (Wright, 2017, p. 92). The novelist and theatre critic Francis King was a stalwart supporter of Wilson's work and wrote to him in 1979 to say how much he had enjoyed *His Monkey Wife* and *Valmouth*: 'why doesn't the Arts Council commission a new musical from *you*?' (letter from Francis King, 1979, Sandy Wilson archive). If the Arts Council did not call to commission a new musical, they did sponsor his next production. In an indication of quite how far Wilson had moved from being the toast of the West End, 'The World Première of Mr. Sandy Wilson's new musical *The Clapham Wonder*' (*The Clapham Wonder* programme, Marlowe Theatre, 1978) took place at the Marlowe Theatre, Canterbury[8] in 1978 for a three-week run, and was not taken up by any commercial theatre management or ever produced in London.

The Clapham Wonder is an anomaly for Wilson, as the only complete work of his based on the work of a woman writer;[9] the 1959 *The Vet's Daughter* by Barbara Comyns. Like John Collier's novella *His Monkey Wife*, *The Vet's Daughter* is a strange novel in its combination of social and magical realism. Especially coming after *His Monkey Wife*, with its celebration of passive femininity, it is difficult to see what it was that appealed to Wilson in Comyns's novel; *The Vet's Daughter* is a feminist parable in which a woman has mystical abilities which enable her to evade male predators. Wilson's musical is set in a historically vague 'early twentieth century' and, while the location is clearly South London, Wilson specifies in his typescript that 'the scenes throughout should be designed in an impressionistic rather than realistic manner' (*The Clapham Wonder*, typescript, Act 1, p. 1, Sandy Wilson archive). Like Sarah Sinquier, of the 1950 musical *Caprice*, Alice Rowlands, the heroine of *The Vet's Daughter*, is the daughter of a professional man and longs to escape the suffocating confines of suburban life, a bullying father and an evil stepmother, Rosa. As the cover of the Virago reprint of the novel puts it: 'Growing up in Edwardian south London, Alice Rowlands longs for romance and excitement, for a release from a life that is dreary, restrictive and lonely' (*The Vet's Daughter*, Virago edition, 2013). Rather than escape to the West End of London, as Sarah does, the heroine seeks refuge in magical levitations, which are as fatal for her as the theatre was for Sarah, Alice is trampled to death, alongside the wicked Rosa, by her audience.

The Clapham Wonder is, as were *Caprice* and *His Monkey Wife*, concerned with the tension between the conventional respectability of middle-class life and the showmanship and magic of performance. The play begins where the novel ends with the announcement of Alice's death at the public event of her levitation on Clapham Common (the Clapham wonder of the title). In the first act, Alice and her mother are seen to be bullied and subdued by Mr Rowlands, the vet of the title of Comyns's original novel. Alice takes comfort in her best friend who cannot speak and they communicate in a private sign language which only Alice can understand. This is a household full of women, dominated by a patriarch. After the death of Alice's mother, the family move to Clapham with Rosa Fisher who is purportedly a housekeeper, but she is in fact Rowlands's mistress and Alice's life is made even more miserable. Her ability to levitate at will is Alice's one form of distinction; in the tradition of magical realism, it is never explained either in the novel or in the musical. Levitation is the only thing that marks Alice out as different from other suburban young women; as she sings in a song:

Then I said to myself,
Well, At least you're different,
You don't have to stay on the ground.
(*The Clapham Wonder*, typescript, Act 11,
Sandy Wilson archive, p. 17)

It is precisely that ability not to 'stay on the ground' that appals her potential romantic interest, Nicholas; when she privately demonstrates her ability to him, his conventional sensibilities are threatened by this display of 'difference': 'Different? It's – it's horrible!' (*The Clapham Wonder*, typescript, Act 11, p. 21, Sandy Wilson archive). Alice's father, on the other hand, determines to exploit her strange gift and promotes a media circus around a levitation on Clapham Common, despite Alice's protests: 'Please, Father! I don't want to be peculiar. I want to be *ordinary!*' (*The Clapham Wonder*, Act 11, typescript, Sandy Wilson archive, p. 30). Alice is content to levitate in private, but the thought of a public demonstration appals her as much as it does Nicholas. It is strongly suggested in both the novel and the musical that the levitation is a silent response to sexual and emotional abuse. Alice's first levitation takes place immediately after she has been assaulted by Rosa's friend Cuthbert, who is aided and abetted by Rosa. Levitation is a means of disassociation from trauma, as Alice describes the experience: 'I just felt very calm and peaceful' (*The Clapham Wonder*, typescript, Act 1, p. 49, Sandy Wilson archive). Each of her levitations occurs at a moment when she is being threatened by an abusive man, either her father or Cuthbert. Alice's story, like Sarah's in *Caprice*, ends in a mysterious death; the magical attractions of show business are shown to be potentially lethal. Despite revisions to the show after the previews, in which three of the original songs were excised, *The Clapham Wonder* had no life beyond the Marlowe Theatre and does not seem to have left a recording behind. As Wright puts it: '*The Clapham Wonder* . . . had no commercial currency. Provincial, undercast, under-reviewed, there was no hope that the miracle of *The Boy Friend* (little show gets taken up and becomes big) would reoccur' (Wright, 2010, p. 91). Wilson clearly cared deeply for *The Clapham Wonder*; he was punctilious in his research on props, itemizing and costing everything that was needed, as his notes on the libretto demonstrate.

Aladdin was the last of Wilson's commissions and his last produced original musical, for which he wrote the book, music and lyrics.[10] It was commissioned in 1979 as the opening show of the newly refurbished Lyric Theatre, Hammersmith, and marked a return for Wilson to the Lyric, which had seen the first productions of *The Buccaneer* and *Valmouth*. The Lyric had asked Wilson to write the show as their annual pantomime, but in the sleeve notes for the original cast recording Wilson wrote: 'Instead of writing a pantomime – a form of theatre about which I know very little – I decided to make *Aladdin* a musical, and based it on the original story in the Arabian nights (*Aladdin*, President Records sleeve notes, 1980)'. *Aladdin* had long been a staple of the Players' Theatre pantomimes, their version based on Victorian scripts found in the British Library, and Cole Porter had written a score for a London production in 1959. Wilson wrote in a programme note that he was concerned to avoid both the Victorian homage of the Players' approach and the commercial pantomime's use of contemporary popular cultural references:

> it seemed to me that the Victorian (pantomimes) written in rhyming couplets and peppered with outrageous puns, were much better left to experts like the Players' Theatre, while the modern versions seemed to be composed of jokes about TV commercials with pauses for pop songs – and that didn't appeal to me at all. I decided instead to go to the source, and bought myself a Penguin edition of *The Arabian Nights*. (*Aladdin* programme, Lyric Theatre, Hammersmith, 1979)

In *Aladdin*, as in so much of his work, Wilson endeavours to steer a path between the modern and the traditional and between the high and low brow. His version, despite his professed research into the original text and his reluctance to write a pantomime, is very traditional in its script, music and lyrics and makes use of many of the tropes of conventional pantomime. Wilson's *Aladdin* opens in an exoticized and mysterious Morocco with Abanazer, who has all the characteristics of the conventional pantomime villain. The second scene is set in the traditional setting for *Aladdin* (a tradition that dates back to the eighteenth century, see Philips, p. 88), the 'Pekin' laundry of Aladdin and his mother, the pantomime dame, played by a man (Joe Melia) in drag. The script does incorporate fairy-tale elements in its plot of an Emperor eager to marry off his beautiful daughter, and of romance, as Aladdin and the Princess Badroulbadour (her original name in *The Arabian Nights*) fall in love at first sight. The final fate of the wicked Abanazar has Gothic echoes of Matthew Lewis's 1796 novel *The Monk*, as he is picked up, as is Ambrosio, the monk in Lewis's novel, in the 'mighty talons of the "Great Roc" (Lucifer in Ambrosio's case) and carried away "beneath the world, to the realms of ice and snow, where he can do no harm to anyone"' (*Aladdin*, typescript, Act 11, p. 34, Sandy Wilson archive).

There is very little intervention from the modern in Wilson's version, but there is a gesture towards gender equality in the casting of the Geni in Wilson's version as 'a petite, female Geni' who is green (*Aladdin*, typescript, Act 1, p. 32, Sandy Wilson archive). There is also a call for colour blindness in the Geni's song:

> Green is Beautiful
> It's as nice as black or brown
> Or yellow or pink.
>   (*Aladdin*, typescript, Act 1, p. 41, Sandy Wilson archive)

The mixed-race singer Elisabeth Welch played Fatimah, the wise beggar woman. In another neat circle in Wilson's career, Welch had appeared in one of his earliest West End revues *Oranges and Lemons* in 1948.

Wright assesses *Aladdin* as 'a pantomime forced to be a musical and a musical trying to avoid being a pantomime' (Wright, 2010, p. 92). He concludes his account of Wilson's oeuvre with this less than celebratory comment on *Aladdin*, and adds:

> It would be disappointing to end on such a note, and there is no need to do so, for Wilson's contribution to the post-war British musical is one of the most distinctive and interesting. There has, of course, been far too much focus on *The Boy Friend* and much tosh talked about it. Set it aside, and let us rediscover the several joys of *The Buccaneer, His Monkey Wife*, and, yes, *The Clapham Wonder*. (Wright, 2010, p. 93)

It is impossible to set aside *The Boy Friend*, the most successful and loved musical that Wilson ever wrote. *The Buccaneer, His Monkey Wife* and *The Clapham Wonder* all have their charms, particularly in their scores, but they also have their problems. In *The Boy Friend* Wilson wrote a perfect small musical that won hearts across the West End, Broadway and the world. He was never able to replicate the magical combination of venue, cast and timing that made *The Boy Friend* such a success, but he never gave up trying.

Conclusion

A young Oxbridge graduate . . . has given the West End theatre the wistful, nostalgic freshness of his long-running little masterpiece

(Wilson and Rose, 1957, p. 38)

it does seem to me that the vitality and intensity of camp and show biz, and the way that in form and style if not in specifically expressed sentiments, it stands outside of the routine and conventional, is preferable to the dreary, conforming and phonily down-to-(middlebrow)-earth of the others.

(Richard Dyer, 1973, p. 8)

The complexity of a culture is to be found not only in its variable processes and their social definitions – but also in the dynamic interrelations, at every point in the process, of historically varied and variable elements.

(Raymond Williams, 1977, p. 121)

Wilson grew up on the musicals of Noël Coward and Ivor Novello and learned his craft as a lyricist and composer in revue. It is now a truism of theatre history that the advent of a new wave of kitchen sink drama staged at the Royal Court signalled the beginning of the end for the light comedies and revues that had been so important in the post-war years. Wilson's entry in the *Encyclopedia of Musical Theatre* serves to confirm this version of theatre before *Look Back in Anger* in 1956 as lacking in any seriousness, describing him only as a 'Versatile British author/songwriter who was able to write both a major international hit and a connoisseur's delight before wit and charm went out of fashion' (Gänzl, 2001, p. 227). However, as Rebellato and Shellard have decisively demonstrated, this version of drama history, which pits the popular theatre of the West End against the radical drama of the Royal Court, promotes the idea that any theatre before 1956 was frivolous, and consigns all earlier plays of the decade (including those of Terence Rattigan and Noël Coward) to darkness. Rebellato cites some of those critics who have derided any post-war theatre that preceded *Look Back in Anger* and points out that 'The scorn heaped on the period can sometimes make it puzzling that anyone ever went to a theatre that was "constricted" . . . "stagnant" and wreathed in cobwebs of despair' (Rebellato, 1999, p. 5). The overly neat division between 'Anger and After', in the title of John Russell Taylor's influential book of 1963, that is so prevalent in cultural history, denies the interconnectivities between people, theatres and forms of drama. Wilson's career exemplifies those connections.

Bauer and Cook have pointed out that a similarly reductive opposition applies to many contemporary histories of sexuality, in which the 1960s are read as a clean break from the conformist repression of the 1950s:

> Histories of sexuality, literature and social change have often located the 1950s as the beginning or end of analysis, the place to stop an examination of the war years, or to start on the 1960s and the social, sexual and cultural changes that are seen to mark that later decade. Until recently, long histories of modern sexuality have tended to give significance to the 1950s mostly in terms of repressive norms against which the gay and women's liberation movements reacted in the decades that followed. (Bauer and Cook, 2012, p. 3)

Again, this is a false division that denies the myriad forms in which men and women resisted those 'norms' and laid the foundations for the liberation movements of 1960s; it is also to undermine the many pleasures and complexities of gay lives in the decade of the 1950s.

In terms of musical theatre, in Wright's estimation, the sensibility of Coward, Novello and Wilson could not survive into the 1970s because their work was so constrained, in contrast to the elaborate spectacles fashionable in musicals of that period: 'The emotional excess that was by now (the 1970s) characterising the most eminently successful British musicals was not in Wilson's armoury. Neither was it in the armoury of Coward, Novello, Ellis[1], Slade or Bart[2], in all of whose work there is a sense of corseting emotions' (Wright, 2010, p. 92). What is unstated here is that all these writers were outside the mainstream, by virtue of their homosexuality, and in Bart's case, his Jewishness. They were writing at a time when they had no choice but to be circumspect, their emotions could not but be 'corseted'.

Sheridan Morley, writing in the programme for the 1997 revival of *Divorce Me, Darling!*, also notes that the gentle camp and wit of Wilson and Julian Slade which had conquered the West End in the mid-1950s seemed to have been displaced, particularly by the blockbuster musicals of Andrew Lloyd Webber in the 1980s, just as the work of Coward and Novello had been overtaken by the American imports in the post-war period. Morley thought however that Wilson would see a revival of his status:

> Just as *Oklahoma!* and *Carousel* arriving in the West End at the end of the war, made Coward and even Novello suddenly non-people, so the

coming of the mega musicals of the 80s made Wilson seem suddenly anachronistic.

Yet time brings its curious revenges, Novello and Slade may still be out there in the dark, but both Vivian Ellis and Noël Coward lived long enough to see a full scale renaissance of their work, and I reckon the same may be about to happen to Wilson. . . . *The Boy Friend* and *Divorce Me, Darling!* conjure up a lost world with something more than just regret or nostalgia. Slyly they comment on their period; these scores are in that sense far more subversive than they first appear, and like elegant time-bombs, they continue to explode just when you least expect them. (Chichester Festival Theatre programme, *Divorce Me, Darling!* 1997)

Wilson never did live to see a 'full-scale renaissance' of his work; although *The Boy Friend* has never been out of production, it is the musical by which he is remembered. If *The Boy Friend* is out of the dark, it is, however, regularly revived as a lost world of the 1920s, rather than as a product of the 1950s. Raymond Williams, in writing of literature, would describe *The Boy Friend* as 'archaic', that is, 'that which is wholly recognised as an element of the past, to be observed, to be examined, or even on occasion to be consciously 'revived', in a deliberately specializing way' (Williams, 1977, p. 123). *The Boy Friend* was 'wholly recognised as an element of the past' at the time of its first production, it was a self-conscious revival of a past that was resonant in the post-war context.

Williams identifies a complex interconnectivity between forms of culture, and argues that dominant forms are always accompanied by 'emergent' new modes, and also by 'residual' forms from the past: 'We have certainly still to speak of the "dominant" and the "effective". . . . But we find that we have also to speak . . . of the "residual" and the "emergent", which in any real process are significant both in themselves and in what they reveal of the characteristics of the dominant' (Williams, 1977, p. 121). Wilson is of course a single individual rather than a cultural movement, but his career, particularly in the case of the production of *Valmouth*, demonstrates that what appear to be decisive breaks are, as Williams suggests, always part of a complex process, in which the dominant is shaped by residual forms, and the emergent is never entirely new. Wilson was so shaped by and attuned to prevailing fashions, and he achieved popular success so young, that his career offers a means of identifying some of the shifts and contradictions in the popular culture of the mid-1950s. Wilson had one brief shining moment as the dominant presence in British musical theatre with *The Boy Friend*, but thereafter he largely retreated to the past, to the work of writers such as Firbank and John Collier who belonged to the 1920s and 1930s and who were by then themselves residual figures. He also retreated to his own moment of dominance with a return to *The Boy Friend* in *Divorce Me, Darling!* There were projects that might have cemented his status, his scripts for *Pygmalion* and Isherwood's *Berlin Stories* were clearly on the mark (both would became major hits in other hands as *My Fair Lady* and *Cabaret*), but these never came to fruition and thereafter his work would be culturally residual, relegated, in the words of Wright's chapter heading, to 'Pastiche and Esoteric' (Wright, 2010, p. 70).

Wilson had modelled himself as a young composer and lyricist on the then dominant theatrical figures Coward and Novello, both in terms of their music and their modes of masculinity. He remained in thrall to them (it was in 1973 that he wrote his hagiography of Novello, *Ivor*), past the point when they had lost their status as dominant stars in theatre or music. He was however unable to detach himself from that mode and to recognize that musical styles had moved on, as his distaste for the jazz sensibility of Cleo Laine and John Dankworth in the row over *Valmouth* demonstrates. There are clues throughout his musical career that he could be musically intransigent, it is telling that George Devine found his music for *Valmouth* lacking in 'satirical ambiguity', and that Hal Prince found his score for *Goodbye to Berlin* 'very nice', but inappropriate for the Weimar sound of *Cabaret*. Musically, Wilson was clearly much more comfortable with the work of Coward and Novello than he was with contemporary jazz.

The gentle camp of Rattigan, Slade and Wilson would be overtaken in the 1960s by the very evident sexual subversion and overt queerness of Joe Orton,[3] whose first full-length play *Entertaining Mr Sloane* was produced in 1964 (and it should be noted that Rattigan was an investor in the production). Nonetheless, Wilson would go on to write and perform with many who would come to be seen as the theatrical avant-garde, including Harold Pinter, N. F. Simpson and the comedian Peter Cook. Wilson had strong personal and professional connections with key figures at the Royal Court, and with the new wave of theatre. He had been a friend and contemporary of Tony Richardson and of Kenneth Tynan at Oxford, George Devine had taught him at the Old Vic Theatre School. Tynan would become one of the most influential figures in contemporary British theatre as the first literary manager of the National Theatre under the directorship of Laurence Olivier from 1963. Wilson understood that, as the writer of a successful West End musical, he was not seen at the time to belong to this new wave of theatre, but he was close to many who were central to it. As he remembered in an unpublished chapter of his autobiography:

Although, as a mere writer of musicals, I was not considered part of it, the British Theatre was having a resurgence and beginning to shrug off the outmoded styles and explore new territories. Ken [Tynan], almost single-handedly, made a success out of new play at the Royal Court, which Jon[4] and I first heard about when we went round one evening to see Kenneth Haigh (who was the first actor to play Jimmy Porter) . . .

I'm playing the lead in a thing called LOOK BACK IN ANGER 'Oh?' I said, 'What's it like?'

'Can't say,' replied Kenneth. . . . 'I just know I've got a bloody lot of lines to learn. I never stop talking!' (unpublished autobiographical chapter, p. 327, Sandy Wilson archive)

It is significant that this episode was not included in the published version of the autobiography, it does not neatly fit with the narrative of the successful West End and Broadway lyricist that structures Wilson's own account of his career.

Although Wilson would never have defined himself as an 'Angry Young Man', he was included as such in press reports. The *Daily Express* reported a punch up after a one-off performance of a play by Stuart Holroyd[5] at the Royal Court in 1958: 'Among those booing the religiosity of the script were, John Osborne, Lindsay Anderson, Michael Hastings and Ken and Elaine (Dundy) Tynan. Sandy Wilson was reported to have said: "I hated the play, but loved all the excitement"' (clipping, *Daily Express*, 10 March 1958, Sandy Wilson archive). In 1970, Wilson was described in a *Guardian* interview as 'an angry middle-aged growler' (*The Guardian*, 14 September 1970, clipping, Sandy Wilson archive), a description he clearly did not object to, as he kept the clipping carefully filed. Wilson was not at all dismissive of Osborne and the new generation of theatre but anxious to work with them, as the correspondence relating to *Valmouth* demonstrates. He describes a very positive relationship with John Osborne and was clearly knowledgeable about movements in contemporary theatre; he remembers a dinner party with John Osborne, Kenneth Tynan and Tynan's first wife Elaine Dundy[6] of which he writes: 'all got very het up and argumentative over Brecht, Milton Shulman and other things' (undated manuscript, Sandy Wilson archive). He did however have his limits, and was unimpressed by the Berliner Ensemble:

The Parties . . . I remember particularly the one for the Berliner Ensemble, on the first night of MOTHER COURAGE (Sept 10th, 1956). We had all been dragooned by Ken into coming to see it, as part of his Brecht Crusade, and this was our reward. I thought, while watching the play, how amazingly plain and unattractive the cast had managed to make themselves. (undated manuscript, Sandy Wilson archive)

Kathleen Tynan[7] asked Wilson to write of his memories of the 1950s after Kenneth Tynan's death in 1980, and his response makes it clear that he had read and admired a new generation of writers: 'It was the time of what were called the Angry Young Men, and of course Ken was a champion of John Osborne and LOOK BACK IN ANGER. But for some reason both he and Elaine detested Colin Wilson (THE OUTSIDER) whom I rather revered – for a while' (undated manuscript, Sandy Wilson archive).

The 1960 satirical revue *Beyond the Fringe* is, like *Look Back in Anger*, seen as a cultural watershed; according to Trussler, it 'gave a new lease of life to revue' (Trussler, 1994, p. 332). In an article titled 'Revue', Wilson himself wrote about *Beyond the Fringe* as ringing the death knell for his kind of musical revue:

> the appearance of BEYOND THE FRINGE (1961), in which four University graduates introduced political satire of a kind hitherto considered unacceptable, made other revues look parochial and insipid by comparison, and when television took up this trend stage revue was more or less doomed. ('Revue', undated, unpublished article, Sandy Wilson archive)

Those involved in *Beyond the Fringe* were of a different generation; they were too young to have fought in the war and had grown up in post-war austerity. While the revue writers of Sandy Wilson's cohort were not directly political, the lack of deference for establishment figures in *Beyond the Fringe* was seen to be cutting edge and radically new. However, as Wilson himself also noted (Wilson, 1975a, p. 129), the form of *Beyond the Fringe* had emerged out of the 'intimate revues' in which Wilson had first started his career in theatre, and, like Wilson, its cast, Alan Bennett, Peter Cook, Dudley Moore and Jonathan Miller had all started out in university revues.[8] Peter Cook had already acquired a professional agent as an undergraduate, based on his work for the revue *Pieces of Eight* (to which Wilson contributed music). It was Kenneth Tynan who ensured the success of *Beyond the Fringe*, as he had for *Look Back in Anger*, with a glowing review. The distinction between 'revue' and the 'satire boom' is another false opposition, which does not recognize the interconnections of forms and people. It also underestimates the satirical edge of the many revue songs which in the early 1950s, to judge from Wilson's lyrics, were very satirical about the heteronormativity of contemporary culture.

Wilson was emotionally conservative, both politically and aesthetically. If his politics were broadly sympathetic to the left (he was a supporter of Neil Kinnock, a friend of the Labour MP Gerald Kaufmann, he detested Margaret Thatcher and subscribed to the *New Statesman*), he could be cloth-eared to shifts in racial, gender and sexual politics, as he was to musical shifts. Wilson, like *The Boy Friend*, was locked into nostalgia for a previous age. Nostalgia features large throughout his work, but while his nostalgia always has a camp edge, it is not necessarily queer, or progressive. There is a cosy nostalgia for imperial masculinity in *The Buccaneer* and an unquestioning acceptance of passive femininity in *His Monkey Wife*. There is also a wilful ignoring of the problematic racial representations in *Valmouth*, and all his work displays some anxiety about the advance of modernity and a mistrust of social change.

The conservative quality of Wilson's music and writing is also evident in his mode of presentation as a homosexual man. Wilson was, if broadly supportive, clearly disconcerted by the public demonstrations of the Gay Liberation movement, as his lyric 'Why Did it Have to be Gay?' indicates:

> In my old-fashioned way,
> I'm all for hi-de-ho and also hi-de-hey.
> But something has gone for ever.
>
> (undated lyric, Sandy Wilson archive)

The 'hi-de-ho' of Gay Liberation challenged, as it did for his friend Peter Wildeblood and for the Homosexual Law Reform Society, the discretion that they had all grown up with and which Wilson had so admired in Coward and Novello. Wilson was of a generation who had had to be circumspect about their sexuality, and were uncomfortable with declaring it; it is significant that in the 1948 version of his unpublished novel *Oxford's Not What It Used to Be* there is no reference at all to the protagonist's sexuality.

Mort has also suggested that the 1960s were not the 'watershed break' (Mort, 2010, p. 4) that is often assumed in histories of sexuality; he argues that it was not the case that

> the rise of the permissive society was a linear and directed force that erupted in the late 1950s and ran its course through the decade that followed, modernizing sexual behaviour in ways that were socially beneficial and qualitatively different from the system of public morality that preceded it.
> . . . the permissive society was neither a revolution in English social life nor a radical break with the sexual cultures that preceded it; rather it was an extremely uneven acceleration of shifts that had a much longer period of incubation. (Mort, 2010, pp. 3–4)

Wilson's unproduced play of 1958 gives some indication of that 'extremely uneven acceleration of shifts'. In *The Way We Are* Wilson writes about youthful

Oxford theatrical ambitions frustrated in adult life in London, and about the current climate of the arrest and harassment of gay men. In a speech Francis, the central male character, suggests that things are worse for gay men in the 1950s than they had once been and, as in Wilson's lyric, wistfully expresses nostalgia for the apparently more innocent period of his youth:

> Why does it all have to change? Why aren't we allowed to have fun anymore? I didn't mean any harm – none of us did. We were just behaving as we always have done. Why does that have to be wrong? Can't it be amusing any more – the way it used to be? . . . it's just as if whatever we do now is suddenly out of date – and illegal as well. . . . Where has it all gone to? Or perhaps it never existed . . . (*The Way We Are*, Act II, pp. 50–1, Sandy Wilson archive)

Wilson never quite was able to escape his own nostalgia, and that would keep him back, professionally, personally and politically.

The Players' Theatre was a space which did allow 'it to be amusing', if the 'way that it used to be' was for the management and audience largely the Victorian period. The theatrical world did offer a relatively safe and welcoming space for homosexual men, as writers, performers and audiences, who were otherwise hounded and demonized in the press, by the law and by the medical profession. Theatricality could also be a means of articulating resistance. Neil Bartlett however makes the salutary point that it would be wrong to understand theatre as a 'natural' professional home for homosexual men:

> There is absolutely no evidence that the performing arts were any more associated with or practiced by or welcoming to homosexual people in the hundred years or so between 1861 and 1968 than (say) ambulance driving, trade unionism, embroidery or motherhood; nor do we know whether theatrical types have been any more legion among our number than non-theatrical types. (Bartlett, 2017, p. 69)

It may be the case that there is no evidence, but it is also true that there are recurrent references to the importance of the theatre in the letters and memoirs of homosexual men of the period. There is little doubt that theatre and the spaces it provided were then key to a sense of homosexual identity in the context of a draconian public and institutional vilification of gay men. As Bartlett himself has acknowledged, homosexual men were central to the development of British theatre, and, in the 1950s, shaped the West End as performers, writers and impresarios (Bartlett, quoted in Sinfield, 1998, pp. 152–3).

In 2017, in celebration of the anniversary of 1967 Sexual Offences Act and the partial decriminalization of homosexuality in Britain, the American poet and novelist, Garth Greenwell, wrote of

> the brilliant, brave, defiant aesthetic that is gay male faggotry. Decades later, the virtues of that aesthetic – extravagance, effeminacy, indulgence, ornament, elegance, sexiness, ferocity, rage – would be a blessed counterpoise to the staid realism that holds sway in many an American writing workshop. . . . This is the whole history of queer art: taking stigma and turning it into style. (Greenwell, 2017, p. 3)

Sandy Wilson's work may not be very brave or ferocious, and he would himself have disdained the term 'faggot'; nonetheless, his work does have something of the aesthetic of 'gay male faggotry'. His work continually refuses the 'staid realism' that became the dominant form of fiction writing in the 1950s, and, from, *Look Back in Anger* onwards, the fashionable mode of the theatre. In 1953 and 1954, Sandy Wilson, Julian Slade and Terence Rattigan represented strong (and popular) voices in theatre that celebrated and made a case for a mode of being that was not comfortable with the Brave New World of respectable post-war consensus and heteronormativity. Among the many strategies for resistance to sexual conformity was subversion in the various forms of camp, another was the use of Polari, the subcultural language that helped to define membership of a community; both camp and Polari flourished in theatre circles. However, as Paul Baker has outlined, camp and the use of Polari were largely repudiated by the new politicized generation of the Gay Liberation Front (see Baker, 2006, pp. 115–16). Wilson is a significant figure for both queer history and musical theatre because he marks that moment of transition. His career demonstrates how far theatrical, musical and queer histories are complicated and shaped not by sudden change, but by incremental processes.

It may seem quaint to celebrate the fey camp of musical theatre in the 1950s in the twenty-first century, but it is important to remember how recent prosecutions for homosexual acts were. It remains the case that many homosexual men continue to take refuge in the bars, clubs and theatres of London's West End, a 2017 report from the campaigning organization Stonewall[9] reported that one in five LGBT people had experienced hate crime or discrimination. Looking back at the brutality of the Metropolitan Police and at the prejudices of the press, parliament and the judiciary, it may seem comforting to consider how far gay rights have come since the 1950s, with the celebration of the fiftieth anniversary of the Sexual Offences Act of 1967. In my lifetime I have seen bars in Soho transform, with plate glass windows and rainbow flags flying, in contrast to the black painted secrecy of before. In this current era of corporate-sponsored gay pride marches, in which registration is required to march, it may be that the police are marching alongside the drag kings and queens through streets adorned with rainbow flags, but it must also be remembered that it once took real courage to take part in a Gay Pride march, or even to attend a meeting of the Homosexual Law Reform Society, as the protagonist of an unproduced play by Wilson demonstrates. The right to march and the equalization of gay rights have been bitterly fought for through reformist and revolutionary campaigns from the Homosexual Law Reform Society through to the Gay Liberation Front. From the Stonewall riots to the campaigns of Stonewall, there have been innumerable acts of political resistance to a dominant sexual conformism; those equal rights were hard won and continue to need defending. As the campaigning journalist Owen Jones angrily wrote in 2017, as the Conservative government gave posthumous pardons to gay men who had been criminalized for homosexual activity during the 1950s:

> It is fashionable now, particularly among those who resent LGBT equality, to claim that the struggle is over. . . . The legacy still looms over us: the damage inflicted on the lives of hundreds and thousands of people . . . the homophobia that underpinned those persecutions has not gone away. . . . The damage will continue for many decades.
> The correct response to these pardons is to pay tribute to those who struggled and to learn from their courage to finish what they started. (Jones, 2017, p. 28)

This book is a part of that response, as a tribute to a figure who was never directly a political activist, but who was one of those who struggled. Throughout Sandy Wilson's music and lyrics, from *The Boy Friend* to *Aladdin*, there is a continuous strand of mischievous camp that subverts and challenges convention, it is not always radical (as camp is not always progressive), but in a period in which, in Barry Cryer's phrase, it 'was an awful, awful time to be gay' it was a necessary defence. Wilson deserves to be remembered for more than *The Boy Friend* and to be understood as more than a footnote in the history of British musical theatre and in queer history.

Afterword

I should declare my interest in Sandy Wilson. I grew up with *The Boy Friend* and the Players' Theatre and both have been important throughout my life. My mother, Ursula Harby, had worked at the Players' Theatre before I was born, she served in the bar and worked in the office, and played the Wicked Fairy to Hattie Jacques's Good Fairy in the pantomime *Sleeping Beauty*. It was a very important place for her, and the Players' was very much part of our lives as children. We went to the Late Joys every birthday, and every Christmas to the pantomime at the Players'; each year a membership card for the Players' Theatre Club would arrive for my mother in acknowledgement of her work with them. My parents had the original cast recording of *The Boy Friend*, and I played it over and over again, and came to know all the words, I am still liable to sing 'All I want is a room in Bloomsbury' and 'It's never too late to fall in love' on appropriate occasions.

After the war, the Players was a club for lost people of all kinds, a place which welcomed gay men, unemployed theatre people and those damaged by the war. My mother remembered an artist who had lost his hands in the war but who painted scenery with his feet. My mother was among those people, an aspiring actress (who was, like Wilson, posted to Egypt during the war) who had come to London in search of theatre work. Her mother suffered a stroke in Norfolk, and it was Reginald Woolley who took care of her. Reggie and his partner Don Gemmell remained close friends of my parents throughout their lives, they often came to dinner at our house, and were always there to greet us with a drink at the Players' bar. I remember Don explaining the mechanics of the flying balloon which spectacularly concluded one pantomime.

While I was at university, the Drama Society put on a production of *The Boy Friend*. My friend Adam Wide was the director, and my good friend Nigel Pugh played Lord Brockhurst (to ovations for 'It's never too late' every night), my flat mate Sue Shepherd was Polly, and Phil Nice played Percival Brown. I was no actor but I did design and paint the sets, complete with a hanging silver moon for the final ball scene. Two years later, Nigel and Adam who had been at school and university together met at the Players' Theatre to attend a revue. As they chatted before the performance, they simultaneously said to one another: 'I have something important to tell you.' They were interrupted by the beginning of the performance and had to wait until the interval before each was able to tell the other that he was gay. The magic of the Players' continued to work its charm, it was still a 'haven for gay men' into the late twentieth century. Nigel and Adam had known one another for over a decade and had never before discussed their sexuality. They both loved *The Boy Friend* but Nigel, certainly, did not realize that its author was gay. It was *The Boy Friend*, Sandy Wilson and the Players' which helped them to formulate an understanding of what it meant to have a camp sensibility. And from childhood, it was the Players' which gave me an appreciation of camp and pastiche, and for that I will always be grateful.

I wrote the final chapters of this book under the lockdown of the 2020 Coronavirus epidemic. Writing of Soho, its bars, restaurants and clubs, the West End of London and theatre, I recognized how intensely I miss them and appreciate them all in ways I had never before understood. Long may Soho reign as a place of 'colour and daring'.

It was a privilege to have access to Sandy Wilson's papers at the Harry Ransom Center, and to be able to follow his meticulously catalogued life and career (catalogued both by him and the Harry Ransom curators). There was a sadness in discovering the number of scripts which never saw production and books that were never published, and many of them deserve to be revisited. Overall, however, there was much pleasure to be found in his writing, in the wit of his letters and in so many of the scripts. I came to understand that he was a much loved man who was surrounded throughout his life by a close and appreciative circle of friends. And he gave us all *The Boy Friend*. Thank you, Sandy Wilson.

Notes

Chapter 1

1 Hugh Paddick played Percival Brown in the first West End production of *The Boy Friend*.
2 Sandy Wilson, interviewed in 1998, demonstrated a knowledge of Polari: 'I was living with a dancer . . . and they all talked it, regardless of sex, it was nothing to do with sex – it was just a kind of professional slang' (Wilson, quoted in Baker, p. 32).
3 According to Barry Cryer, Julian Slade recognized the reference while Wilson did not. Both however were pleased at the tribute.
4 Julian Slade was vice-president of Cambridge Footlights.
5 Wilson does not feature in Pattie's account of *Modern British Playwriting*, nor in O'Connor's *Straight Talking: Popular Gay Drama from Wilde to Rattigan*.
6 *Gay's the Word* is now the name of a gay bookshop in Central London.
7 According to Matt Cook, the association of 'gay' with homosexuality goes back at least to the 1920s, when Noël Coward made use of it: 'Noël Coward used "gay" with evident relish at its new double meaning in "Green Carnation", a number from his musical *Bitter Sweet* (1929)' (Cook, 2007, p.156). Wilson also describes first encountering the term while at Oxford.
8 Vida Hope would become the first director of *The Boy Friend*.
9 Hermione Gingold sat directly in front of Wilson at the first night of *The Boy Friend*, Wilson's response 'her presence nearby seemed like a talisman' (Wilson, 1975a, p. 198) suggests how important she was to him.
10 In the post-war period there were only five women's colleges at Oxford, and men's colleges did not admit women until 1979.
11 Tom Arnold was an impresario and known as the 'King of Pantomime'.
12 Jack Hylton was a band leader and impresario.
13 Bronson Albery was at the time manager of three West End theatres, the Albery theatre in London is named after him.
14 Arthur Miller's *A View from the Bridge* had opened in London in 1956, and Michael Gazzo's *A Hatful of Rain* in 1957, it was made into a film the same year.
15 Michael and Heather Godley were friends from Oxford.

Chapter 2

1 Kinsey and the staff of the Institute for Sex Research, Indiana University, published their study of women's sexuality in *Sexual Behavior in the Human Female* in 1953.

2 This was Montagu's second trial for homosexual offences, he had been arrested and put on trial in 1953, but denied any offence and was not convicted.

3 One of the characters cited in the Julian and Sandy sketches in *Round the Horne* was named 'Pandro Wildebeeste' in a possible reference to Peter Wildeblood (see Baker, P., 2019, p. 168).

4 Wildeblood also wrote a novel in 1958, *West End People*, which was turned into a musical in 1959, a celebration of the diversity of Soho, under the title *Crooked Mile*; it was produced by Players' Ventures (an arm of the Players' Theatre Club) and transferred to the Cambridge Theatre in the West End.

5 This may be the origin of Soho's name, derived from a hunting cry.

6 See www.thehistoryofLondon.co.uk (accessed April 2020).

7 The French House got its name because it was the unofficial base for Charles de Gaulle and the French Resistance during the Second World War.

8 *Absolute Hell* was televised for the BBC in 1991 and staged at the National Theatre in 1995 and again in 2018.

9 Peter Wildeblood wrote a gossip column for the *Daily Mail* and was a sometime theatre critic for the paper before becoming a diplomatic correspondent. Other notable gay gossip columnists in the period included Tom Driberg and Beverley Nichols.

10 Lord Longford would later become a very conservative moral campaigner, voting against the equalization of the age of consent. He supported the Thatcher government's legislation Section 28, which made the 'promotion of homosexuality' by local authorities illegal, which had an impact on schools, libraries and theatres. Section 28 was not repealed until 2003, a repeal which was still resisted by many prominent Conservative politicians. Longford was instrumental in setting up the Festival of Light. He is best known for chairing and giving his name to a 1972 report on pornography, which led to another moral assault on Soho, now focussed on bookshops. Longford maintained his commitment to penal reform until his death, controversially campaigning for the release of Myra Hindley.

11 Like Lord Longford, despite his support for law reform, Dyson became increasingly conservative and was late known for his publication with Brian Cox of the *Black Paper on Education* in 1969 (London: Critical Quarterly Society) which argued against comprehensive education.

12 Dyson and Angus Wilson would later become colleagues at the University of East Anglia.

13 CHE's office in the 1970s was based in Great Windmill Street, very close to Piccadilly Circus and in the heart of Soho.

14 It was not until 1994 that the age of consent for homosexual men was lowered to eighteen, and it was only in 2000 that it was equalized to sixteen years.

15 www.c-h-e.org.uk (accessed April 2020).

16 The first Pride marches took place in several states in the United States in 1970.

17 CHE lost many members over its proposal to lower the age of consent to twelve, when consent could be proved, and, in 1975, when its conference supported the controversial group, the Paedophile Information Exchange (PIE), which campaigned for the abolition of any age of consent. CHE sent a letter to members in 2019 stating: 'CHE's campaigning days are clearly past – the need has changed' (www.c-h-e.org.uk, accessed April 2020). It now focusses on documenting the history of CHE.

18 As far as I can gather, it was never produced on stage or on the radio.

19 www.admiralduncan.co.uk/soho (accessed April 2020).

Chapter 3

1 'No one in the café where they had their table would have known what this meeting was, whether it was an anglers' club, or newspaper sub-editors . . . their style was so correct, their manner reserved and cool, and so discreet their furtive looks at the young men of fashion . . .'
Proust, 1992, p. 25

2 Macqueen-Pope published his own tribute to Ivor Novello in 1951, *Ivor: The Story of an Achievement.*

3 Beryl Samson responded that her memories were too personal and 'not of interest to the general public' (Letter from Beryl Samson, 16 August 1974, Sandy Wilson archive).

4 Beverley Nichols was a contemporary of Wilson's at Oxford, and a prominent figure as an undergraduate, as president of the Oxford Union and editor of the student magazine *Isis.*

5 This was based on Coward's 1936 one-act play *Still Life.*

6 H. M. Tennent's were responsible for the success of Rattigan's early play *French Without Tears* which was one of the plays performed for the troops by ENSA (Entertainments National Service Association) during the war. Beaumont went on to produce Rattigan's, and H. M. Tennent's, biggest success, *The Winslow Boy in* 1946.

7 Rattigan's father was a diplomat, his grandfather a knighted Member of Parliament. Rattigan was knighted in his own right for 'services to theatre' in 1971. Coward had been knighted in 1970.

8 *Victim* was pioneering in 1961 for its sympathetic portrayal of a respectably married barrister (played by Dirk Bogarde) blackmailed over his friendship with a young man. It was a powerful intervention in the debate over homosexual law reform.

9 Rattigan invested in Orton's work, and wrote to congratulate him on
   Entertaining Mr Sloane in 1964; Beaumont co-produced *What the Butler
   Saw* in 1969.
10 Giles Brandreth makes no reference to this in his 'celebration' of Gielgud,
   referring only to Perry as 'a close friend and colleague of John's and Binkie's'
   (Brandreth, p. 73).

Chapter 4

1 It is not coincidental that Heaven, a gay nightclub catering to a younger
   generation, opened directly opposite the Players' Theatre in 1979.
2 ENSA (Entertainments National Service Association) was set up in 1939 to
   provide entertainment for the British armed forces in the Second World
   War.
3 This is an indication of quite how male dominated the theatre production
   world was in 1947, as it largely remains.
4 *The Good Old Days* ran on the BBC until 1983, broadcast not from the
   Players' Theatre Club in Villiers Street but from the Leeds Variety Theatre.
   Don Gemmell was the chair for the first two televised performances, but
   thereafter it was Leonard Sachs.
5 The 'Make Do and Mend' movement was a 'home front' campaign in
   Britain, organized by the British Board of Trade from 1941 as a response to
   the need for rationing during the Second World War.
6 Sandy Wilson's account of the first production of *The Boy Friend* is replete
   with references to the Players' ethos of making do and mending with
   limited resources (see Wilson, 1975a).
7 Despite this apparent diversity, the Players' was not above using minstrels in
   its shows, with white players blacked up to perform minstrel numbers.
8 Princess Margaret regularly attended shows at the Players' and the
   Queen attended a performance of *The Boy Friend*. Wilson was one of the
   signatories to a letter to the *Daily Express* which deplored the Church of
   England's ruling that Princess Margaret could not maintain her royal status
   if she were to marry a divorcé, Captain Peter Townsend (see Kynaston,
   p. 524).
9 Daniel Farson, who wrote his own account of Soho in the 1950s, was among
   the many gay man of the period with a penchant for music hall, 'all his
   money going in a glorious attempt to run a music-hall pub in the Isle of
   Dogs' (Melly, 1987, p. xiv).
10 The first reference to 'fairy' as a slang term for homosexual is dated in the
   Oxford English Dictionary as 1895 in the *American Journal of Psychology*,
   and a citation in the same entry for Evelyn Waugh's *Brideshead Revisited*,
   published in 1945, suggests how widespread the usage was in the post-war
   period (*OED*, Vol.V p. 676).

11 www.playerstheatre.co.uk (accessed April 2020).
12 There never was a woman chair at the Players' Theatre, even while Jean Anderson ran the club during the war.
13 Private telephone conversation with Barry Cryer, 2018.

Chapter 5

1 In the original production the show was in three parts, with the first part a version of the Late Joys music-hall numbers.
2 Kitty Black (Binkie Beaumont's one-time secretary) remembered that 'everyone' – including Princess Margaret – had flocked to see it (Black, p. 220).
3 This was because of the lack of availability of a West End theatre at that time, a process discussed at length in Wilson's autobiography.
4 The 1943 *Late Joys* features Vida Hope in a photograph singing 'Ittle Dirly Dirl' (Sheridan, 1943, p. 58) dressed in Victorian pantaloons; a review of her performing as 'a monstrous child of fabulous proportions' is quoted in the 1952 *Late Joys* (Sheridan, 1952, p. 31).
5 Hattie Jacques appeared regularly in the Joys music hall and had played the good fairy in *The Sleeping Beauty in the Wood* pantomime in 1948. She was already famous beyond the Players' Theatre from her appearances on the BBC radio comedy shows *It's that Man Again* (1939–49) and *Educating Archie* (1950–60).
6 *Oklahoma!* replaced Noël Coward's 1946 *Pacific 1860* at Drury Lane, where Coward's musical had run for only 129 performances.
7 This was more than a little ungracious, the revue *At the Drop of a Hat* was then running successfully in London's West End, a successful double act of Wilson's Oxford friend Donald Swann with Michael Flanders.
8 There are direct references to Cole Porter's 'Let's Do It, Let's Fall in Love', which Coward would later popularize, in Wilson's song 'The Riviera':

> 'Ev'rybody's doing the Riviera
> Multi Millionaires and their little pets do it
> Even maiden ladies who wear lorgnettes
> have taken to it'

9 A reference to Coward's 1925 song 'Poor Little Rich Girl'.
10 The correct French is 'la plage', but, according to Colin Sell who was the musical director for a number of Wilson's productions and revivals, when this was pointed out to Wilson he preferred to keep to his own version.
11 By 1958 the word 'gay' would have been firmly associated with homosexuality, particularly in theatrical circles. Peter Wildeblood remembered encountering the term on meeting an American serviceman while at Oxford (sometime between 1945 and 1948). 'I had not heard

the expression before, but apparently it was an American euphemism for homosexual' (Wildeblood, 1955, p. 23).

12 This was a coded reference to *Caprice* (1950), the musical comedy which had first brought Wilson to the West End, Wilson wrote the lyrics for Geoffrey Wright's music. Wright and Wilson had both contributed to the revue *Oranges and Lemons* in 1948, at the Lyric Theatre, Hammersmith.

13 Nice and the French Riviera would have had a particular resonance for gay men at the time, John S. Barrington, the photographer of 'male physique' images who launched *Male Model Monthly* in 1954, holidayed and took pictures there (see Smith, 1996).

14 The title is an inversion of the title of the 1926 Rogers and Hart musical *The Girl Friend*.

15 According to Colin Sell, the song never fails to rouse an encore.

16 In the 2019 production of *The Boy Friend* at the Meunier Chocolate Factory, Lord Brockhurst is shown as tricked into singing to his disguised wife rather than to Maisie, in the year of the Harvey Weinstein trial and in the context of the MeToo movement, the age differential was too uncomfortable.

17 William Bendix was an American actor known for his 'tough-guy' roles.

18 Wilson went to many amateur productions of *The Boy Friend* and saved all the programmes – including those in Ipswich, the Midland Bank Operatic Society and in 1995, at Edgbaston High School for Girls, in which his great-niece was appearing. He sent good wishes to the programmes of many more.

19 Maria Charles had played Dulcie in the original production. She directed *The Boy Friend at* the Players for a fortieth birthday production in 1994 (the cast included John Rutland, who had first performed Lord Brockhurst, reprising his original role). It went on to tour venues including Sussex, Oxford, Birmingham, York, Norwich and Edinburgh. Maria Charles had appeared in Wilson's 1952 revue *See You Again*.

20 John Bedding worked for Samuel French, the theatre publishers and agents.

21 The relatively small cast and band make *The Boy Friend* particularly appropriate for amateur productions.

Chapter 6

1 This is Wilson's note on the front of the typescript.

2 Approximately £650,500 in 2019.

3 A song from *Oh, Henry!* does feature in a 1972 cabaret recording, *Sandy Wilson at the Players*.

4 Keith Michell was at the time known as a Shakespearean actor but would go on to become celebrated for his portrayals of Henry VIII, most notably in the 1970 BBC television series *The Six Wives of Henry VIII*.

5 Wilson's revues *See You Again* (1951) and *See You Later* (1952) were both produced at the Watergate.

6 Kenneth Williams took over the central role of Montgomery from Peter Bartlett in the move from the Watergate Theatre to the Lyric Hammersmith.

7 Wertham, Fredric *Seduction of the Innocent,* New York: Rinehart 1954.

8 This was organized by the Comics Magazine Association of America in an attempt to fend off government intervention.

9 See Philips, 2012, pp. 143–63.

10 Again, the connotations of the word 'gay' would have been widely known among theatre people and servicemen.

11 Beaton's *My Royal Past* was revised and reissued as a book in 1960.

12 Wilson's first professional involvement with the theatre was writing songs for Hermione Gingold in her 1948 revue *Slings and Arrows.*

13 Julie Andrews was not cast in the film, Eliza was played by the then better-known Audrey Hepburn.

14 *Goodbye to Berlin* and *Mr Norris Changes Trains* were first published together as *The Berlin Stories* in 1954.

15 According to Wilson's notebooks, Andrews was insistent that he keep in the abortion scene that features in the novel.

16 *West Side Story* had come to London in 1958 and *Fings Ain't Wot They Used T'be* from the Theatre Workshop, Stratford East transferred to the West End in 1960.

Chapter 7

1 'Aunt Edna' was the term Terence Rattigan used to describe a 'low brow' member of the theatre public (see Rebellato, p. 153), the name was taken up by Joe Orton who wrote letters to the press from Edna Wellthorpe to provoke controversy over his plays. Joe Orton was another fan of Ronald Firbank and, with his lover Kenneth Halliwell, wrote novels in the style of Firbank.

2 Laurence Olivier had turned down *Look Back in Anger*, as had Terence Rattigan and Binkie Beaumont. (www.royalcourttheatre.com accessed September, 2019).

3 Jon Rose, Wilson's partner at the time.

4 William Chappell, dancer and choreographer.

5 Philip Roberts' 2001 account of the Royal Court Theatre makes no reference to *Valmouth* or to Sandy Wilson.

6 It is clear from the letter that this is Binkie Beaumont.

7 It is interesting to note that Hal Prince's concerns about Wilson's version of *Goodbye to Berlin* also centred on the music rather than the script.

8 Codron produced Harold Pinter's *The Birthday Party* at the Lyric Hammersmith, in 1958.

9   Wright notes that there are musical similarities between the scores of
    Valmouth and *His Monkey Wife*: 'Wilson's tropical sounds pronounce the
    place a sort of cousin to Valmouth' (Wright, 2010, p.89).
10 These are teaching notes which clearly prefigure Dyer's 1992 *Only
    Entertainment*.
11 Mrs Vajnavalkya was played in each production by a black woman, first by
    Bertice Reading in Liverpool and Hammersmith, with Cleo Laine taking
    over in the West End production. Elisabeth Welch sang the part in the
    1975 BBC recording.
12 The Royal Court had a history of challenging the Lord Chamberlain's Office,
    often producing plays as club performances in order to evade censorship.
    Edward Bond's 1965 play *Saved* (produced at the Royal Court) is often cited as
    the play which brought an end to the Lord Chamberlain's powers of censorship.
13 Bertice Reading recorded two songs from *Valmouth* for Parlophone
    in 1958. Elizabeth Welch sang Madame Vajanavlyka in a BBC Radio
    production in 1975.
14 Woodfall Films produced films from key texts of the 1950s reworked for
    the 1960s New Wave cinema, which brought the work of the Royal Court
    and other theatres to a much wider audience; these included *Look Back in
    Anger* (dir. Tony Richardson, 1959), *Saturday Night and Sunday Morning*
    (dir. Karel Reisz, produced by Tony Richardson, 1960), again with a score
    by Dankworth, *A Taste of Honey* (dir. Tony Richardson, 1961) and *The
    Loneliness of the Long Distance Runner* (dir. Tony Richardson, 1962).
15 Kenneth Tynan had also been a contemporary of Wilson's at Oxford, also
    involved with the Oxford University Experimental Theatre Club.
16 The New York production was again directed by Vida Hope, with Bertice
    Reading as Mrs Vajnavalkya and Gail Jones (the daughter of Lena Horne) as
    Niri-Esther.
17 The directors of ALS management included Ray Galton and Alan Simpson,
    Frankie Howerd, Erik Sykes, Spike Milligan and Beryl Vertue, who was the
    agent for all of them.
18 Portmeirion had been the setting for the ITV television series *The Prisoner*
    which broadcast from 1967–8.
19 Fabio Cleto would later become the editor of a collection of essays on Camp
    (Cleto, 1999) and in 2019, an adviser to the Metropolitan Gala Ball which
    was themed around Susan Sontag's essay 'Notes on Camp'. In a continuing
    correspondence, Cleto later writes (23 January 1994, Sandy Wilson archive)
    to ask if Wilson would like to be included in a chapter he is writing on 'the
    tradition of camp'.
20 *Brigadoon*, with lyrics by Alan Jay Lerner and music by Frederick Loewe,
    had opened on Broadway in 1947, and tells the story of a fantasy Scottish
    village which appears for one day every 100 years.
21 If *The Clapham Wonder* had closed the year before, this interview must have
    taken place in 1979.

Chapter 8

1 Peter Maxwell Davies's score was the only Academy Award for *The Boy Friend* in 1972.
2 This is according to Wilson's musical director Colin Sell.
3 www.rogerebert.com/reviews/the-boy-friend-1972.
4 *His Monkey Wife* is not alone in using the metaphor of an ape as a metaphor for a socially taboo relationship. The stage show and film of *Cabaret* (1972, dir. Bob Fosse), which came after the novel but preceded the musical of *His Monkey Wife*, makes use of a similar trope in a sequence in which the Master of Ceremonies sings 'If you could see her through my eyes' to a monkey bride, a song which ends with the line 'She wouldn't look Jewish at all'.
5 Vivian Matalon was then Artistic Director of the Hampstead Theatre Club.
6 Sylvia was the name of Wilson's own cat, and the title is a sly reference to Terence Rattigan's 1950 play *Who is Sylvia*.
7 This was a neatly circular finale for *His Monkey Wife*; as Wilson remembered in a programme note, the theatre was named after the son of Hermione Gingold, for whom Wilson had contributed revue songs for *Slings and Arrows* at the beginning of his career (programme for *His Monkey Wife*, Scarborough Theatre, 1984, Sandy Wilson archive).
8 Wilson had appeared at the Marlowe Theatre the year before in his one-man show *Sandy Wilson Thanks the Ladies*.
9 Wilson had written music for a compilation of Dorothy Parker's writing, *As Dorothy Parker Once Said* in 1966.
10 The musical arrangements were by Colin Sell who had worked with Wilson on *The Clapham Wonder* and on a 1977 revival of *The Boy Friend*.

Conclusion

1 Vivian Ellis, lyricist and composer, whose musicals spanned the 1920s to the late 1950s.
2 Lionel Bart, lyricist and composer, most widely known for *Fings Ain't Wot They Used T'Be* (1959, for Joan Littlewood's Theatre Workshop, Stratford East) and *Oliver!* *(1960).*
3 Orton contributed a sketch to Kenneth Tynan's revue *Oh! Calcutta!* which was performed in London in 1970 after his death.
4 Jon Rose, Wilson's then partner.
5 *The Tenth Chance*, Stuart Holroyd's only play.
6 Author of *The Dud Avocado*.
7 Tynan's second wife, Kathleen Halton.
8 *Beyond the Fringe* brought together sketches and performers from the Cambridge Footlights and the Oxford Revue, and was first performed at the Edinburgh Fringe Festival, hence its title.

9 Stonewall, named after the New York Stonewall riots of 1969, was founded in 1989 in response to the Thatcher government's implementation of Section 28, which banned the 'promotion of homosexuality'. A number of its founding members were actors: Sir Ian McKellen, Pam St. Clement, Michael Cashman and Simon Fanshawe.

Bibliography

Ackland, Rodney. *Absolute Hell*. London: Oberon Books, 2017.

Ackroyd, Peter. *Queer City: Gay London from the Romans to the Present Day*. London: Vintage, 2001.

Aldor, Francis. *The Good Time Guide to London*. London: George G. Harrap, 1951.

Babuscio, Jack. 'Camp and the Gay Sensibility', in David Bergman (ed.), *Camp Grounds: Style and Homosexuality*, pp. 19–38. Amherst: University of Massachusetts Press, 1999.

Baker, Paul. *Polari: The Lost Language of Gay Men*. London: Routledge, 2006.

Baker, Paul. *Fabulosa!: The Story of Polari, Britain's Secret Gay Language*. London: Reaktion Books, 2019.

Baker, Richard Anthony. *British Music Hall: An Illustrated History*. Stroud: Sutton Publishing, 2005.

Bartlett, Neil. 'Theatrical Types', in Clare Barlow (ed.), *Queer British Art 1861-1967*, pp. 68–93. London: Tate Publishing, 2017.

Bauer, Heike and Cook, Matt (eds.). *Queer 1950s: Rethinking Sexuality in the Postwar Years*. Basingstoke: Palgrave Macmillan, 2012.

Benedick, Adam. 'Obituary: Reginald Woolley', *The Independent*, 20 March 1993.

Bengry, Justin. 'Scandal and the Origins of Legal Reform in Britain', in Heike Bauer and Matt Cook (eds.), *Queer 1950s: Rethinking Sexuality in the Postwar Years*, pp. 167–82. Basingstoke: Palgrave Macmillan, 2012.

Bergman, David. 'Introduction', in David Bergman (ed.), *Camp Grounds: Style and Homosexuality*, pp. 3–16. Amherst: University of Massachusetts Press, 1999.

Black, Kitty. *Upper Circle: A Theatrical Chronicle*. London: Methuen, 1984.

Bourne, Stephen. *Brief Encounters: Lesbians and Gays in British Cinema 1930-1971*. London: Cassell, 1996.

Brandreth, Giles. *John Gielgud: A Celebration*. London: Pavilion Books, 1985.

Brown, Ivor. *Theatre 1954-1955*. London: Max Reinhardt, 1955.

Carpenter, Humphrey. *OUDS: A Centenary History of the Oxford University Dramatic Society 1885-1985*. Oxford: Oxford University Press, 1985.

Cleto, Fabio. 'Introduction: Queering the Camp', in Fabio Cleto (ed.), *Camp: Queer Aesthetics and the Performing Subject*, pp. 1–42. Edinburgh: Edinburgh University Press, 1999.

Clum, John M. *Acting Gay: Male Homosexuality in Modern Drama*. New York: Columbia University Press.

Conekin, Becky, Mort, Frank and Waters, Chris (eds.). *Moments of Modernity: Reconstructing Britain 1945-1964*. London: Rivers Oram Press, 1999.

Cook, Matt. 'Queer Conflicts: Love, Sex and War, 1914–1967', in Matt Cook
    (ed.), *A Gay History of Britain: Love and Sex Between Men Since the Middle
    Ages*, pp. 179–214. Oxford: Greenwood World Publishing, 2007.
Coward, Noël. 'Foreword' to Peter Noble. *Ivor Novello: Man of the Theatre, The
    Authorised Biography*, pp. ii–iii. London: The Falcon Press, 1951.
Coward, Noël. *Future Indefinite*. New York: Doubleday, 1954.
Coward, Noël. 'Foreword' to Raymond Mander and Joe Mitchenson. *Musical
    Comedy: A Story in Pictures*, pp. 6–8. London: Peter Davies, 1969.
Coward, Noël. *Autobiography*. London: Methuen, 1986.
Cryer, Barry. *You Won't Believe This: An Autobiography of Sorts*. London: Virgin
    Publishing, 1999.
Curran, James and Seaton, Jean. *Power Without Responsibility: Press,
    Broadcasting and the Internet in Britain*. London: Routledge, 2018.
Davies, Russell, ed. *The Kenneth Williams Diaries*. London: Harper Collins, 1993.
Davies, Russell, ed. *The Kenneth Williams Letters*. London: Harper Collins, 1994.
Day, Barry. *The Essential Noël Coward Companion*. London: Methuen, 2009.
Day, Barry, ed. *The Letters of Noël Coward*. London: Bloomsbury, 2014.
Day, Gary, ed. *Literature and Culture in Modern Britain, Vol. 2 1935–1955*.
    Harlow: Longman, 1997.
Dorney, Kate. *The Changing Language of Modern English Drama 1945–2005*.
    Basingstoke: Palgrave Macmillan, 2009.
Dorney, Kate and Gray, Frances. *Modern Theatre in 100 Plays*. London: Methuen
    2013.
Dorney, Kate and Gray, Frances. *Played in Britain: Modern Theatre in 100 Plays*.
    London: Bloomsbury, 2014.
Dowling, Brian. 'Customs of the Players', in *Late Joys Past and Present: Players'
    Theatre Souvenir*, pp. 13–15. London: Players' Theatre, 1951.
Dundy, Elaine. *Life Itself!* London: Virago, 2001.
Dyer, Richard. 'The Hollywood Musical: Some Notes towards a Study Project',
    Paddy Whannel Archive, North Western University, 1973.
Dyer, Richard. *Only Entertainment*. London: Routledge, 1992.
Dyer, Richard. *The Culture of Queers*. London: Routledge, 2002.
Dyer, Richard. *Pastiche*. London: Routledge, 2007.
Ebert, Roger. Review of *The Boy Friend*, 8 February 1972, https://www.rogerebert.
    com/reviews/the-boy-friend-1972 (accessed September 2019).
Elsom, John. *Post-war British Theatre*. London: Routledge and Kegan Paul,
    1979.
Farson, Daniel. *Soho in the Fifties*. London: Michael Joseph, 1987.
Foucault, Michel. 'Other Spaces: The Principles of Heterotopia', *Lotus
    International: Quarterly Architectural Review* 48/49 (Milan: 1986), pp. 9–17.
Freedland, Michael. 'Obituary, Sandy Wilson', *The Guardian*, 28 August 2014,
    p. 35.
Fryer, Jonathan. *Soho in the Fifties and Sixties*. London: National Portrait Gallery
    Publications, 1998.

Gänzl, Kurt. *The British Musical Theatre*. Basingstoke: Macmillan, 1986.

Gänzl, Kurt. *The Encyclopaedia of the Musical Theatre Volume III*. New York: Schrimer Books, 2001.

Gardiner, James. *A Class Apart: The Private Pictures of Montague Glover*. London: Serpent's Tail, 1992.

Garland, Rodney. *The Heart in Exile*. London: W.H. Allen, 1953.

Gordon, Robert, Jubin, Olaf and Taylor, Millie. *British Musical Theatre since 1950*. London: Bloomsbury, 2016.

Gottfried, Martin. *Broadway Musicals*. New York: Harry N. Abrams Inc. 1980.

Gowing, Laura. 'LGBT Histories and the Politics of Identity', in Anna Maerker, Simon Sleight and Adam Sutcliffe (eds.), *History, Memory and Public Life: The Past in the Present*, pp. 294–316. London: Taylor and Francis, 2018.

Grainge, Paul. 'Reclaiming Heritage: Colourization, Culture Wars and the Politics of Nostalgia', *Cultural Studies* 13, no. 9 (October 1999), pp. 621–38.

Green, Benny (eds.). *The Last Empires: A Music Hall Companion*. London: Michael Joseph, 1986.

Greenwell, Garth. 'At Last I Felt I Fitted In', *Guardian Review*, 1 July 2017, p. 3.

Harradine, Archie. 'The Story of the Players' Theatre', in *Late Joys At the Players' Theatre*, pp. 8–38. St Albans, Herts: Staples Press Ltd, 1943.

Hewison, Robert. *Culture and Consensus: England, Art and Politics since 1940*. London: Methuen, 1995.

Hope, Vida. 'Preface' to Sandy Wilson. *The Boy Friend: A Play in Three Acts*, pp. 11–14. London: Andre Deutsch, 1955.

Hopkins, Harry. *The New Look: A Social History of the Forties and Fifties in Britain*. London: Secker and Warburg, 1963.

Hornsey, Richard. *The Spiv and the Architect: Unruly Life in Postwar London*. Minneapolis: University of Minnesota Press, 2010.

Houlbrook, Matt. *Queer London: Perils and Pleasures in the Sexual Metropolis*. Chicago: University of Chicago Press, 2005.

Howard, Diana. *London Theatres and Music Halls 1850–1950*. London: The Library Association, 1970.

Huggett, Richard. *Binkie Beaumont: Eminence Grise of the West End Theatre, 1933–1973*. London: Hodder & Stoughton, 1989.

Ibell, Paul. *Theatreland: A Journey through the Heart of London's Theatre*. London: Continuum, 2009.

Innes, Christopher. 'Terence Rattigan: The Voice of the 1950s', in Dominic Shellard (ed.), *British Theatre in the 1950s*, pp. 53–63. Sheffield: Sheffield Academic Press, 2000.

Isherwood, Christopher. *The World in the Evening*. Harmondsworth: Penguin, 1966.

Isherwood, Christopher. *Diaries. Volume I 1939–1960*, ed. Katherine Bucknell. London: Methuen, 1996.

Jackson, Stanley. *An Indiscreet Guide to Soho*. London: Muse Arts Limited, 1946.

Jones, Owen. 'Why this Pardon for Britain's Gay Men Is so Inadequate', *The Guardian*, 2 February 2017, p. 28.

Kift, Dagmar. *The Victorian Music Hall: Culture, Class and Conflict*. Cambridge: Cambridge University Press, 1996.

Kinsey, Alfred C., Pomeroy Wardell, P. and Clyde, Martin E. *Sexual Behavior in the Human Male*. Bloomington: Indiana University Press, 1948.

Kynaston, David. *Family Britain 1951–57*. London: Bloomsbury, 2009.

Lahr, John. *Automatic Vaudeville: Essays on Star Turns*. London: Methuen 1984.

Lane Clark, William. 'Degenerate Personality: Deviant Sexuality and Race in Ronald Firbank's Novels', in David Bergman (ed.), *Camp Grounds: Style and Homosexuality*, pp. 134–55. Amherst: University of Massachusetts Press, 1999.

Lewis, Brian, ed. *British Queer History: New Approaches and Perspectives*, pp. 109–33. Manchester: Manchester University Press, 2013.

Linkof, Ryan. '"These young men who come down from Oxford and write gossip": Society Gossip, Homosexuality and the Logic of Revelation in the Interwar Popular Press', in Brian Lewis (ed.), *British Queer History: New Approaches and Perspectives*, pp. 109–33. Manchester: Manchester University Press, 2015.

Long, Scott. 'The Loneliness of Camp', in David Bergman (ed.), *Camp Grounds: Style and Homosexuality*, pp. 78–91. Amherst: University of Massachusetts Press, 1999.

Macqueen-Pope, Walter James. *An Indiscreet Guide to Theatreland*. London: Muse Arts, 1947?

Macqueen Pope, Walter James. *The Melodies Linger On: The Story of Music Hall*. London: W.H. Allen, 1950.

Macqueen-Pope, Walter James. *Ivor: The Story of an Achievement*. London: W.H. Allen, 1951.

Mander, Raymond and Mitchenson, Joe. *British Music Hall: A Story in Pictures*. London: Studio Vista, 1965.

Mander, Raymond and Mitchenson, Joe. *Musical Comedy: A Story in Pictures*. London: Peter Davies, 1969.

Mander, Raymond and Mitchenson, Joe. *The Theatres of London*. London: New English Library, 1975.

Marshall, Norman. *The Other Theatre*. London: John Lehmann, 1947.

Medhurst, Andy. 'In Search of Nebulous Nancies: Looking for Queers in Pre-gay British Film', in Robin Griffiths (ed.), *British Queer Cinema*, pp. 21–34. London: Routledge, 2006.

Medhurst, Andy. *A National Joke: Popular Comedy and English Cultural Identities*. London: Routledge, 2007.

Melly, George. 'Introduction' to Daniel Farson. *Soho in the Fifties*, pp. xi–xv. London: Michael Joseph, 1987.

Metcalf, John. *London A to Z*. London: Thames and Hudson, 2016.

Meyer, Moe (ed.). *The Politics and Poetics of Camp*. London: Routledge, 1994.

Meyer, Moe. *An Archaeology of Posing: Essays on Camp, Drag and Sexuality*. Madison: Macater Press, 2010.

Morley, Sheridan. *Spread a Little Happiness: The First Hundred Years of the British Musical*. London: Thames & Hudson, 1987.

Morley, Sheridan. *The Private Lives of Noël and Gertie*. London: Oberon Books, 1999.

Mort, Frank. *Cultures of Consumption: Masculinities and Social Space in Late Twentieth-Century Britain*. London: Routledge, 1996.

Mort, Frank. *Capital Affairs: London and the Making of the Permissive Society*. London: Yale University Press, 2010.

Muñoz, José Esteban. *Cruising Utopia: The Then and There of Queer Futurity*. New York: New York University Press, 2009.

Napper, Lawrence and Williams, Michael. 'The Curious Appeal of Ivor Novello', in Bruce Babington (ed.), *British Stars and Stardom from Alma Taylor to Sean Connery*, pp. 42–55. Manchester: Manchester University Press, 2001.

Newton, Esther. *Mother Camp: Female Impersonators in America*. New Jersey: Prentice-Hall, 1972.

O'Connor, Sean. *Straight Acting: Popular Gay Drama from Wilde to Rattigan*. London: Cassell, 1998.

Pattie, David. *Modern British Playwriting: The 1950s*. London: Methuen Drama, 2012.

Payn, Graham and Morley, Sheridan (eds.). *The Noël Coward Diaries*. London: Macmillan, 1983.

Pimlott, Ben. *The Queen: Elizabeth II and the Monarchy*. London: Harper Press, 2012.

Price, Reynolds. *Ardent Spirits: Leaving Home, Coming Back*. New York: Scribner, 2009.

Philips, Deborah. *Fairground Attractions: A Genealogy of the Pleasure Ground*. London: Bloomsbury, 2012.

Porter, Kevin and Weeks, Jeffrey (eds.). *Between the Acts: Lives of Homosexual Men 1885–1957*. London: Routledge, 1991.

Proust, Marcel. *À la recherche du temps perdu, Volume IV, Sodome et Gomorrhe*. Paris: Éditions Gallimard, 1992.

Rattigan, Terence. *Collected Plays*. Volume II. London: Hamish Hamilton, 1953.

Rebellato, Dan. *1956 and All That: The Making of Modern British Drama*. London: Routledge, 1999.

Richardson, Nigel. *Dog Days in Soho: One Man's Adventures in Fifties Bohemia*. London: Victor Gollancz, 2000.

Rider Haggard, Henry. *King Solomon's Mines* (1885). London: Harmondsworth, Puffin, 2018.

Roberts, Philip. *The Royal Court Theatre and the Modern Stage*. Cambridge: Cambridge University Press, 2001.

Robertson, Pamela. 'Mae West's Maids: Race, "Authenticity" and the Discourse of Camp', in Fabio Cleto (ed.), *Camp: Queer Aesthetics and the Performing Subject*, pp. 393–408. Edinburgh: Edinburgh University Press, 1999.

Roen, Paul. *High Camp: A Gay Guide to Camp and Cult Films*, Vol. 2, San Francisco: Leyland Publications, 1997.

Ross, Andrew. 'Uses of Camp', in David Bergman (ed.), *Camp Grounds: Style and Homosexuality*, pp. 54–77. Amherst: University of Massachusetts Press, 1999.

Russell, Ken. *The Lion Roars: Ken Russell on Film*. London: Faber and Faber, 1993.

Shellard, Dominic. *British Theatre Since the War*. New Haven: Yale University Press, 1999.

Shellard, Dominic. '1950-1954: Was It a Cultural Wasteland?' in Dominic Shellard (ed.), *British Theatre in the 1950s*, pp. 28–40. Sheffield: Sheffield Academic Press, 2000.

Sheridan, Paul. *Late Joys at the Players' Theatre*. London: T.V. Boardman and Company, 1943.

Sheridan, Paul. 'The Players' Theatre of "Joys"', in *Late Joys Past and Present: Players' Theatre Souvenir*, pp. 3–12. London: Players' Theatre, 1951.

Sheridan, Paul. *Late and Early Joys at the Players' Theatre*. London: T.V. Boardman and Company, 1952.

Sherrin, Ned. *Ned Sherrin: The Autobiography*. London: Little, Brown, 2005.

Sinfield, Alan. 'The Theatre and Its Audiences', in Alan Sinfield (ed.), *Society and Literature 1945-1970*, pp. 173–98. London: Methuen, 1983.

Sinfield, Alan. *Literature, Politics and Culture in Postwar Britain*. London: The Athlone Press, 1997.

Sinfield, Alan. *Gay and After*. London: Serpent's Tail, 1998.

Sinfield, Alan. *Out on Stage: Lesbian and Gay Theatre in the Twentieth Century*. London: Yale University Press, 1999.

Smith, Rupert. *The Life of John S. Barrington*. London: Serpent's Tail, 1996.

Snelson, John. '"We said we wouldn't look back": British Musical Theatre, 1935-1960', in William A. Everett and Paul R. Laird (eds.), *The Cambridge Companion to the Musical*. Cambridge: Cambridge University Press, 2008.

Sontag, Susan. 'Notes on "Camp"', in *Against Interpretation and Other Essays*, pp. 275–92. Harmondsworth: Penguin, 1983

Stirling, Richard. *Julie Andrews: An Intimate Biography*. London: Piatkus Books, 2007.

Taylor, Affrica. 'A Queer Geography', in Andy Medhurst and Sally Munt (eds.), *Lesbian and Gay Studies: A Critical Introduction*, pp. 3–19. London: Cassell, 1997.

Taylor, John Russell. *Anger and After: A Guide to the New British Drama*. Harmondsworth: Penguin, 1963.

Thorndike, Sybil. 'Foreword' to Paul Sheridan. *Late and Early Joys at the Players' Theatre*, ed. John Courtney Trewin, p. 9. London: T.V. Boardman and Company, 1952.

Trewin, John Courtney. *The Gay Twenties: A Decade of the Theatre*. London: Macdonald, 1958.

Trussler, Simon. *The Cambridge Illustrated History of the British Theatre*. Cambridge: Cambridge University Press, 1994.

Walkowitz, Judith R. *Nights Out: Life in Cosmopolitan London*. London: Yale University Press, 2012.

Warner, Philip. *The Best of British Pluck: The Boy's Own Paper*. London: MacDonald and Jane's, 1976.

Waters, Chris. 'Disorders of the Mind, Disorders of the Body Social: Peter Wildeblood and the Making of the Modern Homosexual', in Becky Conekin, Frank Mort and Chris Waters (eds.), *Moments of Modernity: Reconstructing Britain 1945–1964*, pp. 134–51. London: Rivers Oram Press, 1999.

Weeks, Jeffrey. *Coming Out: Homosexual Politics in Britain, from the Nineteenth Century to the Present*. London: Quartet Books, 1977.

Weeks, Jeffrey. *The Languages of Sexuality*. London: Routledge, 2011.

Whitehouse, Edmund. *London Lights: A History of West End Musicals*. Cheltenham: This England Books, 2005.

Wildeblood, Peter. *Against the Law*. London: Weidenfield and Nicolson, 1955.

Wildeblood, Peter. *A Way of Life*. London: Weidenfield and Nicolson, 1956.

Wildeblood, Peter. *West End People*. London: Weidenfield and Nicolson, 1958.

Williams, Raymond. 'Dominant, Residual and Emergent', in Raymond Williams (ed.), *Marxism and Literature*, pp. 121–8. Oxford: Oxford University Press, 1977.

Wilmut, Roger. *Kindly Leave the Stage! The Story of Variety 1919–1960*. London: Methuen, 1985.

Wilson, Sandy. *This Is Sylvia: Her Life and Loves*. London: Max Parrish, 1954.

Wilson, Sandy. *The Boy Friend: A Play in Three Acts*. London: Andre Deutsch, 1955.

Wilson, Sandy. *I Could Be Happy: An Autobiography*. New York: Stein and Day, 1975a.

Wilson, Sandy. *Ivor*. London: Michael Joseph, 1975b.

Wilson, Sandy. *The Roaring Twenties*. London: Eyre Methuen, 1976.

Wilson, Sandy. *Divorce Me, Darling!: A Musical Play*. London: French, 1981.

Wilson, Sandy and Rose, Jon. *Who's Who for Beginners*. London: Max Parrish and Co. Limited, 1957.

Woolf, Michael. 'In Minor Key: Theatre 1930–1955', in Gary Day (ed.), *Literature and Culture in Modern Britain Vol. II 1930–1955*, pp. 86–99. London: Longman, 1997

Wright, Adrian. *A Tanners' Worth of Tune: Rediscovering the Post-War British Musical*. Woodbridge: The Boydell Press, 2010.

Wright, Adrian. *West End Broadway: The Golden Age of the American Musical in London*. Woodbridge: The Boydell Press, 2012.

Wright, Adrian. *Must Close Sunday: The Decline and Fall of the British Musical Flop*. Woodbridge: The Boydell Press, 2017.

Index

Ackland, Rodney   35, 43, 129
Against the Law (P. Wildeblood)
        25, 32
Aladdin (S. Wilson)   143–4
Albery, Bronson   10, 74
Anderson, Jean   58
Anderson, Lindsay   8, 10, 19, 121, 151
Andrews, Julie   88, 101, 103, 130, 132
'angry young men', the   14, 151, 152,
        see also avant-garde theatre;
        Royal Court Theatre
avant-garde theatre
    challenge to West End theatre
        17, 53, 147–8 (*see also*
        Royal Court Theatre)
Ayckbourn, Alan   140

Beaumont, Hugh 'Binkie', *see also*
        musicals
    'camp intellectual'   49–50, 55
    class   46–7
    with Coward and Novello   40–5,
        49, 51, 54–5
    decline in popularity   51–2, 53, 76
    discreet sexuality   2, 33, 45, 48,
        55, 153
    humble origins   46
    powerful figure   39, 41, 44–5,
        54, 55
    producer for Wilson
        The Buccaneer   93–4
        Divorce Me, Darling!   106
        Oh Henry   92
    support for new productions
        53, 76
Beaton, Cecil   99, 100
Bedding, John   90
Bennett, Joan Sterndale   5, 75
Berlin Stories (C. Isherwood)
    Wilson's adaptation   102–4

Beyond the Fringe   18, 152
Black, Kitty   40, 44, 50, 52, 74, 84
The Boy Friend (film-K. Russell)
        129–55
    critical reception   133–4
    1930s setting   131, 132, 133
    pastiche   131
    plot   132–3
    Wilson's dislike of   129–31,
        133, 135
The Boy Friend (play-S. Wilson)
    Britishness   70, 73–4, 80
    camp   65, 70, 75, 84–5, 86–7, 99,
        134, 148
    class   79–80
    Coward and Novello inspiration
        78–9, 90
    critical reception   88, 89–90
    New York production   87–9
    1920s setting   70–1, 75, 77, 78–9,
        80–5, 133, 134, 149
    originality of   73, 80
    pastiche   1, 65, 70, 71, 78, 85–6,
        87, 88, 89, 109, 131, 134
    plot   79–80
    post-war context   75–6, 81–4,
        87, 149
    success of   73–5, 87, 91, 144–5
    wide appeal   89, 90, 109
Boy's Own Paper, The   95, 96, 97,
        99, *see also* comic book,
        the
Brideshead Revisited (E. Waugh)   7,
        see also Wilson, Sandy, at
        Oxford
The Buccaneer (S. Wilson)
    plot   96–8
    reviews   93–5, 98
    sexual politics   98, 153
Burgess, Guy, *see* Cambridge spies

Cabaret, (B Fosse)   102–3, 150,
        see also Berlin Stories,
        Wilson's adaptation
Cambridge spies   23, 24, 31
Cambridge University, *see* Oxbridge
camp, *see also under* Firbank,
        Ronald; Players' Theatre
        Club; *Salad Days*
    definitions of   65, 68, 86, 125–6
    High Camp   47, 85, 87, 125, 134
    shift away from   17, 34–7,
        148–50, 155
    as a strategy of identification
        36–7, 65, 155
    in Wilson's works   2, 17, 91, 156
        (*see under The Boy Friend;*
        Valmouth)
Campaign for Homosexual Equality
        (CHE)   35–6
Caprice (S. Wilson)   11, 99–100, 142
censorship   11, 33, 48, 59, 119–20
Charles, Maria   90, 104
Churchill, Winston   44, 45
The Clapham Wonder (S. Wilson)
        99, 126, 141–3
Codron, Michael   113, 124, 140
Coghill, Nevill   8–9
Collier, John   135, 140, 141, 149
comic book, the   95–6, *see also The*
        Buccaneer
Cook, Peter   17–18, 150, 152, 153
Coronation, the (1953)   62, 70–1,
        75, *see also* 1950s
Coward, Noel, *see also* musicals;
        Wilson, Sandy, Coward
        and Novello, influence of
    with Beaumont and Novello
        40–5, 49, 51, 54–5
    'camp intellectual'   49–50, 55
    class   46–7
    decline in popularity   13, 51–2,
        76, 100, 148–9
    discreet sexuality   2, 33, 45,
        55, 153
    humble origins   46

pastiche   78, 86
patriotism during WWII   43–4
powerful figure   39, 41, 45, 47,
        49, 54, 55
Cryer, Barry   66, 68, 156

Dankworth, John   120–1, 150
Delaney, Shelagh   34, 52
Devine, George   8, 17, 52, 53,
        110–13, 150
Divorce Me, Darling!   104–8
    1930s setting   104–5, 106–7,
        108, 131
    pastiche   106, 108
    at the Players' Theatre   104,
        105–6
    plot   105
    reviews   106–7
    revival   148–9
Dundy, Elaine   83, 123, 151–2
Dyer, Richard   36–7, 54, 64, 65, 86,
        111, 114

English Stage Company, *see* Royal
        Court Theatre
Entertaining Mr Sloane (J. Orton)
        53, 150
ETC, *see* Oxford University
        Experimental Theatre Club
Eyre, Richard   89–90

Farjeon, Gervase   60, 75
Farson, Daniel   28, 31–2, 37–8
Ferrier, Brian Stratton   19
Festival of Britain (1951), the   62, 63
Feuer, Cy and Martin, Ernest H.
        87–8, 129
Firbank, Ronald
    camp   111, 119, 125
    'niche taste'   110, 112, 122
    Wilson's adaptations of   11, 99,
        110–13, 123, 127 (*see also*
        Valmouth)
Flanders, Michael   11, 18, *see also*
        Swann, Donald

gay history   2, 21, 51, 148, 155–6,
    see also homosexuality;
    queer culture(s)
gay men, *see also* homosexuality
    harassment of   23–5, 36, 45–9,
        82, 154
    safe spaces for   8–9, 30, 48–9, 51,
        53–4, 64, 68
Gay Liberation Front (GLF), *see* Gay
        Liberation movement
Gay Liberation movement   2, 35–6,
        55, 153, 155–6
Gemmell, Don   59, 60, 70, 106, 157
Gielgud, John   44, 45, 46, 48, 50,
        51, 53
Gingold, Hermione   5, 11, 101
The Good Old Days (BBC)   58, 69
Gray, Dulcie   12, 19

Hampstead Theatre Club   139–40
Harradine, Archie   59, 62
Heal, Joan   105–6
The Heart in Exile (Garland)   25
His Monkey Wife (S. Wilson)   135–42
    critical reception   139–41
    plot   136–9
    sexual politics in   137, 139, 141
Hobson, Harold   14, 71, 106, 121
homosexuality
    decriminalization of   32–6, 42, 155
    in 1950s   23–4, 32–4, 35–6,
        45–6, 55, 68, 82, 148,
        154, 156
    prosecution of   23–5, 65, 155
    and the theatre   24–7, 48–9,
        54, 154
Homosexual Law Reform Society
        34–6, 153, 156
Hope, Vida   5, 74, 84–5, 88, 92, 101,
        113, 127, 131

Isherwood, Christopher   16, 84–5,
        87, 99, 102, 103–4, *see also*
        Berlin Stories, Wilson's
        adaptation

Ivor (S. Wilson)   39, 42, 85, 150, *see*
        also Wilson, Sandy, Coward
        and Novello, influence of
Ivy restaurant, the   39–41, 53–4

'Julian and Sandy'   1, 78

Kander, John and Ebb, Fred   102–3
Kinsey, Alfred C.   24, 33
kitchen sink drama, *see* avant garde
        drama
Korda, Alexander   92

Laine, Cleo   115, 120–1, 124, 150
'Late Joys', *see under* Players' Theatre
        Club
Leigh, Vivien   14, 123
Linkof, Ryan   32–3
Lister, Laurie   11
Littler, Prince   50, 52
Lloyd Webber, Andrew   148
Longford, Lord (Frank Pakenham)
        33, 35
Look Back in Anger (J. Osborne)   17,
        52–3, 152, 155, *see also*
        avant-garde theatre; Royal
        Court Theatre
Lyric Theatre, Hammersmith, the
    Aladdin   143
    The Buccaneer   93–4
    Oranges and Lemons   11
    Valmouth   113, 121–2

MacDonald, Jeanette   100, 101
Maclean, Donald, *see* Cambridge spies
MacQueen-Pope, Walter James   40,
        59, 67
Masteroff, Joe   102–3
Metropolitan Police, the   23, 28, 46, 82
MGM (Metro Goldwyn Mayer)
        129–30, 134
Miller, Johnathan   18, 20, 152
Montagu trial, the   24–5, 32, 33,
        45, 47, 55, 82, *see also*
        Wildeblood, Peter

Moore, Dudley   18, 152
Morley, Sheridan
    The Boy Friend   74, 87, 131–2, 134
    Divorce Me, Darling!   148–9
Mort, Frank   24–5, 27, 29–30, 34,
        35–6, 63, 64, 153
musicals   1, 51–3, 76–7, 108, 122,
        130, 147–9
music hall, *see under* Players' Theatre
        Club
My Fair Lady (Lerner & Loewe)   53,
        101, 150
My Royal Past (C. Beaton)
    Wilson's adaptation   100–101

1950s, the, *see also* Coronation (1953);
        homosexuality, 1950s
    austerity   28, 30, 65, 75–6, 81,
        83, 133
    conformism   11, 28, 36, 65, 148
1960s, the   107–8, 130, 132, 141,
        148, 150, 153
Novello, Ivor, *see also* musicals;
        Wilson, Sandy, Coward
        and Novello, influence of
    with Beaumont and Coward
        40–5, 49, 51, 54–5
    'camp intellectual'   49–50, 55
    class   46–7
    decline in popularity   13, 51, 76,
        100, 148–9
    discreet sexuality   2, 33, 55, 153
    entourage   42
    humble origins   46
    pastiche   78, 86, 101
    patriotism during WWII   43–4
    powerful figure   39, 41, 42, 45, 54
    prison sentence   43

Oh, Henry! (S. Wilson)   92–3, 95, 101
Oranges and Lemons (L. Lister, S.
        Wilson)   11, 144, *see also*
        revue
Orton, Joe   49, 52–3, 125, 150, *see*
        also avant-garde theatre;
        Royal Court Theatre

Osborne, John   17, 110, 111, 121,
        151–2, *see also* avant-garde
        theatre; Royal Court Theatre
Oxbridge   1, 9–10, 24, 50
Oxford Circus (ETC)   10, 11, 110
Oxford University, *see* Oxbridge;
        Wilson, Sandy, at Oxford
Oxford University Dramatic Society
        (OUDS)   8–9
Oxford University Experimental
        Theatre Club (ETC)   1,
        8–10, 11, 18, 99

pantomime, *see Aladdin;* Players'
        Theatre Club
pastiche   64, 78, 85–6, *see also*
        under Coward; *Divorce Me,*
        Darling!; Novello; Players'
        Theatre Club; *Salad Days;*
        The Boy Friend (film and
        play); *Valmouth*
Perry, John   48, 50, 51, 93
Piccadilly Circus   4, 23, 27, 28–9,
        see also Soho
Pieces of Eight   17, 18, 152
Pinter, Harold   18, 150
Players' Theatre Club, the
    The Boy Friend   57, 62, 69, 70–1,
        73, 74–5
    camp   64–5, 68–70
    diversity of patrons   63–5
    Divorce Me, Darling!   104,
        105, 106
    history of   57–8, 69
    innovative theatre   59–60, 62, 71
    'Late Joys'   5, 56, 58–63, 157
    music hall   1, 58–9, 61, 64–5,
        67–9, 70, 78
    pantomime   59, 62, 68, 78
    pastiche   64, 68, 78–9, 158
    rituals   65–8
Polari   1, 26, 28, 34, 36, 55, 155
Prince, Hal   102, 103–4, 140, 150
Princess Margaret   63, 123
Pygmalion (G. B. Shaw)
    Wilson's adaptation of   101, 150

queer clubs   31, 37, *see also* Soho,
      private clubs and pubs
queer culture(s)   24, 29, 45, 54, 155,
      see also gay history
queerness
   in Orton's work   52, 150
   in Wilson's work   97, 99, 112

Rattigan, Terrence
   and avant-garde theatre   52–3,
      147, 150, 155
   dominance of West End theatre
      45, 48–9, 155
   at Oxford   7, 8
Rebellato, Dan   17, 47, 50, 51, 53,
      119–20, 147
Rees, Joan   102, 130–1
revue   10–11, 76, 110, 152, *see also*
      Beyond the Fringe; Wilson,
      Sandy, writing revue
Richardson, Nigel   28, 75
Richardson, Tony   8, 9, 17, 109,
      110–12, 121, 150, *see also*
      Royal Court Theatre;
      Valmouth
Ridgeway, Peter   57, 59
The Roaring Twenties (S. Wilson)
      80, 82, 85
Rose, Jon   13–16, 17, 100
Round the Horne (BBC)   1, 78
Royal Court Theatre
   avant-garde theatre at   17, 53,
      147, 151
   production of *Valmouth*
      109–13, 120
   Wilson's links with   8, 17, 53,
      109–10, 121, 150–1
   Wilson's rift with   113, 120–1,
      see also avant-garde theatre
Russell, Ken   130–5, *see also The
      Boy Friend* (film)

Sachs, Leonard   57, 58, 60, 62
Salad Days (J. Slade)
   Britishness   73, 77
   camp   17, 65, 150, 155

decline   148–9, 150
   pastiche of 1920s   78
   success   1, 73, 77
Schlesinger, John   8, 9, 17
Second World War   5, 7, 30, 43, 44
*Sexual Behaviour in the Human Male,
      the 'Kinsey' report, see*
      Kinsey, Alfred C.
Sexual Offences Act of 1967   35,
      36, 155
Sheridan, Paul   66
Sherrin, Ned   18
Shulman, Milton   139, 140, 151
Simpson, N. F.   18, 150
Slade, Julian   1, 8, *see also Salad Days*
Slings and Arrows (H. Gingold)
      11, 51
Soho   27–38, *see also* gay men, safe
      spaces for
   bohemianism   28, 39
   history   27–8, 29
   private clubs and pubs   30–2,
      37–8, 155
   'vice spots'   23, 28, 31, 83
Sontag, Susan   65, 68
Stonewall   155, 156
Swann, Donald   8, 10, 11, 12, 18,
      see also Flanders, Michael

A Taste of Honey (S. Delaney)   34
Tennent Ltd., H. M.   44, 45, 92,
      93, 112
Thatcher, Margaret   20, 152
That Was the Week That Was   18
This Is Sylvia (S. Wilson)   107, 137
Twiggy   130, 132, 133, 134
Tynan, Elaine, *see* Dundy, Elaine
Tynan, Kathleen   9, 152
Tynan, Kenneth   8, 9, 10, 12, 17, 53,
      81, 110, 150–2

Valmouth (S. Wilson), *see also* Royal
      Court Theatre
   camp   111, 119, 122, 124–6
   class   113–14, 115, 119
   exoticism   114–15, 118

mixed reactions to   121–4
pastiche   122
plot   116–17
race   111, 117, 119
revival   124–5
sexuality   117, 118
Van Druten, John   102, 103
Villeneuve, Justin de   130
Voices in the Air (BBC)   18

Watergate theatre, the   11–12, 38, 93
A Way of Life (P. Wildeblood)   25,
        33, 34, 35
Who's Who for Beginners (Wilson &
        Rose)   14–15, 17
Wildeblood, Peter
    being gay in 1950s   25, 32–5, 153
    imprisonment   33
    Montagu trial   24–5
    nostalgia for 1920s   82–3
    rejection of camp   34–6
Williams, Kenneth   1, 6, 18, 93–4, 97
Williams, Raymond   149
Wilson, Sandy
    adaptations of gay writers   2, 91
    conservatism   121, 152–4
    Coward and Novello, influence
        of   2, 12–13, 17, 39–42,
        55, 78, 108, 131, 147, 150
    early life   3–5, 10, 29, 40, 95, 97–8
    end of West End career   108,
        109, 113, 126, 141

friendships   4, 8, 9, 16, 18–19,
        20, 32, 33, 38, 70 (*see under*
        Royal Court Theatre,
        Wilson's links with)
homosexuality   2, 8–9, 13,
        16, 21, 33, 36–7, 54, 55,
        153, 155
left-wing sympathies   19–20,
        152
nostalgia for 1920s   82–3, 85, 90,
        153–4
at Oxford   1, 6–10
problems with projects   101–6,
        112–13, 120
relationship with Jon Rose
        13–16
wartime service   5–6
writing for TV and radio   18
writing revue   9–12, 18, 152
Wolfenden Report, the   24, 33, 34,
        35–6
Woolley, Reginald
    director at the Players' Theatre
        60, 106
    set designer   60, 62–3, 69–70, 74,
        75, 84, 88, 104, 131
Wright, Adrian   20, 64, 73, 77–8,
        85–6, 99, 100, 104, 108
Wright, Geoffrey   11, 99
Wyndham's Theatre, the   29, 74

Yui, Chak   13, 16–17